The Law Revolution

BOOKS BY MELVIN M. BELLI

The Adequate Award
Belli Looks at Life and Law in Japan
Belli Looks at Life and Law in Russia
The Law Revolt (2 Vols.—legal edition of *The Law Revolution*)
Medical and Tort Year Book
Medical and Criminal Year Book
Modern Damages (3 Vols.)
Modern Trials (3 Vols.)
Ready for the Plaintiff
Trial and Tort Trends (18 Vols.)

The Law Revolution

by Melvin M. Belli

(Volume One—Criminal Law)

Introduction by
Erle Stanley Gardner

Sherbourne Press, Inc., Los Angeles

Library of Congress Catalog Card Number 67–21874

Manufactured in the United States of America by the Kingsport Press, Inc., Kingsport, Tennessee

First Printing

To those tough cases which made the five to four decisions. They controverted, fomented, and promoted the Law Revolution, thereby making a better life and law for all of us. Furthermore, they're a lot more interesting than those bland nine to zero sandlot baseball games.

Introduction

Melvin Belli is a *great* showman. Moreover he has all of the self-effacing modesty of a steam calliope in a circus parade. These dominant qualities tend to make the casual appraiser fail to appreciate the fact that the man is also a legal genius.

For years Belli has violated many of the traditions of the conservative lawyer—and has made the program pay off.

Where the average member of the legal profession would retire in conservative seclusion behind a modest legend on the door of a quiet office, Melvin Belli screams his name to the public in offices in the Belli Building and even charges the public admission to see where the great man works.

People who pay the price of admission and enter the office will find a profusion of law books, some of which are arranged with careful casualness in eye-catching positions.

These books will be by the master himself.

What escapes the casual observer, however, is the fact that these books are as different from the traditional law books as is Belli's personality different from that of the average lawyer.

Where most legal books deal with abstract principles, illustrated with key cases, Belli's books present a whole new, down-to-earth approach to the practice of law.

The average law student can probably learn more practical law, increase his legal efficiency in the courtroom, and do more to double his earnings by reading Belli's books than those of any other legal writer.

The books are crisp. They are crackling. They pull no punches, and they are intensely practical.

There can be no doubt but that we are engaged in a legal revolution. This revolution reaches from the reasoning of the Chief Justice of the United States Supreme Court down to the long-haired, raucous-voiced hippie who is screaming at a gathering of college students from a soapbox.

I can't look upon this legal revolution with the equanimity or perhaps the admiration indicated by Melvin Belli. On the other hand, I know of no other author who more pungently sums up that revolution in terms of actual, factual appraisal.

This man has made a terrific impact upon the administration of justice in this country, and, while the showman part of his makeup would probably resent the implication, he is a great teacher.

Today the whole practice of law in the field of civil liability has become changed because of the things Melvin Belli has done. He can no more be ignored or brushed under the rug than the atomic bomb can be locked in the closet.

Here is a great man, flamboyant, purposely dramatic, probably conceited, with a minimum of personal modesty, but one of the truly great legal authors, one of the outstanding trial lawyers of all time.

The lawyer who hasn't read Melvin Belli's books simply isn't up-to-date.

Erle Stanley Gardner

CONTENTS

FOREWORD

The Law Revolution: What Revolution? Whose Revolution?

How is it possible to have a Law Revolution? The two words are as compatible as cold fire and dry water.

The essence of the law is consistency, predictability, and constancy, as those ideas are summarized and intended in the words *stare decisis* (reliance on previously decided cases). A revolution is accompanied by plots and coups d'etat, by gunfire and barricades in the streets. Has this pattern begun in the American legal system? Not in the literal sense, certainly. But a review of the decisions of the United States Supreme Court—and of many of the highest state courts—of the past few years should argue that the winds of change are blowing strongly in the land.

For many attorneys and laymen, recent developments in the law have come as a shock. "What's happening to the law?" some ask. Others wonder: "is the law becoming a happening?"

Precedents are being discarded with what critics of the trend term a great casualness, and one member of the United States Supreme Court was so upset by current developments that he was moved to remark that his court's decisions were taking on the character of a railroad ticket: "good for this date and train only."

But the crucial factor that all critics of the Law Revolution ignore is that the primary genius of American law is its own ability to grow and to conform. This built-in capacity enables it to adapt to the changed sociological and technological era that we have entered.

This flexibility has always been fundamental to our legal system. But in previous generations, change has come with glacial movement—measured in slow inches. This was the law evolution, and has been a part of the system since Chief Justice John Marshall told the Congress in *Marbury* v. *Madison* (1803) that the Supreme Court, not the legislature, would decide what the Constitution said—and what it meant.

Today, one hundred sixty-five years later, the Supreme Court is still doing that job, called judicial review. But today, and for the past half-dozen years, the court's interpretations of the Constitution have at last begun to take account of the realities of the world outside the courtroom.

In its broadest terms, this has been the Law Revolution. Abstract legalisms, the Supreme Court has been saying, are all very well. But how well do these legalisms serve the needs of society as we enter the last third of the twentieth century? An unimplemented, academic clause guaranteeing "due process of law" cannot of itself be taken home in the market basket, nor can it guarantee a home next door to a more (or less) worthy neighbor. All of the individual's relationships, as they are affected by the law, are being reexamined in the light of dramatically different constitutional standards and theories.

The Law Revolution is here, like it or not, and it is important that everyone be aware of it. When you have finished reading this book, I'm sure you will agree with me that today's law is "where the action is." It's happening now.

Melvin M. Belli
San Francisco, California

CHAPTER ONE

Where the Action Is

Soon there will be a man on the moon—a live earthman. Passenger airplanes will fly faster than sound. Doctors will "grow" arms, legs, and other anatomical appendages. There will be voice writing and photo-telephoning. There already is "the pill" to interfere with human conception. Scientists are working in laboratories the world over to make other pills for faster human thinking, memory, and analysis to supplement the already mechanical brains, which unravel mathematical problems faster than ever we dreamed.

This world of science, engineering, and medicine is not based on *status quo* nor upon the law's *stare decisis* need to examine every past performance and decision. There's no dust on modern medicine's test tubes or space-shot machinery.

But what shall we lawyers suggest to the curious and imaginative youths who wish to choose a challenging, vital, and modern profession? What can we offer in the way of a profession that looks forward, not back; a discipline that ranges edges of frontiers, not somnolent courthouses?

Science? Medicine? Engineering? Pathology? Communications? Architecture? Yes, all of these, but why not the law?

Are we afraid to suggest our law as a profession for modern imaginative youth because, by comparison with other endeavors and disciplines, it's cobwebbed and unchallenging? It's not socially servicing? It's a remnant of old pettifogging?

Today's lawyer who thinks antiquity in law is its essential ingredient, who feels that law is and must forevermore remain a laggard in its discipline to perform primarily a braking purpose, has not read the opinions of courts of last resort during the last ten years. He continues to regard law as his particular servant, that law is for and serves him, not the layman.

But the true modern trial lawyer can recommend, without fear that his discipline will suffer by comparison with science and the other professions, his modern law as something that is as consonant with modern man's complex living as anything that's coming off the drawing boards or out of the test tubes. And we're just as *avant* in protecting the individual and his right to be, think, do, act, and live like one, as the most fervent pleas of the most offbeat, bearded protester. Indeed, that's the most complained of philosophy and opinions of the United States Supreme Court, that it takes too much care of the least of us.

The individual really has no place else to turn for redress than the law—the courts. An individual can't go to Congress or his state legislature without a lobby, a pressure group, or "friends!" Could Gideon, the individual, have gotten a hearing before the Florida legislature? Lenny Bruce's brand of individualism a listen anywhere but in a court?

Legislatures do legislate for the biggest of us but I don't think it too dramatic to say that as long as the Supreme Court gives its attention to the least of us, all of us will be safe. Certainly we can tell those student marchers at the University of California whose main and most modern complaint was placarded as "Don't turn us into IBM machines" that our law and courts are the only institutions today who are dedicated to preventing just that. And I do believe that the true spirit of the common law is: respect for the individual.

In its essence, the Law Revolution is about people with a grievance, people who have managed to have their grievance removed from the obscurity of some local trial court and elevated into the national arena of constitutional litigation.

Who are these people? Their names—Gideon, Mapp, Miranda, Escobedo, Murphy, Malloy, and many others—mean little if anything to the average citizen as he pursues salvation, or happiness, or both. To lawyers, however, each of these names is (or ought to be) fraught with significance. Each of these names represents a classic landmark in America's continually developing constitutional history.

In addition to having a grievance, all of the persons named had something else in common: they were unwilling to accept the judgment of a trial court where their grievance was disposed of in accordance with precedent and *stare decisis*. Because of this fact, and because the persons involved were willing to pursue their legal remedies to exhaustion—the story of the Law Revolution can be written.

The Supreme Court is the end of the road for all litigants. It is the Holy of Holies of the American legal system. Of the more than one million cases which are heard and decided in the American trial courts each year, less than one hundred fifty ultimately receive the benefit of a Supreme Court opinion during each term of the court. Of these one hundred fifty decisions only a few qualify as true Law Revolution cases. But it has been these few cases—perhaps a half dozen a term—which have made the revolution. And it is these cases which the Law Revolution is all about. The cases and the litigants who made the cases happen. For some it has been a bankruptingly expensive process; for others, who were indigent when they started on the long and torturous road to the judicial summit, it has meant just time, patience, and an unwillingness to quit when the odds were incredibly long. Before the revolution only the great corporate entrepreneurs fought their way up the ladder of the appellate process. Today, in our age of revolution, the great corporations are still there to be sure, but they are apt to find themselves on the same docket with a man who has never earned more than $50 per week in his life.

Heretofore equality of the law was for "everyone." By the language of state and federal constitutions, and from inscriptions on the facades of public buildings, one at least had the academic impression that everyone stood equal before the law. But before the Law Revolution, law was for the rich; not merely because they were rich but because they had the capacity to bend the law toward their own property rights with proper preparation purchased with ample funds.

The Law Revolution has changed that. The poor have become so protected that they've almost, by comparison with the rich, gotten more than their share of "equal protection." Judges politically are loath to "trample a worker's rights, stifle a picketing striker's boycott," or shortcut an individual from a minority group's professed rights. Indeed, now in some of our large cities, bar associations are loath to go after individual lawyers belonging to minority groups for unprofessional practices, i.e., Negroes, because of their immediate and embarrassing complaint of "persecution of minority."

In early times there was considerable special law consisting of rules and procedures applicable to the poor as a distinct class, but now there is a new concept in treating with the poor as a special class both for compensation and for raising their social as well as economic status in the American welfare system.

There's been more revolution in America's common and statutory law and constitutional law, federal and state, within the last ten years than ever before in our history excepting our initial revolutionary beginning!

But is it heresy for a lawyer to ascribe "revolution" to his profession that speaks primarily of *status quo* and *stare decisis?*

Law encompasses all man's complex and conniving doings. The sparks of all the sciences of the world may be raked up in the ashes of the law. And law is the cement that holds civilization together. So to be *cohesive,* there must *be certainty, predictability* in that law. The rules governing a contract made today must be just as valid and respected tomorrow.

If the certainty and predictability commodities of *stare decisis* and *status quo* are the essential ingredients of law, how then can we say a "revolution" within this law is consistent with its essence? Isn't "revolution" negation of law?

The answer is, at least for me, that we've had a "revolution" within our law but with due process. Predictability and certainty (*stare decisis* and *status quo*) are not absolute immutable terms. They are relevant and relative to the changed social, economic, and moral conditions of the times during which they are applied. They are immutable but at the same time must have a built-in commodity of growth to be consonant with modernity, otherwise they wouldn't be compatible; they'd be an out of context compatibility. Therefore, our law contemplated, necessarily considering not merely the exact moment of decision, but tomorrow, and itself gave birth to this built-in capacity of development—"revolution."

But most lawyers and judges refuse to admit there has been a "revolution" in our law. The very word "revolution" as with "overruled" in the law is anathema to the *status quo* and *stare decisis* thinking of out of context judges and lawyers of ancient bent. Revulsion at the thought of "revolution" causes some judges to torture constitutional language and language of prior decisions to say "We distinguish" or "We discover a different interpretation of that which was always there." They cannot bring themselves honestly to say "We reject" or "We overrule" even if these pronouncements are necessary to keep law from being archaic and impractical.

California's esteemed Roger Traynor, chief justice of the State Supreme Court, concurred with the majority of that court in the matter of *Escola* v. *Coca Cola,* a damage suit as a result of an exploding bottle. Liability, Justice Traynor said, rested with the manufacturer. This came at a time when the states were divided just about twenty-four to twenty-four in their thoughts about imposing liability on a manufacturer. (There is as much division between the courts of last resort in the several states sometimes as there is between individual United States Supreme Court justices.) Though writing with the majority, his reasons prognosed and prophesied that tort law in this country would abruptly "revolt" toward absolute liability, imposing responsibility for compensation upon him best able to stand the risk (perhaps by way of "warranty").

But that is the civil portion of the Law Revolution, and while that revolution comes first in chronology, we'll save that for another volume and move on to a 1964 California case, *People* v. *Pierce,* in which Chief Justice Traynor of the California Supreme Court brought his earlier prophesy to full flower when he expressed in the following words the spirit of the common law to hold that husband and wife could "conspire." They were to be henceforth no longer "one" as the common law had held to deny the operation of the law of conspiracy to them: defendants finally contend that the long-established rule formulated by this court would afford them immunity, should not now be overruled except by the legislature. In effect, the contention is a request that courts abdicate their responsibility for the upkeep of the common law; that upkeep it needs continuously as this case demonstrates.

If, indeed, our law has this built-in capacity to grow, to keep modern, then the priests of the law, the lawyers, may take heart that theirs is a noble and essential and modern and inspiring and imaginative profession serving all classes of mankind everywhere now, not historically and academically.

Were we not to take Justice Traynor's view of the future of the law that we, not necessarily legislatures, are charged with its upkeep, then the course of lawyers would be clear. It would be stilted *stare decisis* with the IBM machine substituting for the thinking of human brains. With *uniformization* and the present penchant for *standardized* rather than *imaginative* or *curious individual* thinking, the lawyer of the future would be but an adjunct to this IBM machine. He could be one of the similarly-dressed-standing-in-line-gray-flanneled-clerks to corporations, banks, and insurance companies where the real decisions and law upkeep is made at the lay level. His most imaginative task might be the occasional searching for a "loophole" in the old law.

I recall not long ago in Prague, Czechoslovakia, I spent a sober (without slibovitz) Sunday afternoon with the dean of the law school. He told me how he had just advised his daughter to leave the law school and go into engineering because lawyers under the Communist regime could look forward to nothing more stimulating than the drawing of an occasional contract between cooperative hog farms, setting up of accounting procedures, and being loaned from one department of government to the other to draft regulations of policies already determined.

But if Justice Traynor's injunction is to be followed, then the course of future law students is clear. It is the position of regained leadership.

Who shall set the morality of the community, temper its ideals, its ethics, and delineate its customs and business conditions other than the lawyer as the steward of the common law, that cement that holds all of us into communal living? The modern lawyer must zealously guard *stare decisis* and *status quo* where it is essential to understanding tomorrow of today and the sanctity of today's agreements tomorrow, whether private, contract, or statutory, but he must nurture his common law so that it will be the fairest flower in the garden—a consonant and relative flower not an ice age fern.

So I have no difficulty telling law students that their law is now searching for the stars, just as is engineering and architecture and space design. I can sincerely tell law students to study *ethics* and *philosophy* and *semantics* and *psychology* and *psychiatry* and *medicine* as adjuncts to their study of the law. I tell them that first they must be curious and imaginative to enter our temple.

Are these the qualities of the *stare decisist?* I tell them no longer are we like the ancients who argued all day about how many teeth a horse had, no one thinking of the expedient empirically of examining and counting them. I tell them that really there is a revolution, but an orderly and needed one, *naturally developing*, and torture is not done to human rights and vested interests but rather that human rights and vested interests are constantly protected—*with due process.*

We're not *coddling criminals* with our recent United States Supreme Court decisions, we're *protecting the individual accused* as never before, and, God forbid, maybe even you and me. And the fact that many thinking lawyers and judges now oppose capital punishment is to the credit of our law for, in opposing capital punishment, we admit that one of the biggest arguments against it is the capacity for error in this law of ours, that the all too final imposition of its sentence may be upon an innocent man.

Is it a deficit in our discipline to admit the capacity of our law to err? Not at all; it is a belated recognition that law, like humans, can err and when erring it expresses its greatest attribute—its *consonance with humanity.*

This recognition of this capacity of our law to err is another noble expression of our modern law, that of the now *humility* of those on high—judges and justices. No longer is there the arrogance of the Star Chamber king in our law, the implacable fiat of a Louis XIV—though perhaps some advocates of the old *stare decisis* and *status quo* might still desire even these ancient rules that were often more arbitrary than equitable, more often errant than "divinely right."

What is partly correlative and partly causative, but also most important to our revolution, is that a more knowledgeable layman is beginning to understand our law and its modernity. He is beginning to study it. Union men and lay leaders are no longer satisfied with esoteric terms and the "Oh, it's too complicated for you to understand." Our lawyers, too, are now beginning to explain controversial court rulings, what's back of them, what history provoked them, what economic conditions foster them.

And our "revolution with due process" has spanned the whole *corpus juris*, civil and criminal, domestic relations, tax law and administrative law, civil liberties, even the old no due process domain of immigration law and military law. It is just beginning to enter the domain of psychiatry and the law. All of this we shall see *infra*.

The historical restriction on the development of law which is embodied in the quotation carved on the National Archives Building in Washington, "Past is Prologue" from Shakespeare's *The Tempest*, is no longer relevant. Past is no longer prologue. Precedent for precedent's sake is no longer sanctified.

Our law is for the new and great society. As my Bishop-lawyer-theologian friend Pike says, it's "*where the action is.*"

CHAPTER TWO

Making a Revolution—Judicial Review

A. Am I Appealing? In 98 per cent of the cases which are tried in the law courts of the United States, there is no appeal taken nor any form of judicial review given. There are many reasons why this is so, primarily the cost to an appellant. But it is fortunate for all of us that the remaining 2 per cent exists because it is out of this selected group of litigants—a substantial number even so—that the substance of the Law Revolution has been made. This substance is a unique product of the Anglo-Saxon/American system of jurisprudence, and it arrives only when a judicial decision becomes "visible" to other members of the bench and bar. Visibility, in our system, means that the case is reported (published) in one of the official volumes of cases which appear with increasing frequency each year. As soon as a case is reported, it has meaning to and application for all of us even though we were not parties to the original litigation.

Collected in numbered volumes on the lawyer's shelves, these somber-hued tomes are The Law, because they contain the last or latest word concerning what the lawmakers (legislature, Congress) really meant when they wrote the law. This applies to the statutes, ordinances, regulations, and administrative rules which purport to govern our relations with government and our fellow man.

Collectively, these accumulated reported decisions are the

substance of the law: the flesh and blood hung on the skeleton which our elected officials have constructed while in Congress or assembled by legislature. Anyone with access to a law library can tell you what the law says, but it takes a judge from an appellate or higher court to tell you what the law means.

This brings us back to that dissatisfied 2 per cent who appeal cases which went against them in lower courts. In order for an appellate judge to interpret a law or laws in a visible, reported fashion, it is necessary that a litigant carry his case out of the trial court and into the appellate courts. Does this mean that every time a trial court decision is appealed a new law or interpretation will be made? Far from it. In perhaps 75 per cent of the cases which are appealed, the higher courts affirm the decision reached by the jury or the judge in the trial court. This is the appellate court's way of saying that the trial court's decision was the correct one, based on prevailing legal rules. In three-fourths of the remaining cases, where the trial court is reversed, the appellate court is merely saying that some error occurred in the course of the trial which made the outcome questionable. But in a few cases—really very few—new law is made.

This is known as judicial review, and it is a particularly sensitive field in the law because the judiciary alone, of the three branches of government, is supreme: the justices, not the legislators or executives (governors or the President), will say what is the law.

The layman complains "Why should our elected representatives in our state and national legislatures give us the laws we want only to have nine men (sometimes five to four) hold them unconstitutional?" This question was asked and answered a long time ago. It was answered even before Chief Justice John Marshall gave us our definitive answer in this country in *Marbury* v. *Madison.*

Every constitutional law book and the judicial review

decisions show that there was, long before the United States Supreme Court and our Constitution, a concept of a "natural law," a *de rerum natura,* a feeling that judges were the ones to say what was the law; that is, if anyone other than the king (in a non-democracy) was to say it.

The question was never practically put as to what the legislature (or the Executive) would do if they did not want to follow the "perverse" holding by a judge that their law was unconstitutional. Call out the militia? (The Supreme Court, of course, has no militia.)

President Lincoln sought practically to avoid judicial review by "packing the court." Probably the greatest criticism of judicial review came during the time of President Franklin Roosevelt. He, too, proposed "packing (enlarging) the court" with favorable justices so that the "will of the people would not be thwarted."

In retrospect, we see how the NRA and some of the other New Deal legislation really was unconstitutional as held by the United States Supreme Court.

Recently, a federal court enjoined a Congressional Un-American Activities Committee from proceeding. Right or wrong, it had the "power" so to order. And, what's more important, the exercise of this power by the courts has been accepted by "we the people" in whom sovereignty ultimately resides in this country.

Ultimately, any "unconstitutional" law may be made constitutional by amending the Constitution and submitting it to the voters, but even then, the Supreme Court will have a crack at the language, i.e., its interpretation.

Somewhat of a novelty in our Law Revolution has been the congressional hearing. Because of radio and television and other communications, the congressional hearing has become far more than a mere hearing—it has become a pillory. At any event, the congressional investigation has become high drama on television and of high publicity value to the legislators, who depend upon keeping their name and image before their constituents. However, considerable law has grown from these congressional hearings, e.g., the Fifth Amendment ramifications, waivers, contempt.

The fact remains that "new" law can be made and has been made when a case is affirmed on appeal. An excellent example of this involved the matter of *Gottschalk* v. *Cutter Laboratories,* the noted "polio case." (A fuller version of this case will be found in the civil law volume of *The Law Revolution.*)

The Cutter case was really a number of cases in which children had been given the Salk poliomyelitis vaccine. But the vaccine was more "Cutter" than "Salk" although Cutter confessedly was attempting to make Salk vaccine.

Somehow live virus remained in the vaccine and this was at a time when only the dead—killed with certainty—vaccine was being administered. The live attenuated vaccine had not been invented. The children got the dread disease from the vaccine, the very disease the vaccine was to prevent.

We sued Cutter Laboratories principally in breach of warranty rather than in negligence. The distinction is that we did not have to show, suing in warranty, that anyone was at fault. All we had to prove was that Cutter came to market with an unwholesome product and that this product was the proximate cause of the injuries.

Cutter fought this case through every court, although Cutter had agreed to abide by a first decision. On the side of Cutter was every medical and surgical society in Canada and the United States. This came as a shock to me because I felt that doctors and surgeons would want to be sure, for the benefit of their patients, that a substance they injected from a vial was safe and "wholesome." But apparently an unholy spirit of the medical fraternity (see Volume Two, *The Law*

Revolution on the medical conspiracy of silence) was stronger than the doctor-patient obligation.

When one starts a law suit, he looks for a comparable law. If he can find a case that stands up, then he's "home free." But, with Cutter, not only were there no such cases in world jurisprudence in all its history, there wasn't even a comparable case. So we had to make "new law." And new law was made when the cases were ultimately settled at around two million dollars after we had sustained the trial court verdicts through every court in California.

As a result of these cases, men, women, and children can now at least rely on monetary recovery if their drugs are not wholesome, and I am convinced that this warning to pharmaceutical manufacturers has made their supervisorial conduct more stringent.

In Volume Two, we'll see how this law has extended itself to automobiles, steering wheels, tires, inflammable clothes. In fact, the old adage "We stand behind what we sell" has now become the law rather than a huckster's blandishment. Now, Madison Avenue with its promises can create contracts along with purchasing desire.

I walked into a United States Circuit Court not long ago seeking to sustain $500,000 in a Quadrigen Vaccine case. That case is still *sub judicae* (under the court's consideration), so I'll only comment now that there were at least half a dozen major premises which some six years ago would have been bitterly contested as "not the law" but which now because of the Law Revolution were accepted without argument. This is a trend toward absolute liability, manufacturer to consumer, and this part of the Law Revolution was made by state courts and lower federal courts, very few of these cases having even reached the United States Supreme Court and little tort law in the Law Revolution actually has been made "on high."

Across the nation several thousand appellate decisions are reported annually. Merely to read them all would occupy the average lawyer full time; fortunately, the great majority can be ignored. Most attorneys read or scan quickly the only reported decisions of their own high state courts and the federal courts of their own district. Many attorneys rely on digests of legal or publication services which summarize important new decisions.

So here is the firing line of the Law Revolution: the fashioning of new legal rules by appellate court judges in the context of the appellate process which in turn affect (or control) the decisions of thousands of trial courts and other thousands of lawyers and litigants.

Many clients have walked out of their lawyer's office completely mystified after being advised that they had no chance to win in some potential litigation. The client was probably mystified because the lawyer had told him that *Jones* v. *Smith*, a case decided in 1919, would govern the result of his own litigation.

"So where's the Law Revolution that I read about," Mr. Prospective Plaintiff asks himself and his attorney, "if something that happened fifty years ago is affecting my rights now?"

A valid question. But the answer lies in the nature of the law's fundamental approach to problem solving, or case resolving. In the legal shorthand this is the concept of *stare decisis* which means that the courts will abide by or adhere to previously decided cases, at least insofar as the same principle of law is involved. To determine whether a given set of facts comes within an established rule of law or precedent is the substance of most litigation, from the trial court on through the appellate process.

In the most simplified form, the great majority of trials are simple "fact-finding" processes. Once the facts of the dispute are established, the law which is to be applied is easily seen. In criminal cases this takes the form of attempting to determine whether the particular accused defendant did the acts charged. If he did and he has no legal (i.e., lawful) defense, such as consent in a charge of rape of an adult, his guilt is established. This may sound neat and simple, but in practice the problem of distinguishing factual questions from legal questions can be quite complicated. The distinction is important, however, because the basic rule of appellate procedure is that the appellate court will not re-try the factual issues in a case. Thousands of litigants, convinced of the justice of their cause, have not been able to understand why their attorneys advised them to not waste their money on an appeal when the only issue in the case was a factual one.

But even with the noted limitation, many thousands of litigants are willing to bear the expense of taking their problem to an appellate court. In spite of the harsh reality of appealing, the appellate courts of the states are busier than ever. And the docket of the Supreme Court of the United States, the last stop on everybody's litigational highway, sees more cases filed on it each term than on each previous term.

And it is here that we find the stuff and substance of the Law Revolution. Because it is only when a legal decision becomes visible, that is—published in one of the official reports, that it becomes a part of the continually expanding legal structure.

A published opinion of a court becomes a new precedent (*stare decisis*) on which other courts and other judges can be expected to rely when reaching a decision in the cases before them. If a published opinion is the product of an appellate court in your own state, it is binding on the trial courts of that state—unless, of course, distinguishable on its facts from your case.

The essence of the American Law Revolution of the recent past has been the readiness, if perhaps not the eagerness, of the appellate courts across the nation to reexamine decided cases and the rules of law they contain. This reexamination has been undertaken by the judges in the light shed by advances in scientific, medical, and psychiatric knowledge, and in view of the changing conditions of society.

B. Fifty Sovereign States—but *One* Sovereign Supreme Court. Everyone who has taken a basic civics course knows that the United States is composed of fifty sovereign states—and the federal government. The state governments are organized very much like the federal government: each has an executive, legislative, and judicial branch. At the top of the judicial branch is the state supreme court (not always called that, but the idea is there) which is for that state the last stop on the litigational road for those who take their grievances into the law courts.

However, just as the federal Congress is paramount in certain specified situations (e.g., the power to declare war, coin money) the United States Supreme Court is also empowered to oversee (the polite word is "review") the activities and decisions of the fifty state "supreme" courts. This power is not absolute, to be sure, and is theoretically exercisable only in certain clearly defined kinds of cases. These are cases which present a "substantial federal question" or which arise under the Constitution or "laws of the United States," that is the enactments of the federal Congress. The Supreme Court derives this authority from the document which transformed thirteen more or less independent colonies into a nation—the United States Constitution.

But the Constitution, like all products of the hand of man, is a document composed of words, and words must inevitably be interpreted by other men using other words. In essence, this is a brief description of the Supreme Court's appellate jurisdiction. (The Supreme Court also has "original" jurisdiction in certain cases which are set out in the Constitution, but this type of jurisdiction has had little importance to the Law Revolution and does not need consideration here.)

The whole area of jurisdiction (especially federal jurisdiction) is one in which lawyers delight in arguing. For our purposes, however, it is enough to realize that the United States Supreme Court has the power in a proper case, to review the laws, ordinances, administrative regulations, and court decisions of all the fifty states and local political subdivisions, as well as the laws and administrative rules of the federal government. But it doesn't have to review any of these. Although there is a limited class of cases which are entitled to review by the Supreme Court as a matter of right (most often where a federal or state law is declared unconstitutional by a lower state or federal court), most of the Supreme Court's business is the result of granting a writ of *certiorari,* which it grants in a small percentage of the cases which are presented to it via petition during each term.

The writ of *certiorari* (latin for "to be informed of" or "to be made certain in regard to") is granted when the complaining, i.e., appealing, party to a lawsuit can convince at least four of the nine Supreme Court justices that his case is worthy of a full dress review by the court. But the writ is used sparingly, and is often denied in cases where the lower court's decision was obviously in error. Fred Vinson, a former chief justice, put it this way in a speech, "To remain effective, the Supreme Court must continue to decide only those cases which present questions whose resolutions will have immediate importance far beyond the particular facts and parties involved."

By thus limiting itself ("judicial abstention" it's called), the Supreme Court has managed to keep its work load at a manageable level—and also keep its relations with the state courts and the states themselves on a friendlier basis. The furor that has greeted many recent Supreme Court decisions, such as school segregation and those concerning police interrogation practices, illustrate the late Chief Justice Vinson's comment quoted above, while also revealing why the Supreme Court is necessarily the storm center of the Law Revolution, at least insofar as that revolution involves basic reinterpretations of constitutional requirements and doctrines.

But to a lawyer—and his long suffering client—the magic words "writ granted" by the Supreme Court of the United States is the ultimate accomplishment. The granting of the writ merely means that four of the nine justices believe the case presents a question or questions which are of sufficient importance to be worth review. It does not necessarily mean that four justices believe in the rightness of the appellant's cause, or the wrongness of the decision that is being attacked. It does mean, however, that the lawyer will have his opportunity to tell the court—through brief and oral argument—how and why his client was denied justice in a lower court.

But what are the odds against getting to the Supreme Court of the United States? Of the more than one million cases which are tried in the courts of the United States each year, less than two hundred are heard in the Supreme Court during its nine-month term. But the precedent value of these cases—the most visible of all decisions—is incalculable since each decision affects the course and outcome of hundreds or thousands of litigational situations prospectively.

The awesome power and authority of the Supreme Court is largely taken for granted by those involved in the judicial process, but the power is not explicitly conferred on the court by the Constitution as it might seem. The power resides in the court as a result of the court's own decisions. These decisions were reached in the context of cases which did not directly challenge the authority of the court, but did require the court to define its own powers relative to other branches of the federal government as well as the state governments. One of the Supreme Court's most critical powers—the right to review (and therefore decide differently) decisions of the highest state courts is a congressionally authorized power. It is called judicial review and is apparently completely misunderstood by some politicians, i.e., California's Governor Reagan.

The Judiciary Act of 1789—the law which established the federal court system—grants this power specifically to the court. During the nineteenth century a number of unsuccessful efforts were made to repeal this grant of authority and at least seven state supreme courts denied the constitutional validity of the grant of authority. However, the question has become moot since the ratification of the Fourteenth Amendment to the Constitution since, by judicial interpretation, no arm of the state government, including its courts, may deprive its citizenry of either "due process" or equal protection of the laws. With these highly elastic concepts at hand, the grant of authority from Congress is in all probability no longer necessary to give the court the power to intervene in state court determinations.

In theory the three branches of the federal government are coequals, bound together with the glue of the United States Constitution. It was settled early by the Supreme Court that the final authority on interpreting the Constitution had to reside in the court itself, thereby implying that acts of Congress could be—and would be—declared null when the court chose so to declare. The principle was announced in 1803 and has never been challenged seriously even though this decision, like all Supreme Court decisions, rests on the voting majority of the court at any given date.

The history of the court has been a sparing use of the powers it has claimed for itself. During the first half century of its existence (mostly under the leadership of Chief Justice John Marshall who served thirty-four years between 1801 and 1834), the judicial branch of the government entrenched itself solidly but carefully.

C. The Law as "Due Process." Although it was clear from the earliest days that the Supreme Court would be the "last word" on what the Constitution said (or meant) in any given situation, the range of the court's power was still limited in scope by the concept of state autonomy in its relations with its citizens. It should be remembered that the men who established the national government were concerned primarily with limiting the power of the federal government in its relations with the citizens of the states. The general feeling was that the states presented no problem as potential tyrants since the voters could easily correct any local abuses by and through the electoral process.

The Bill of Rights—the first ten amendments to the Constitution—was ratified in 1791 and was felt to provide all the protections needed against a tyrannical central government. But what happens when a state does violate one of the rights guaranteed by the Bill of Rights? Where may the aggrieved party go to get justice?

Prior to the Civil War, the court was able to read the "Great Instrument" as containing some protections for the individual against the activities of the state, most notably in the Dartmouth College case where a state law was held to violate the Constitution because it impaired the sanctity of a private contract. In other cases the court protected or limited state authority in areas primarily relating to commercial activities. Early court decisions construing the Commerce Clause of the Constitution made the United States a common market and prevented the raising of artificial tax and custom barriers among the states. But all this had little to do with human rights and the Supreme Court had, in so many words, rejected the idea that the Bill of Rights represented any limitation on the power of the states.

In *Barron* v. *Baltimore* (1833), Chief Justice Marshall could not find any language in the Constitution by which the Fifth Amendment's guarantee of due process could be extended to limit any other governmental body except the national government. So when plaintiff Barron alleged that certain actions of the city of Baltimore had deprived him of property without due process of law, the question before the Supreme Court was: does the city have to give such to Mr. Barron? Indeed not, thought the chief justice. The only restrictions on the actions of state (and lesser) governments was found in the Constitution's Article I, Section 9, which prohibits the passage of any Bills of Attainder or *ex post facto* (a "now" law to apply retroactively) legislation.

The problem was not as severe as it might seem, however, since many states had adopted constitutions which embodied the same guarantees as those found in the Bill of Rights. But not all the states had all these protections, so that when the Louisiana legislature acted to disenfranchise a number of slaughter house operators shortly after the Civil War, the Supreme Court again found itself contending with the problem first raised in *Barron* v. *Baltimore.*

The year was 1873 and the Civil War, less than ten years concluded, was fresh in the minds of the nine men of the court. Five years previously, the still-truncated union had ratified the second of the Civil War Amendments, the fourteenth. The abolition of slavery and involuntary servitude had been ratified in the Thirteenth Amendment in 1865. The thirteenth was the first addition to America's "Great Instrument" in sixty-one years. The thirteenth was clear and direct: it prohibited slavery or involuntary servitude (except as punishment for crime) and gave the Congress the power to enforce the amendment by appropriate legislation.

The Fourteenth Amendment presented a large grab bag of ideas which are still, after one hundred years, emerging from the language in constitutional litigation. The greatest bulk of controversy about the fourteenth has centered on Section 1, which contains four major components. First, the amendment provides a definition of citizenship—both state and national. It then lists three limitations on the powers of the states in relation to citizens of the United States. "No state shall make or enforce any law which shall abridge the privileges and immunities of citizens of the United States; nor shall any state deprive any person of life, liberty, or property, without due process of law; nor deny to any person within its jurisdiction the equal protection of the laws."

The New Orleans butchers, in the famed Slaughter House case, provided the first Supreme Court test of one of the amendment's key phrases, the privileges and immunities clause, as well as the other language of Section 1.

The Louisiana legislature had granted an exclusive charter to a corporation to provide slaughterhouse and butcher services in the city of New Orleans. Independent butchers, in order to operate, were required to pay fees to the chartered corporation. In a court test of the law, the Louisiana Supreme Court upheld its constitutionality; the independent butchers appealed to the United States Supreme Court, relying principally on the theory that the Louisiana law abridged their "privileges and immunities" as citizens of the United States. The language of the Fourteenth Amendment had been a part of the Constitution only five years when the case was decided by the Supreme Court.

The butchers argued that the Louisiana law so infringed on their right to make a living that it abridged one of the privileges and immunities of national citizenship. Their argument said that the right to ply their chosen trade was an incident of citizenship. But this argument did not appeal to a majority of the Supreme Court. By the narrowest of margins —five to four—the court upheld the Louisiana law on the ground that the right to work as a butcher or baker or candlestick maker was not one of the incidents of national citizenship. The butchers were asking the Supreme Court to spread over them an umbrella of "national" protections which would guard them against state action which was discriminatory or otherwise disagreeable.

As the majority of the court saw the question, the butchers were asking the Supreme Court to find in the language of the new amendment the authority to transfer to the federal government all the protections of civil rights which were formerly the concern of state governments. This concept was rejected out of hand as a step that would profoundly alter the relationship between the federal government and the states, reducing the states to the status of legislating with one eye on Congress and the federal courts.

The butchers also urged that the "due process" and "equal protection" clauses of the new amendment also required the court to hold the state Slaughter House Law unconstitutional. This theory got short judicial shift from the judges. In that era the idea that government should intervene in commercial affairs for the purpose of regulating economic relationships seemed to the court highly distasteful. The prevailing social philosophy of the day was Herbert Spencer's laissez faire individualism, buttressed by the new theories of evolution being circulated by the English biologist, Charles Darwin. The situation of the plaintiffs in the Slaughter House cases was to the learned judges of the Supreme Court a practical and real-life illustration of Darwin's theory concerning the survival of the fittest. The court's decision, it is important to note, was an opinion in context with the prevailing social thought of the times.

As to the argument of the butchers that the Louisiana law constituted a denial of due process, the author of the opinion, Mr. Justice Miller, threw in a classic piece of dictum relating to the purpose and reason for the inclusion of this language in the Fourteenth Amendment. It was, he felt, exclusively designed to protect the recently freed Negroes of the country from laws of the state governments which discriminated against them. In Justice Miller's words, "We doubt very much whether any action of a state not directed by way of discrimination against the Negroes as a class, or on account of their race will ever be held to come within the purview of this provision."

As a consequence of the Slaughter House cases decision, the "privileges and immunities" section of the Fourteenth Amendment has never bulked large in constitutional litigation; the "equal protection" clause has found application in a variety of situations (most notably the 1954 school desegregation decisions), but the "due process" clause has since become the touchstone of the whole Law Revolution. By it and through it, the entire panoply of "rights" which protect the individual from the intrusion of any overreaching government have been grafted onto the American legal structure. The mechanism in use here—the due process clause of the Fourteenth Amendment—has been successively held to incorporate the basic protections of the Bill of Rights. This process, which proceeded gradually during the amendment's first eighty-five years, has picked up momentum during the past fifteen years—the era of the Law Revolution.

The history of the due process clause in the years immediately following the decision in the Slaughter House cases is something of a study in judicial irony. In 1877, the court was again called upon to invalidate a state law on the ground that it violated the protection of this clause. However, in this later case, *Munn* v. *Illinois,* the economic shoe was pinching the other party's foot. Illinois had a statute which permitted regulation of the rates charged for transporting and warehousing grain. The big money was behind the grain storage and transporters, primarily the railroads. The court was consistent in its holding that even though the power to regulate rates could be abused, thereby denying a fair return on investment, it was not the problem of the Supreme Court to protect the railroads and warehouse owners. The polls, not the courts, was the place to look for help, the court said.

This decision so outraged the Establishment, according to legend, that it led to the formation of the American Bar Association—whose initial membership sought to protect their big business clients from the confiscatory tactics of Populist-oriented legislatures. (And it is only in recent years that the American Bar Association has been forced by some of its more "liberal" members to concern itself with human versus property rights.)

It did happen finally that the doctrine of the *Slaughter House Cases* v. *Illinois* was overruled—at least insofar as the right of business to operate without the constrictions of "socialistic" legislation, which became popular in the wake of the post-Civil War industrial expansion.

The related questions—first raised by the New Orleans butchers—concerning the relationship between the due process clause and the rights of an individual as against, or in relation to, his government was left in some constitutional limbo for many years. The "personal" due process question did get before the Supreme Court in 1884 when defendant Hurtado challenged the California procedure of using a district attorney's information to charge an "infamous (felonious) crime." The Bill of Rights (Fifth Amendment) specifies that such a charge may only result from a grand jury indictment. The court reviewed the California practice and, finding nothing in it that was repugnant to the current theories of due process, added this prophetic language: "The due process clause, by reason of its operation upon all the powers of the government, legislative as well as executive and judicial, could not be appraised solely in terms of its sanction of settled usage."

The court went on to note that arbitrary power, even when it is the will of the multitude, could not operate to deprive any citizen of his basic rights under the Constitution. Unfortunately for Hurtado, the right to indictment by a grand jury is not one of these basic rights, and an information—a written complaint issued by a district attorney—did the job just as well.

For many conservatively oriented years, however, the principal application of the due process clause was in the business sphere, as the court shot down law after law which meddled with the prevalent theories of laissez faire economics.

Individuals, primarily defendants in state court proceedings, got little of value from the Fourteenth Amendment in their relations with the authorities, in spite of the language found in Hurtado. At one time or another, convicted criminals attempted to graft one or more of the protections of the Bill of Rights onto the states, but with virtually no success until 1961 when *Mapp* v. *Ohio* showed the way. As late as 1947, in *Adamson* v. *California,* the court held that the self-incrimination provisions of the Fifth Amendment do not apply to the states. As late as 1958, that the double jeopardy provisions of the Sixth Amendment are not violated when a defendant is prosecuted in consecutive trials for the robbery of four persons, all at the same time.

The great constitutional debate of the past twenty-five years has centered on what has become known as the "incorporation" question. Stated in its simplest terms, it asks only:

which of the provisions of the Bill of Rights are incorporated into the Fourteenth Amendment's due process clause and thereby are operative on the fifty state governments? The Law Revolution has principally been concerned with finding more and more of these rights until today the incorporation is virtually complete. The revolution has in a large sense been of, by, and with due process of law. In the chapters that follow we will examine the landmark cases that have made the revolution and reshaped American constitutional theory. If the revolution can be summarized in a few words these might be: "the Bill of Rights is now a code of criminal procedure for all citizens, whether in state or federal court."

CHAPTER THREE

You Can't Come In!

The six members of the Cleveland, Ohio police department who forcibly entered a private residence one pleasant spring day in 1957 certainly did so without any notion that they were to become principal actors in a great constitutional drama.

Acting on information that the home of a Mrs. Doralee Mapp and her daughter harbored a fugitive who was being sought for questioning about a recent bombing, the officers acted. Armed with further information that Mrs. Mapp's home contained a quantity of gambling paraphernalia linked to a numbers game, the police asked permission to search the home. They had no search warrant with them and were promptly refused admittance by Mrs. Mapp. But enter they did, nevertheless, and in the course of an extended search of the house they found an assortment of books they judged to be lewd and lascivious. Since possession of this material is a crime under Ohio law, Mrs. Mapp was arrested. She was later tried and convicted for the possession of lewd and lascivious material, thereby setting the stage for the first great engagement of the Law Revolution.

Police assertions about the presence of a "fugitive from justice," "illegal numbers game material," and the actual discovery of contraband on the premises might have added up toward making Mrs. Mapp sound like a modern Ma Barker. But in fact Mrs. Mapp was a rather mild-mannered proprietress of a boarding house who claimed to be innocent in fact and knowledge of all the charges.

Her sense of outrage at the arrest and conviction led her through successive appeals in Ohio courts. She lost all of them. Ultimately, her case was heard by the United States Supreme Court, which granted a writ of *certiorari* primarily on the basis of her claim that the Ohio law which made possession of lewd books and pictures a crime was unconstitutional because it violated the First Amendment's guarantees of freedom of speech. Although the Fourth Amendment question was raised and argued, it was apparent that Mrs. Mapp's attorneys felt they were on firmer ground with a First Amendment challenge. Only eight years prior to Mrs. Mapp's arrest, the Supreme Court had decided, in *Wolf* v. *Colorado,* that the Fourth Amendment's protections—the right of citizens to be free in their persons, property, and effects from unreasonable searches and seizures—did not apply to the states through the Fourteenth Amendment's due process clause. This was not a right which was "implicit in a concept of ordered liberty," as Justice Cardoza had phrased it twenty-five years earlier when attempting to cope with the question of which of the rights guaranteed by the Bill of Rights were also binding on the states.

In the Wolf case, the court had been presented with the problem and had flatly declined to extend the rule with its protections. The crux of the problem, as the court viewed it in Wolf, was that in order to make the protection of the Fourth Amendment meaningful to those criminal defendants who had been victims of illegal searches, it would have to announce a basic rule of evidentiary exclusion binding on all state courts. In deference to the federal system, it declined to take this step.

So this background here: in 1914 the court did create such an exclusionary rule, but it had limited its application to the *federal* courts, even though it had blandly said at the time that the rule was of constitutional origin.

At the time it decided Wolf, the court, through Justice Frankfurter, told the states that they should reexamine their procedures and, in effect, encouraged them to adopt the Weeks rule, a much earlier Supreme Court decision which had held that the federal government could not use the product of illegal search and seizure in a federal prosecution. The opinion noted that thirty of the then forty-eight states did not adhere to Weeks. Typical was New York, which, in 1926, had rejected the exclusionary rule in a classic opinion by one of the great judges of the American judiciary. In *People* v. *Defore,* Judge Cardoza asked the famous question: "is the criminal to go free because the constable has blundered?" He answered his question with a large *no.*

Progress in this area of search and seizure was slow and uncertain but some states did change the rules as time and experience accumulated. California "bought" Weeks in 1955 when the conviction of a Los Angeles bookmaker by the name of Cahan got to the State Supreme Court. Associate Justice (now chief justice) Roger Traynor served notice on law enforcement officials that henceforth they must act within the law in their efforts to control crime.

No one involved in the original "bust" of Mrs. Mapp knew it, but the winds of constitutional change were soon to blow strongly in the land. In 1960 the court discarded the so-called silver platter doctrine when it held (*Elkins* v. *United States*) that a state official could not turn his illegally seized evidence over to a federal official on a silver platter to use in a federal court prosecution—or vice versa (*Rea* v. *United States*) four years before that.

Into this constitutional setting came Mrs. Mapp—her

broken front door, her dirty pictures, and her lawyers. The opinion of the court was written by the recently-retired, often-conservative Texan, Justice Tom Clark. Never noted for a passionate espousing of causes of persons accused of crimes, Mr. Justice Clark on this occasion looked deeply into the Constitution and found a pervasive "right of privacy" whose protection it was the obligation of the Supreme Court to enforce. And enforcement of this right could only come by closing the courtroom door to evidence obtained by official lawlessness in flagrant abuse of the constitutional rights. Justice Clark was moved to comment upon Judge Cardoza's lament about blundering constables in the following rhetorical flourish. "The criminal goes free, if he must, but it is the law that sets him free. Nothing can destroy a government more quickly than its failure to observe its own laws, or worse, its disregard of the charter of its own existence."

In this way the protections of the Fourth Amendment became "implicit in the concept of ordered liberty," and thereby applicable to the individual states through the Fourteenth Amendment. But not without a fight! Three and perhaps four justices dissented in an opinion by Justice Harlan which sharply criticized the majority for judicial adventuring, deciding cases on a basis that it could easily have avoided. But subsequent decisions of the court in this area have reinforced the original decision.

The problem that a case such as *Mapp* v. *Ohio* presents to the Supreme Court is a great deal wider than the immediate problems of Mrs. Mapp and her dirty pictures. In the prisons of thirty states, at the time the case was decided, were men whose convictions were based on evidence which was obtained in violation of the rules laid down in Mapp. Logically (and the law is nothing if not logical), the prison doors should have swung wide for this great mass of criminals, at least to the extent of providing them a new trial without the tainted evidence. However, when squarely confronted with the problem, the Supreme Court, seven to two, said, in effect, "too bad" (*Linkletter* v. *Walker*). The irony of Mr. Linkletter's plight was found in the fact that his conviction had been affirmed by the Louisiana Supreme Court prior to the time that the Ohio Supreme Court had affirmed Mrs. Mapp's conviction, even though his crime was committed after Mrs. Mapp's. The question before the house is therefore: does the Supreme Court "make" law or discover the law that is? By denying Mr. Linkletter's petition for a writ of *habeas corpus* (his time for a direct appeal to the Supreme Court via the customary writ of *certiori* had long since run out), the court in effect said: "we *make* the law."

A. Bugs, Finks, and Wiretaps—Somebody Out There Is Listening. Recently there was a considerable stir created by the revelation of Hal Lipsett, a San Francisco private eye testifying before Congress, that the state of his art of electronic eavesdropping had reached the point where it was possible to "bug" the olive in a martini. The news made good cocktail party conversation ("Do two olives give you stereo reception?") for a time, but for most of us that was the end of it.

Not for our Supreme Court, however, and much as they might like the problem to go away, it won't. Or it hasn't. At every term of court since 1927, there has been presented at least one case which causes the justices to walk a judicial tightrope between the anchor points of the constitutional protection of privacy and the need for efficient law enforcement.

The problem was first put into the constitutional focus in 1928 when an assortment of bootleggers (the country was in the midst of the "noble experiment") got to the Supreme Court after their federal court convictions of violating the

Volstead Act. Olmstead and his co-defendants were not small-timers with a backwoods still; they were Big Business, running booze in fast boats from Canada into Washington state. Their downfall came about because much of their business was conducted via telephone (one line of which, with a high degree of accuracy, ran directly into the Seattle police station!). The feds got most of the evidence they used to convict the rumrunners via wiretaps. For a minority of the court the case offered a clear-cut situation in which the justices were able to philosophize at length on the constitutional questions involved. However, the convictions were affirmed on the simple theory that no Fourth Amendment search and seizure right was violated by federal telephone tapping, since such activity could not be considered either a "search" or a "seizure" within the meaning of the amendment.

Of course, the fact that the framers of the Bill of Rights neglected to mention the telephone as a protected area may have weighed heavily in the majority's decision. The fact that the telephone was almost one hundred years away from being invented at the time the Fourth Amendment was adopted did not disturb the author of the prevailing opinion, Chief Justice Taft, former President of the United States.

Olmstead is still interesting today because it was one of the first cases to come to the Supreme Court in which the new age of technology clashed head-on with traditional human and personal values. The court's handling of the problem was disappointing, but hardly unexpected considering the nature of the case (big time bootleggers, police collusion) and the times. Subsequent developments robbed the case of most of its vitality as a constitutional precedent, but it remained on the books as good law until June, 1967, when the Supreme Court reexamined the basic question of the Fourth Amendment and wiretapping in *Berger* v. *New York.* There, a state law which permitted wiretapping on the authority of a judicial warrant was invalidated as violating the "penumbral" right of privacy which is now implicit in the protections of all the Bill of Rights' amendments.

During the years between the Olmstead and Berger cases, the court was called upon to cope with this basic problem in the context of increasingly sophisticated electronic detection and surveillance equipment. The Supreme Court's Monday morning "quarterbacks"—the erudite gentlemen who write for the law reviews produced by the nation's law schools—found the court's decisions in this area to be a fertile source of generally critical comment. For the most part, the decisions created a patchwork of rules and regulations that really did not limit the practice of bugging, wiretapping, or electronic eavesdropping—merely made it more complicated to use the evidence which was obtained in this way. Thus, the states were left largely to make their own rules, if any at all, and enforce them as they saw fit. Most of the cases which reached the court during this interval originated in the federal courts and were concerned with the "white collar" defendant: tax evaders, customs avoiders, and other managerial kinds of criminals.

The Law Revolution finally came to grips with the technological revolution on the last decision day of the 1967 Supreme Court term. On that date the court, through retiring Justice Tom Clark, gave its decision in the case of *Berger* v. *New York*, another constitutional landmark. Berger did at last what dissenting justices since Oliver Wendell Holmes and Louis Brandeis had been suggesting. It overruled *Olmstead* v. *United States* (1928) by holding that telephone conversations, as well as other forms of private communication, are protected by the Fourth Amendment. And, by applying *Mapp* v. *Ohio*, it held that these same limitations on wiretapping applied to state as well as federal action.

The problem in the Berger case was presented by a New

York law which very broadly permitted almost any law enforcement official, on a minimal showing of need or probable cause, to get judicial authorization to bug a home, office, or other theoretically private place. In its five to four decision, the court held that the law was unconstitutional because of its broad sweep and lack of protection for the individuals affected.

The defendant Berger was one of a number of persons involved, according to the New York district attorney, in a conspiracy to bribe the chairman of the New York Liquor Authority for the purpose of obtaining favorable treatment on liquor license applications. Berger was not one of the victims of the wiretapping-eavesdropping operation, but information obtained through this means was essential to gain his conviction for participation in the plot. His role in the proceedings is not entirely clear, but as a public relations man he was apparently cast as a go-between, or perhaps the word is fall guy. Whatever his relationship to the alleged shady doings, his conviction by the New York courts at last provided the vehicle for the Supreme Court to ride into the twentieth century—the century of Big Brother.

In a sentence that provides the keynote to the opinion Justice Clark notes that: "The law, though jealous of individual privacy, has not kept pace with advances in scientific knowledge." This Supreme Court judicial confession was followed by a historical review of the Fourth Amendment, its pre-Colonial antecedents in England, and its incorporation into the Bill of Rights as a prophylactic measure designed to prevent the notorious English Writs of Assistance which permitted the authorities to make a general search for incriminating materials. The Fourth Amendment's requirements of particularity and definiteness, Justice Clark pointed out, were a free society's most effective guarantee of continued freedom.

After reviewing the principal cases which have refined the doctrines of the Fourth Amendment, Justice Clark points out that the New York wiretap law involved in the Berger case has a great deal in common with the despised Writs of Assistance. At this point the opinion moves into the kind of balancing act which has been popular in the court's opinions in recent years: the need for wiretaps as a tool to combat organized crime versus the right of the individual to be free in his home, office, etc., from the intrusions of governmental authority.

The scales of justice in this situation come down on the side of the individual: the New York law is too broadly drawn, too general in its application, and contains no safeguards for protecting the privacy of individuals who are not guilty of anything.

Whether or not a permissive wiretap law *could* be written which would satisfy the court's requirements is an open question. In the view of the dissenting Justices Black, White, and Harlan, the answer is no. It is doubtful that many state legislatures will feel it worth the effort even to try, although this door was left slightly ajar.

In the view of Justice Hugo Black, the constitutional literalist, the court's decision is wrong because in order to reach the result that it did it was necessary either "to rewrite the Fourth Amendment or rewrite the New York wiretap law," neither of which is proper. The other dissenters agreed that there was nothing constitutionally defective about the New York legislation.

Does the Berger decision answer all the questions that the various privacy invasion situations have presented to the Supreme Court—as well as to the state courts? Probably not, in view of the special factual background of Berger and the sometimes confusing "privacy" decisions of the court during the preceding years. In a series of cases involving Jimmy Hoffa, his friends, and his troubles with the law, the court has had to grapple with an assortment of challenges to the use of evidence gathered via a variety of devices, including planted informers with tape recorders. The court, in deciding these cases, fell back on the verbal formula which it had announced in 1963 in the case of *Lopez* v. *United States:* "it has been insisted only that the electronic device not be planted by an unlawful physical invasion of a constitutionally protected area."

B. Merely Evidence—or the Real Thing? The Fourth Amendment has been somewhat complicated by an exception carved out of the body of knowledge dealing with three categories of objects that the courts have traditionally held exempt from search and seizure rules. Stated generally, the courts have tended to uphold the seizure of items which are actual fruits of the crime (stolen goods), instruments of a crime, or contraband.

Let's look for a moment at a hypothetical case that, in fact, occurs with surprising frequency. Assume that the police have reliable information that your home contains merchandise taken in a recent burglary. Armed with a search warrant that has been properly drawn and executed, the police present themselves at your front door. You have no choice except to allow them to enter and search. In the course of their pawing through your belongings, they come upon a quantity of a ground-up green substance that has been left there unknown to you by a friend. Sure enough, the substance is marijuana. You are promptly arrested for possession, and the stolen goods, which actually gained police entry into your home, are forgotten.

Your subsequent conviction for possession of the marijuana will stand up since the officers have legally entered your home, even though marijuana may have been the last thing on their minds when they entered. Marijuana is contraband, and as such, it is legally seizable.

But suppose the situation is different. The police have

information that you are a marijuana dealer. They enter with a warrant that claims information that a quantity of marijuana is to be found on the premises. Instead of finding any marijuana they find instead a personal diary in which you have recorded your transactions as a peddler. May this be seized and used in evidence against you?

The answer depends on whether the officers were federal agents or state officials and further on which state you live in. Some states would characterize such a record as "mere evidence" and refuse to admit it at a trial; others would ignore the so-called mere evidence rule and allow it to be introduced. At this stage of the Law Revolution there are no uniform federal standards on this question. A federal court would probably not permit the evidence to be used, but even that question is not free from all doubt. Two Supreme Court cases, apparently undistinguishable on their facts, reached opposite conclusions in similar situations, *Marron* v. *United States* (1927) and *United States* v. *Lefkowitz* (1932). In California, the diary would be admissible but in New Jersey probably not.

This kind of inconsistency is probably unavoidable in a federal system, but it seems that some uniform rules are necessary or desirable—especially when constitutional issues are involved. This is one of the open-ended battles of the Law Revolution still to be fought and settled by a Supreme Court position that comes down unequivocally. The court will have to decide whether the so-called intimate relationship between the Fourth and Fifth Amendments operates to exclude "mere evidence" of a crime—even when it is acquired through an otherwise legal search and seizure.

CHAPTER FOUR

"I Wanna Lawyer"

"See my lawyer" is an expression of majestic finality. Likewise, the activity occasioned by that ultimately desperate plea "Get me a lawyer!" has caused more legal and lay comment than perhaps any other expression of current time. And, at least to me, quite naturally, the next great change in law took place with respect to the Sixth Amendment, right to counsel.

The landmark case of *Betts* v. *Brady* held that the Sixth Amendment and the right to counsel did not extend to the states through the Fourteenth Amendment. Thus, a defendant in a criminal case in a state court did not have the absolute right to counsel. (*Betts* v. *Brady* was a six to three decision.)

Not until 1963 in *Gideon* v. *Wainwright* did the United States Supreme Court reverse itself and overrule *Betts* v. *Brady*.

Gideon v. *Wainwright* (seven to two) held that the defendant in a criminal case in a state court has an absolute right to counsel. The court held that the Fourteenth Amendment extended the right to counsel to the states and that the Sixth Amendment thereby had full application in state proceedings. As a practical result of the decision, *Gideon* v. *Wainwright*, courts are providing counsel in all criminal (misdemeanors as well as felony) cases. But the full impact of

Gideon really is not yet clear. For example, does it have application to traffic citations, etc.? (My prognosis: it does.)

"I refuse to answer that question on the ground that it might tend to incriminate me." This is an expression of no less majestic finality than the request of a client for a conference with his lawyer, because one of the first things an individual is told upon his arrest is that he does not have to say anything which might incriminate himself. In fact, he is usually told this even before he is told that he may have a lawyer, or that a court will appoint a lawyer for him if he is not able to afford one of his own choosing.

So closely linked are these two functions, the right to counsel and the immunization against self-incrimination, so well interwoven are these constitutional guarantees—they are derived from the Sixth and Fifth Amendments, respectively—that I am going to discuss them in the next two chapters.

I've heard lawmakers and attorneys call the Fifth Amendment to the Constitution an important advance in the development of liberty and one of the great landmarks in man's struggle to make himself civilized. But I can remember back to the days when a great many million Americans who witnessed the congressional committee hearings of the fifties wondered about the wisdom of having the privilege against self-incrimination in the Constitution.

In spite of the fact that those witnesses who "took the Fifth" were known hoodlums or persons suspect of destroying the very Constitution they hid behind, the self-incrimination privilege of the Bill of Rights survived the fifties without a serious threat.

Now, in the era of the Law Revolution, the Famous Fifth not only remains as one of the most vital principles of American democratic government, it has been broadened in scope and infused with even more remarkable vigor by recent United States Supreme Court decisions.

The privilege of immunity from self-incrimination was a part of the English common law derived from an equitable maxim, "no man is bound to accuse himself." It was originally adopted because the chancellors of the ecclesiastical courts had the habit of putting a defendant under oath whether he liked it or not. At earlier common law, the accused in a felony case was considered incompetent to testify on his own behalf. Compelling a man to *testify* against himself offered a poor set of choices: self-accusation, perjury, or contempt. However, because the rules of evidence permitted testimony to be received in a trial concerning statements (admissions) of the defendant made at prior occasions, the defendant's immunity from compulsory testimony lost most of its significance when officers of the law told juries that the defendant had "copped out" while he was being interrogated about the crime. For this reason the Supreme Court very early established the rule that when a defendant's admissions amounted to a full confession of guilt, it became the burden of the prosecutor to convince the judge that the confession was in fact free and voluntary, *Bram* v. *United States* (1897).

The Bram case, however, was mostly forgotten by later courts because the rules concerning the admissibility of confessions were thought to be governed by the court's general supervisory power over the lower federal courts and its power to regulate conduct of prosecutors and judges in those courts. This supervisory power avoided the need to decide self-incrimination questions on constitutional grounds—an approach the court much preferred.

Still the question of the relationship between the Fifth Amendment, the Fourteenth Amendment, and state criminal proceeding would not just go away. The question was given an extended analysis for the first time just sixty years ago in *Twining* v. *New Jersey*.

In that case the defendants failed to testify in their own

behalf in a theft prosecution and the state commented on this fact in closing argument as was permitted by local law. Was this comment on the exercise of the privilege a denial of due process of law as required by the Fourteenth Amendment? After an exhaustive review of the history of the privilege and how it got put into the federal Constitution, the court concluded that there was no reason to conclude either that (1) the privilege was an essential component of due process of law, or (2) comment upon its exercise by the prosecution was, as such, an infringement upon the assertion of the privilege.

The Twining point of view prevailed as settled constitutional doctrine without serious question until 1964, when the Law Revolution at last caught up with the Fifth Amendment. In *Malloy* v. *Hogan,* the Twining case was finally overruled, in principle, although the specific question raised in Twining was not answered in the defendant's favor until *Griffin* v. *California* (1965). In the meantime, the court had been confronted with a series of cases that raised the self-incrimination problem—primarily those involving confessions obtained through outright torture. The first of these was *Brown* v. *Mississippi* (1922) in which a conviction was reversed because "compulsion by torture to exhort a confession is a different matter."

In case on case the court adhered to its original constitutional viewpoint: the privilege against self-incrimination was not a part of the Fourteenth Amendment's rights imposed upon the states. This was the rule as late as 1961, but then the court decided *Mapp* v. *Ohio* and, with that case as the thin end of the wedge, the solid doctrinal front of *Twining* v. *New Jersey* was split open, permitting all sorts of new doctrinal theories to spill through. Mapp, it should be remembered, was a Fourth Amendment (illegal search and seizure) case which had elements of the Fifth Amendment mixed into it. The court had reached back to a case of where a far more conservative court had seen the Fourth and Fifth Amendments "almost running into each other" to prevent unreasonable invasions of the individual's privacy by agencies of the government—federal or state. The worst of the state abuses were corrected through the basic due process clause, and the court uniformly reversed state court convictions based upon "coerced" confessions when the activities of the local gendarmes got too far out of hand.

The court kept telling state law enforcement agents that "ours is an accusatorial, not inquisitorial" system, and as such the devices used to extract a confession from a suspect must conform to those standards "implicit in a concept of ordered liberty." In spite of all the flowery words, however, cases reached the court at every term in which some variation on the coerced confession theme was played. Holding a suspect incommunicado for periods of days while relays of police interrogators worked him over was a favorite theme of the cases. Physical abuse was common in the earlier days and in the cases coming out of the South. In the more sophisticated North, the usual complaint was about psychological coercion. Police interrogation manuals of recent years have suggested various methods of extracting information from reluctant suspects—methods which do not involve the classic third degree. The most favored is known generally as "Mutt & Jeff." A team of questioners works on the suspect. One of the two plays the hard, brutal type and the other, the nice guy. The nice guy explains to the suspect (when the hard guy has left the room) that he (nice guy) is afraid for the suspect's well-being because his partner is such a monster, etc. The suspect will normally make a full confession to the nice guy—if only out of gratitude for a few kind words. Is this coercion? Probably yes, but more on this below.

The case that finally settled the question—*Malloy* v.

Hogan—arose out of a criminal contempt conviction in the state of Connecticut. The defendant Malloy had been convicted of a gambling offense some years prior to the present situation. He had done his time (ninety days) and was apparently free of further problems. The state, however, was making a general inquiry into the subject of gambling and felt that Malloy had information which it could use. Malloy, standing on a claim of self-incrimination privilege (guaranteed by Connecticut law), declined to answer a number of questions concerning his prior gambling connections and activities. He was adjudged to be in contempt and was committed to prison until he could see the error of his ways.

The Supreme Court threw out his contempt conviction on the theory that the state had violated the Constitution by failing to apply the "federal standard" as the test of whether Malloy had properly asserted the self-incrimination privilege. The federal standard in these matters differs from the state standard for invoking the privilege, and the Supreme Court was persuaded (or persuaded itself) that the local standard was the wrong one. Although the language of the Fifth Amendment section relating to the self-incrimination problem is plain, numerous Supreme Court decisions have refined the nature and extent of the privilege—all in federal cases and for the guidance of the federal courts and federal administrative bodies. The most recent of these definitions (at the time Malloy was decided) was found in *Hoffman* v. *United States* (1961) where the court said: the privilege afforded not only extends to answers that would in themselves support a conviction . . . but likewise embraces those which would furnish a link in the chain of evidence needed to prosecute . . . if the witness, upon interposing his claim, were required to prove the hazard . . . he would be compelled to surrender the very protection which the privilege is designed to guarantee. To sustain the privilege, it need only be evident from the implication of the question, in the setting in which it is asked, that a responsive answer to the question or an explanation of why it cannot be answered might be dangerous because injurious disclosures would result.

Connecticut argued that its own standard was not different than the federal standard and also that Malloy was running no risk of self-incrimination because the matters into which the inquiry was being pressed were beyond the one year statute of limitations for misdemeanors, and also Malloy could plead the defense of double-jeopardy in any possible prosecution based on his answers. Fiddle-faddle, said the court. The questions were designed to determine who Malloy had been working for when he was convicted on the gambling violation. This information, the court figured, could lead to other information which might reveal evidence of more recent crimes by Malloy. Again, quoting from the Hoffman case, the court ruled that the federal standard required the judge to be "*perfectly clear* from a careful consideration of all the circumstances in the case, that the witness is mistaken, and that the answer(s) *cannot possibly* have such a tendency to incriminate."

Malloy was a pure "incorporation" decision, but of and by itself made little difference to the states. Although it held that the due process clause of the Fourteenth Amendment incorporates the self-incrimination provision of the Fifth Amendment and thereby applies to the state criminal procedures, no great hue and cry was raised about the decision, primarily because every one of the fifty states had, either by constitution or statute, adopted this "landmark in man's struggle to make himself civilized." For this reason the decision made virtually no practical difference in the administration of criminal justice in the states. It merely gave state court judges a uniform national standard to apply when attempting to determine whether a given individual was correctly claiming the privilege. Superficially, the decision in Malloy could be viewed as a logical extension of the new ground that had been broken by *Mapp* v. *Ohio* decided in 1961. The Mapp case in fact had some Fifth Amendment (self-incrimination) overtones—at least for several of the justices who wrote concurring opinions.

The idea that an illegal search and seizure (at least of private papers) and their use in a criminal prosecution was a *de facto* form of self-incrimination had been suggested as far back as 1886 and cited with strong approval in Mapp.

With the decision in *Malloy* v. *Hogan,* the privilege against self-incrimination in the Fifth Amendment was clearly extended to the states by means of the Fourteenth Amendment. However, there remained still one other obstacle. This was the so-called *comment rule.*

In forty-four of the states, the rule was that the judge and the district attorney could not comment on the failure of a defendant to take the stand to testify. That is, they could not infer (comment) that by the defendant's refusal to take the stand he was guilty.

However, in six states, including California (the latter by state constitutional amendment), the judge and the district attorney were allowed to comment on the failure of the defendant to testify.

After the United States Supreme Court made its decision in *Malloy* v. *Hogan,* the California Supreme Court faced the problem as to whether the decision in *Malloy* v. *Hogan,* extending the Fifth Amendment privilege to the states, made unconstitutional the California rule allowing comment on the failure of the defendant to explain or deny any evidence produced against him.

An excellent example of this conflict in action came in 1936 when I tried my first case before a courtroom situation filled with ironies. My client was Louis Gosden, on trial for his life in a homicide case. My antagonist was district attorney of Alameda County, one Earl Warren. The case, known in legal records as *People* v. *Gosden,* was the first decision under the then new California constitutional provision permitting the judge to "comment on the failure of the defendant to take the stand." The comment in Gosden was not only the *facts* but the *punishment.* The judge told the jury, after defining the law for them, that they must find "extenuating circumstances" to reduce capital punishment to life in prison. The judge then stated, *"I have been unable to find any."*

Today, as the result of *People* v. *Friend,* a California case of 1957, even an instruction to a jury that they must find "extenuating circumstances" in order to reduce capital punishment to life in prison is considered a reversible error. A jury can reduce a sentence without facts or reason and do so *arbitrarily.* (This brings up the interesting question: is a juror, therefore, qualified who arbitrarily disbelieves in capital punishment? And I answer now, reading this query in manuscript before the latest Supreme Court opinions—Yes.)

The Gosden comment on evidence and on the punishment is one of the most brutal we have seen in modern American jurisprudence. Defendant Louis Gosden was executed. He appeared before the courts just thirty years too soon for his life to be saved. The then district attorney, Earl Warren, who vigorously urged defendant Gosden's conviction and execution would now have had to reverse it as chief justice of the United States! I had appealed to that very court on the grounds now recognized. We were turned down. The Law Revolution had not yet started.

But more help is now on the way. In *People* v. *Morse,* decided in 1964, the California Supreme Court, overruling many prior cases, held that in the penalty phase of a first degree murder, it was reversible error to give an instruction and to allow evidence in argument which invited the jury's consideration of the possibility that the Adult Authority might at some future date grant parole to a defendant if he were given a life sentence.

Whether or not the prisoner is granted parole is a matter lying within the expert judgment of the Adult Authority, not within the jury's province. Instructions or evidence on the authority's possible granting of a parole invite speculative argument to the jury and surmise by it of the possible and probable release of a defendant on society in the future. (It's interesting to note here that over on the civil side a somewhat analogous problem presents itself. Can a jury be instructed that a personal injury award is income-tax exempt, or is that too speculative?)

The doctrines of the Fourth and Fifth Amendments "apply to all invasions on the part of the government and its employees of the sanctity of a man's home and the privacies of life. It is not the breaking of his doors, and the rummaging of his drawers, that constitutes the essence of the offense, but it is the invasion of his indefeasible right of personal security, personal liberty and private property. . . . Breaking into a house and opening boxes and drawers are circumstances of aggravation, but any forcible and compulsory extortion of a man's own testimony or of his private papers to be used as evidence to convict him of a crime . . . is within the condemnation . . . (of those amendments)." It was here that the Supreme Court—in 1896—found that the Fourth and Fifth Amendments ran into each other.

However for the dissenting justices in Malloy, the problem was not that easily solved. Justice Clark, who wrote the opinion of the court in Mapp, dissented from the conclusion reached in Malloy and joined an opinion written by Justice Harlan which was highly critical of the majority holding. Justice Harlan pointed out that as recently as 1961 (the year of Mapp) the court had flatly stated that the Fifth Amendment did not apply to the states. Now, a mere three years later, the court reversed itself. The casual attitude toward precedent did not concern Justice Harlan as much as the extension of the new doctrinal theories into previously sacred areas. "The ultimate result [of this approach] is compelled uniformity, which is inconsistent with the purpose of our federal system and which is achieved either by the encroachment on the states' sovereign powers or by dilution in federal law enforcement of the specific protections found in the Bill of Rights," according to Harlan.

The old standard of due process of the law is all that is needed to answer the question: did the defendant get a square deal in the state proceeding? The rule requires the states to deal with their citizens in a spirit of fundamental fairness. "Such an approach may not satisfy those who see in the Fourteenth Amendment a set of easily applied absolutes which can afford a haven from unsettling doubts. It is, however, truer to the spirit which requires this court to constantly reexamine the fundamental principles and at the same time enjoins it from reading its own preference into the Constitution."

The real significance of the Malloy case did not become apparent until two years later, when the United States Supreme Court gave forth its decision in the matter of *Miranda* v. *Arizona,* which, in my opinion, may be the most significant decision in the field of criminal law ever written by an appellate judicial body.

With one mighty blast, the Supreme Court rewrote the entire book of police custodial interrogation techniques. The exact grounds for the decision in Miranda were not made crystal clear in the opinion of the court which was written by Chief Justice Warren. Nevertheless, Mr. Chief Justice Warren noted that "the reasoning in Malloy made clear what had already become apparent—that the substantive and procedural safeguards surrounding the admissibility of confessions in state cases had become exceedingly exacting, reflecting all the policies embedded in the privilege . . . The voluntariness doctrine in state cases, as Malloy indicates, encompasses all interrogation practices which are likely to exert such pressure upon an individual so as to disable him from making a free and rational choice."

Miranda is important, heady stuff, and I'm going to devote an entire chapter to the magnificent implications of it. But before we move on to Miranda, I think we should investigate two other decisions of the Supreme Court which anticipate it, were further logical extensions of the *Malloy* v. *Hogan* rule, and are true Law Revolution cases.

A. My Kingdom for a Lawyer. The need of a king for a horse was once so great that in depreciation he offered his whole kingdom in exchange. Some defendants find themselves in positions where they would gladly exchange all their worldly goods for a lawyer—at least the Supreme Court now supposes that the United States Constitution so considers.

In *Escobedo* v. *Illinois* the defendant, Danny Escobedo, was implicated in the gunshot death of his brother-in-law. Chicago police took him into custody and interrogated him in a police station. He was handcuffed, forced to remain standing, and questioned by police officers during a four-hour period.

In the meantime Escobedo's attorney had been contacted and had arrived at the police station asking to see his client. The request was refused, even though the defendant was at that same time asking the officers to permit him to consult with the lawyer. Eventually he confessed to the crime. At his trial the confession was admitted into evidence, and he was convicted of the crime. The Supreme Court reversed the conviction, but in doing so broke some new constitutional ground—apparently. The reversal could have been based on the finding that the confession was involuntary. "The ultimate test remains, that which has been the only clearly established test in Anglo-American courts for over two hundred years: the test of voluntariness. Is the confession the product of an essentially free and unconstrained choice by its maker? . . . If it is not, if his will has been overborne and his capacity for self-determination critically impaired, the use of the confession offends due process."

This was Justice Frankfurter's language in one of his last opinions rendered in 1961, and in this very area just before his retirement from the court.

Three years later, the court abandoned this two-hundred-year-old standard of the Anglo-American legal system in favor of a radically new standard. Or was it a new standard? The Escobedo decision said something different to everyone who read Justice Goldberg's finely-reasoned prose. The Supreme Court said, in a frequently quoted paragraph: "We hold only that when the process shifts from the investigatory to the accusatory—when its focus is on the accused and its purpose is to elicit a confession—our adversary system begins to operate, and, under the circumstances here, the accused must be permitted to consult with his lawyer."

Some courts took this to mean that the Sixth Amendment's guarantee of the right to have counsel, made mandatory on the states through the 1962 Supreme Court decision of *Gideon* v. *Wainright,* applied as soon as the individual was taken into custody—providing he asked for such help. Others found that Escobedo can be interpreted as a logical extension of the Malloy theory of the Fifth Amendment right. Still others regard the case as just another reversal based upon the use of an involuntary confession admitted at trial in error.

Whatever the court or Justice Goldberg may have actually intended to mean, the decision became a kind of do-ityourself kit for lawyers, police, and judges. If the case were limited to its facts, it would only have application when the defendant was in custody, being questioned, or asking for his attorney, and the attorney was outside banging on the door to get to his client.

Some states—notably Alabama, Florida, Illinois, Nebraska, Nevada, and New Jersey—took the position that the right enunciated in Escobedo applied only when the defendant expressly requested counsel.

One of the state courts which gave the broadest and most liberal meanings to Escobedo was California. This came up in 1965 in *People* v. *Dorado*. Bobby Dorado was a San Quentin convict who was involved in the stabbing death of a fellow inmate. Prison authorities (and members of the local district attorney's office) investigated the crime, primarily by interrogating the defendant. The California Supreme Court, promising its holding on *Escobedo* v. *Illinois,* found that a confession was improperly secured, chiefly because Dorado was never advised by the interrogators that he had a right to remain silent and not answer any questions concerning the crime. So far as is known Dorado never asked for the help of a lawyer. It is a safe guess that Dorado had played the interrogation game before, yet the court was successfully persuaded that if the elements of "custody," "focus," and interrogation were present, the right to have counsel present arose, *ipso facto*. Since Dorado was not advised of this right (although arguably he was well aware of it), his confession was improperly used at his trial. Conviction reversed.

To show the exactness of the Supreme Court's frame of mind in the matter of right to counsel, even a lawyer is entitled to a lawyer. And in California this right is passed along as the court's affirmative duty to ascertain whether the defendant desires counsel and to assign counsel if defendant is unable to procure representation.

As this text is being written, former Los Angeles County Deputy District Attorney Jack Kirshke stands convicted of the first degree murder of his wife and her boyfriend, Orville Drankham. At one point during his trial in the Los Angeles County Superior Court, defendant Kirshke did represent himself. But it was implicit at all times that Kirshke was entitled to counsel and that the court was bound to appoint one for him if he lacked the necessary funds to hire one. Also at this writing, the Kirshke case is on appeal.

To quote from the appeal record of a relevant California case, "Under the [United States] Constitution and law, a lawyer who is accused of a crime is equally entitled in every stage of his trial to the presence and aid of counsel . . . with other persons. . . . The rights of individuals in this respect are not to be gauged by their profession or occupation."

The outcry which greeted the Dorado decision in California reached classic dimensions. Police and prosecutors uniformly viewed it as the beginning of the end of effective law enforcement. The late Chief William Parker of Los Angeles—a tough cop of the old school—called the idea that modern investigative techniques could substitute for the lack of a confession "absurd!" (his exclamation mark).

But in support of its decision to extend the Escobedo rule before being compelled to do so by the Supreme Court of the United States, the California court said that its function was not merely to follow a Supreme Court opinion but "to enforce it in situations wherever it logically applied." Morever, the California court was concerned that if it waited several years for the Supreme Court of the United States further to define the Escobedo rule, convictions had in California in the interim might be subject to reversal, and the work of law enforcement officers would "come to naught."

Subsequent California cases have indicated that there are four points necessary to invoke Dorado. These are: (1) investigation must no longer be a general inquiry into an unsolved crime but must begin focus on a particular suspect; (2) the suspect must be in custody; (3) the authorities must have carried out a process of interrogation that lends itself to eliciting incriminating statements; (4) the authorities must not have effectively informed defendant of his right to counsel or of his absolute right to remain silent and no evidence must have been established that he waived these rights.

One of the consequences here is the elaborate lengths such semidocumentary television shows as *Dragnet 68* use to warn the accused of his rights to remain silent and to have a lawyer present. Although such dramas with police protagonists may seem to labor these points with a bit of heavy sarcasm, it is a fact that California police are bound to inform suspects and individuals who are arrested of their rights. Copying from a card offered by the San Francisco police, I present here their "Specific Warning Regarding Interrogations:

1. You have the right to remain silent.
2. Anything you say can and will be used against you in a court of law.
3. You have the right to talk to a lawyer and have him present while you are being questioned.
4. If you cannot afford to hire a lawyer, one will be appointed to represent you before any questioning, if you wish one."

There is a space for signature, and a box which the interrogating officer may check if the suspect refuses to sign the card. In the matter of making the waiver of rights stick, there are these words addressed to the interrogators:

After the warning and in order to secure a waiver, the following questions should be asked and an affirmative reply secured to each question:

1. Do you understand each of these rights I have explained to you?

2. Having these rights in mind, do you wish to talk now?

The police interrogation room is not the only place where the individual is able to protect himself with silence. The language of the United States Supreme Court in *Griffin* v. *California* defined the issue and answered a very basic question: what about the defendant who does not take the stand on his own behalf?

"Comment on the refusal to testify," the court said, "is a remnant of the 'inquisitorial' system of criminal justice [citing cases] which the Fifth Amendment outlaws. It is a penalty imposed by the courts for exercising a constitutional privilege . . . [and] cuts down on the privilege by making its assertion costly."

The court recognized that there are a number of reasons why a defendant might prefer not to testify at his trial. These reasons might have no relation to the guilt or innocence of the particular charge. For example, evidence of a defendant's prior criminal record may not be presented to a jury by the prosecution, except in certain limited situations. However, if a defendant chooses to testify in his own behalf the prosecution is permitted to impeach his credibility (i.e., attack his truthfulness) by presenting evidence of any prior felony convictions. The theory behind permitting such impeachment is grounded on the premise that any man who has committed a felony is less apt to tell the truth under oath. Whether or not this theory is correct, the usual effect of having the defendant's prior convictions before the jury is to convince them that the defendant is a "bad guy" and convict on that basis.

Even where defendant has no prior criminal record, defense attorneys often, as a matter of trial strategy, prefer to protect their clients from the rigors of cross-examination. A defendant who is slow-witted (really most criminals are not too bright) or who angers easily will make a bad impression on a jury. And cross-examination is the heart and guts of the American adversary system, both civil and criminal. The most effective prosecutors are the most adept cross-examiners and defense attorneys realize that their clients are no match in a battle of wits with an experienced district attorney.

Before Griffin, the defense lawyer was put between the rock and the hard place when deciding whether to permit his client to testify. If he chose to keep him off the witness stand, he was apt to hear something like the following in the prosecutor's closing argument: "This defendant had the right to take the witness stand, it is a privilege afforded to him and he did not do it. You can consider that with all the testimony, and I ask you to consider it. In conclusion . . . does the defendant get on the witness stand and say under oath, 'I am not guilty?' Not one word from him, and not one word from a single witness."

The preceding, by the way, was not made up by me for this book. It is taken from the prosecutor's final argument to the jury in the California case of *People* v. *Adamson* (1946). The defendant was convicted of murder. His death sentence was affirmed by the California Supreme Court without a dissent. References by the prosecutor (District Attorney Ernest Roll of Los Angeles County) to Adamson's failure to testify were made seven times during his summation to the jury, but Adamson's attorney had failed to make any objection. This was good enough for the Supreme Court of California: failure to make objection at the time waives the right to object to the conduct on appeal. The court could say this, even though it knew that such an objection by an attorney merely calls attention to the statement and emphasizes it to the jury.

To be sure, Adamson fared better in the Supreme Court of the United States: his conviction was affirmed by a five to four decision. Unfortunately, being close only counts in horseshoes not in courts of law. Adamson was twenty years ahead of the particular aspect of the revolution that would have kept him out of San Quentin's Green Room. His plea—that California's rule permitting comment on his failure to testify violated his Fourteenth Amendment rights—was accepted by Justices Black, Douglas, Murphy, and Rutledge. The majority opinion, written by Justice Reed, could find nothing constitutionally obnoxious in the California law which was attacked: "The due process clause [of the Fourteenth Amendment] forbids compulsion to testify by fear of hurt, torture, or exhaustion. It forbids any other type of coercion that falls within the scope of due process."

Merely to permit the jury to consider the natural inference that can be drawn from the failure to testify was no due process violation. In the words of Justice Reed: "It seems quite natural that when a defendant has opportunity to deny or explain facts and determines not to do so, the prosecution *should* bring out the strength of the evidence by commenting upon defendant's failure to explain or deny it [emphasis added]."

The court reaffirmed the rule of the Twining case (similar fact situation) decided thirty years earlier, although it did have the grace to point out that if the same situation had occurred in federal court, the conviction would have been reversed as a violation of the Fifth Amendment right. But Twining had held that privilege against self-incrimination was not one of the privileges or immunities of national citizenship and the individual states could, if they chose, abolish it entirely.

As for the objection on due process grounds, the court could rely on Justice Cardozo's opinion in *Palko* v. *Connecticut* (murder prosecution, state appealed from a finding of second degree homicide, new trial ordered, defendant convicted of first degree murder, sentenced to death, appeal based on violation of Fifth Amendment double jeopardy provision, conviction affirmed). Justice Cardozo reached the conclusion that the second prosecution of Palko did not deny him due process of law because the double jeopardy prohibition of the Fifth Amendment was not one of those guaranteed freedoms which are "implicit in a concept of ordered liberty" —the so-called natural law formulation of the problem. This approach left the court free to make up its mind, on a case-by-case basis, whether a given confession was the product of coercion or whether a certain state procedure measured up to the standards of due process that the particular Supreme Court majority found acceptable at the time.

In the course of adhering to this approach (starting with *Brown* v. *Mississippi* in 1936, where the defendant's confessions were admittedly the result of blatant torture), the Supreme Court agreed to hear (i.e., review) better than thirty "confession" cases—mostly in capital punishment situations —and reversed the state court ruling in most of them. The progression in the many cases that reached the court for decision showed the following characteristic: the forms of coercion became increasingly more subtle by the police officers. The court became more willing to find the necessary due process violation in its review of the "totality of the circumstances" of the confession objected to. In theory each decision of the court in this sensitive area redefined the rules for local police agencies as they pursued their duty of apprehending criminals.

A few of the totality of the circumstances that the court was finding important during its thirty-year sojourn through the wilderness of police practices included: length of time of questioning, denial of opportunity to call or speak to family, education (or lack of same) of the suspect, type or nature of the coercion employed.

The problem with such an approach was the inconsistent results created. But then, a consistent rule for inconsistent human conduct is perhaps asking too much. For example, a young man who was arrested for the homicide of his sometime landlady-mistress, and who had the misfortune to have completed one year of law at UCLA saw his conviction affirmed by the Supreme Court because "he knew his right" to keep silent during the eight or ten hours he was held incommunicado and questioned by relays of police officers (see *Crooker v. California,* 1958).

However, three years later a case reached court in which a younger man confessed to a brutal murder-robbery at a gas station after a period of prolonged detention. This conviction was reversed because (although the majority opinion by Justice Frankfurter does not expressly so state) the defendant was mentally defective—a moron who had spent six years in the third grade and finally gave up on schooling at sixteen (*Columbe* v. *Connecticut,* 1961).

The two cases contained many other factual distinctions, but in reading the opinions disposing of them, it seems apparent that Crooker's death certificate was signed when he completed that first year of law school; Columbe's freedom was assured when he dropped out of school at sixteen. The irony of the cases is that from a reading of the record and the various court opinions it seems clear that the Los Angeles police had enough circumstantial evidence to see Crooker convicted, without a confession. In Columbe's case virtually all of the evidence used was a product of the defendant's various confessions. Without them he would have probably never been charged with the crimes. Although the guilt of each man was not seriously questioned, the results that were reached could not have offered much help to local law-enforcement agencies in their need to operate down at the nitty-gritty level within the court's variable rules.

The Crooker-Columbe cases present fairly clear-cut situations: Crooker "knew" he had an absolute right to remain silent while being questioned by the police—because of his law school training. (However, constitutional law—where he would have learned this interesting fact—is not taught in most law schools until the second year!) Columbe, because of mental retardation, may never have heard of the Bill of Rights or the Fourteenth Amendment. But what of a suspect who is a graduate student in engineering? Or one who has had three years of college? Or less?

This variable standard, applied by the court whenever it was confronted with a confession case in which a Fourteenth Amendment (due process) violation was alleged, was dubbed the "totality of the circumstances" test and had as its underlying theory the premise that the reason coerced confessions should not be relied upon for conviction is because they are "untrustworthy evidence." This was the idea advanced in *Lisenba* v. *California* (a 1941 case where the defendant killed his wife by forcing her foot into a rattlesnake cage. She didn't die quickly enough after the rattlesnake named "Lightning" bit her, so he drowned her!) and relied upon by the court in the great bulk of confession cases decided after that.

In 1964, however, (the year of Escobedo and Malloy) the court came to grips with a situation that had long disturbed their poise and decisions: the problem of the confession which is the product of effective psychological coercion. In *Jackson* v. *Denno,* the court recognized in so many words that law enforcement had become too sophisticated to be governed by the rules of the earlier, cruder era. Although the case was actually only a way station along the road to a much more spectacular destination and has much less impact in light of recent decisions, the case is worth examining in some detail both for the light it sheds on prevailing police interrogation procedures and for the concepts about the nature of custodial interrogation and its effect on the person being questioned.

The defendant, Jackson, had been convicted of first degree murder in New York after a trial in which his confession had been an important element of the prosecution case. After running the gamut of direct appeals from his conviction (the Supreme Court had refused to hear his appeal), the defendant launched what is known as a collateral attack on the conviction by petitioning a federal district court for a writ of *habeous corpus,* contending that the New York procedure for determining the voluntariness of a confession violated the Fourteenth Amendment. After losing in both the District Court of Appeals and the Circuit Court, Jackson again petitioned the United States Supreme Court for a hearing. On his second try, he was successful.

What had happened in Jackson's case was the following. Jackson and a lady friend had gone to a hotel in Brooklyn at about one in the morning. After registering, the lady friend left the hotel and Jackson drew a gun and took money from the room clerk. As he left the hotel the defendant came upon his female companion and a police officer. Both men drew their guns and the police officer was shot and killed. Jackson was seriously wounded by two shots in the body. He hailed a cab and was taken to a nearby hospital. The hospital reported the condition of the patient to the police and a detective questioned him there shortly after his arrival. At 4:00 A.M. of that same morning and despite his wounds, Jackson was administered demerol and scopolamine and was questioned by an assistant district attorney. The conversation was recorded by a stenographer. During the course of it Jackson admitted the shooting and admitted that he "got the drop" on the dead cop. Jackson underwent a three-hour operation for his own bullet wounds shortly after this brief interrogation—and, remarkably, lived to stand trial.

At his trial he could not recall the conversation with the district attorney, but he did testify in his own behalf to the effect that the dead police officer had pulled his gun first and shot first. The confession was admitted into evidence without objection by Jackson's attorney.

When Jackson was tried, New York had an unusual procedure to be followed in criminal trials when a confession was introduced in evidence by the prosecution. If the defendant, by his own testimony or other evidence, challenged the confession as being the result of coercion, the court (judge) was required to instruct the jury concerning the use they could make of the confession as evidence. The jury first had to find that the statements made by the defendant amounted to a confession. That if this fact were found, then that the confession was true. And finally that the confession was voluntary—i.e., not coerced.

If they found the confession was coerced, they were instructed that they must "disregard" it and reach their decision in the case based upon the other evidence, if any, which was presented in the trial. The judge did have the initial burden of deciding whether "in no circumstances the confession could be deemed voluntary," in which case it could not be used in the trial. But if reasonable men could differ as to whether the confession was voluntary, it became the jury's job to decide both voluntariness and the weight to be given the confession. (Most American states required the trial judge to give a full hearing, out of the presence of the jury, on the voluntary question. This hearing was "on the record," so to permit a reviewing court to determine whether the question of voluntariness was fully considered before the ultimate question of guilt or innocence was decided.)

The practice followed in *People* v. *Jackson* in 1960 had received the court's seal of constitutional approval as recently as 1953 in the case of *Stein* v. *New York* where an identical question had been raised. At that time the court affirmed three first degree murder convictions with the words: "The people of the state are also entitled to due process of law."

In the era of the Law Revolution a somewhat differently constituted court could easily find that the Stein decision rested upon some unsound assumptions, particularly the one that any jury could reach the conclusion that a confession was involuntary, exclude it from consideration, and thereupon convict the defendant solely on the other evidence in the case. But the court said this is unreal: "If it finds the confession involuntary, does the jury—indeed, can it—then disregard the confession in accordance with its instructions? If there are lingering doubts about the sufficiency of the other evidence, does the jury unconsciously lay them to rest by resort to the confession?"

The mere fact that a confession may be truthful is not enough to justify its use in a trial: "It is now inescapably clear that the Fourteenth Amendment forbids the use of involuntary confessions not only because of the probable unreliability of confessions that are obtained in a manner deemed coercive, but also because of the 'strongly felt attitude of our society that important human values are sacrificed where an agency of the government, in the course of securing a conviction, wrings a confession out of an accused against his will,' and because of the deep-rooted feeling that the police must obey the law while enforcing the law; that in the end life and liberty can be as much endangered from illegal methods used to convict those thought to be criminals as from the actual criminals themselves."

The court wrapped up its opinion by noting that often the only way a defendant can dispute the issue of voluntariness is through his personal testimony—and putting on him this burden is hardly fair since once he takes the witness stand he becomes fair game for impeachment on his prior criminal record if he has any. Further, since there can be no recorded information concerning the jury's resolution of the question of voluntariness, the judge's initial determination takes on aspects of finality for purposes of appellate review. The effect here is to make it even more difficult for the defendant to reach the constitutional issue on appeal. The jury's verdict does not state: we found the confession involuntary, but there was enough evidence to convict, even without it. The verdict is merely guilty or not guilty. The defendant has no way of knowing (for appeal purposes) whether his claim that the confession was coerced was accepted by the trier of fact.

After its review of the New York procedure, as it was employed in the Jackson case, the Supreme Court found the method was not constitutionally sound. Nevertheless, it did not reverse the conviction out of hand. Instead the case was remanded (sent back to the state court) with the instruction that the question of the voluntariness of the confession be subjected to a full hearing—either by a judge, or judge and jury. If the confession was then determined to be voluntary, the original conviction would stand and Jackson would suffer the penalty originally imposed. However, if the confession was determined to have been involuntarily obtained, he was entitled to a new trial—but without the use of the confession by the prosecution.

Since the days of the Inquisition, the confession was the ticket of verity. Yet in the Law Revolution we've learned that man's words about his own self are not necessarily legal, nor are they necessarily accurate psychologically. Physical and mental torture, fear, self-destruction, and confabulation—the inventing of additional details which may or may not be true —are just some of the aspects that make a confession anything but accurate.

That's one side of the problem the layman, who has been complaining about the Supreme Court and the Law Revolution, is not familiar with. But what this individual "knows" is that the Supreme Court has been "coddling criminals" and making it so tough on the police that all the guilty are going free. Sheer rubbish. But too many police and law enforcement officials have spread the word. Mr. J. Edgar Hoover has been the most vocally errant.

The *Jackson* v. *Denno* decision gave the Law Revolution a healthy shot in the arm in this matter. It spelled out to the states once again the news of the Supreme Court's attitude toward state criminal prosecution procedures. The protections of the Fourteenth Amendment were being drastically extended (overextended, according to some critics) to guarantee state criminal defendants something called "fundamental fairness" in their prosecutions. One problem created by this new view was summarized by Justice Harlan in his dissenting opinion in Denno: "If the concept of due process has a little stability as this case suggests, so that the states cannot be sure from one year to the next what this court, in the name of due process, will require of them, surely they are entitled at least to be *heard* on the question of retroactivity."

Another consideration—one more basic to the entire concept of federalism or of parallel federal-state judicial systems—was also pointed up by Harlan's dissent. "It should not be forgotten that in this country citizens must look almost exclusively to the states for protection against most crimes. The states are charged with responsibility for making the area of criminal conduct when it occurs, and preventing its recurrence. In this case, for example, the crime charged—murder of a policeman who was attempting to apprehend the defendant in flight from an armed robbery—is wholly within the cognizance of the states. Limitations on the states' exercise of their responsibility to prevent criminal conduct should be imposed only where it is demonstrable that their own adjustment of the competing interest infringes rights fundamental to a decent society."

Justice Harlan felt that this change of approach in deciding constitutional issues would do a "serious disservice to the healthy working of our federal system in the criminal field."

The decision in *Jackson* v. *Denno* was announced on June 22, 1964, a fateful day for law enforcement in the United States. *Escobedo* v. *Illinois* had been announced the same day. Both cases had been under consideration by the court for several months, Jackson since December, 1963. That same month of June produced another decision which cut deeply into the fabric of American jurisprudence, overturned existing precedents, and generally signaled the birth of a whole new era in constitutional theory. The case itself—*Murphy* v. *Waterfront Commission of New York Harbor*—was not a dramatic new departure simply by reason of its holding. In the Murphy case, the issue was the right of a witness testifying at an administrative hearing to claim the privilege against self-incrimination (and thus refuse to answer questions) when he had been granted immunity from state prosecution, but not from possible federal prosecution.

The case arose when Murphy and an associate were subpoenaed to testify at the bi-state Waterfront Commission hearings into the causes of a work-stoppage at a Hoboken, New Jersey pier. The commission offered the witnesses immunity from prosecution by New York and New Jersey but could not extend this immunity to any potential violation of federal law that might be revealed. The witnesses refused to answer certain questions and were subsequently adjudged to be in contempt.

The Supreme Court, in a rare (these days) nine to zero decision, reversed the convictions although four justices concurred in the judgment on less sweeping grounds than the opinion of the majority advanced. That opinion said, in substance, that since the Fifth Amendment's self-incrimination privilege was binding on the states through the due process clause of the Fourteenth Amendment, it must consistently follow that no one jurisdiction in the United States could compel a witness to give testimony which would incriminate him in any other jurisdiction, notwithstanding a local grant of immunity.

A considerable amount of history and theory went into the majority opinion, written by Associate Justice Goldberg. Boil it down and you have the court saying that the Fifth Amendment privilege is an absolute one. Any limitation on it or qualification of it constitutes an impermissible invasion of a constitutionally protected right. This view of the privilege as an absolute, not a relative or qualified right, made the case important for decisions to follow, *Griffin* v. *California* (1965) among the most notable of these.

It was not until June 13, 1966, that it became apparent to lawyers, Supreme Court buffs, and constitutional theorists that the past was merely prologue. On that date the court decided four cases consolidated for purposes of the decision and opinion under the name of *Miranda* v. *Arizona*. The four cases presented similar fact situations for review. In each of them, the defendant had been arrested on information furnished police concerning a recent crime or series of crimes. In each, the suspect was interrogated over a period of hours and eventually either signed a written confession or made oral admissions of guilt which were recorded by the interrogating officers. In each case these confessions or admissions were used by the prosecution in the course of the defendant's trials. Each was convicted of the crimes to which a confession had been given.

At the outset of his opinion for the five-justice majority, Chief Justice Warren notes that the court's decision in *Escobedo* v. *Illinois* of two years earlier had been the subject of "spirited" legal debate. He adds: "We granted *certiorari* in these cases . . . in order to further explore some facets of the problems, thus exposed, of applying the privilege against self-incrimination to in-custody interrogation, and to give *concrete* constitutional guidelines for law enforcement agencies and courts to follow."

Escobedo, although having Fifth Amendment overtones, was primarily a Sixth Amendment or Right to Counsel case. Even though decided one week after *Malloy* v. *Hogan,* the opinion in Escobedo does not cite the Malloy case possibly because of an uncertainty at the time Escobedo opinion was being prepared by Justice Goldberg. He did not know which way the Malloy case would be decided, although seven of the nine justices of the court accepted the basic theory of the decision: the privilege against self-incrimination should apply to the states as well as the federal government.

Typically, the four individual cases that were consolidated for decision under the general title of *Miranda* v. *Arizona* were very much ordinary crimes of violence that showed no spectacular features in this day of usual violence. Rape, robbery, and murder were the crimes involved. Three states—Arizona, California, and New York—and the federal government had prosecuted in the original trials of the defendants. In one of the cases (*California* v. *Stewart*), the appeal to the Supreme Court had been taken by the state through the Attorney General's Office because the State Supreme Court had reversed the defendant's conviction (and death penalty sentence) on the basis of the court's holding in *Escobedo* v. *Illinois.* The state court had ordered the defendant to be retried but without the use of certain admissions secured during extended police questioning.

In none of the cases was it alleged that the police had been guilty of brutality or undue coercion. At most, the interrogations of the various defendants had been prolonged. (Stewart had been questioned while in custody over a five-day period on nine different occasions. In the other cases questioning had lasted less than one day, although apparently it had been continuous. Ernesto Miranda's confession had been secured by Phoenix police after only two hours in custody.)

But in reaching its decision in these cases the court largely ignored these factors, although they were mentioned in passing. The crucial question in each was not denial of the right to consult with an attorney as it had been in *Escobedo* v. *Illinois* (where the police had prevented Danny Escobedo from consulting with his lawyer even though the attorney was in sight of his client), but whether the police had advised the arrested suspect that he not only had a right to have an attorney present during questioning, that he had an absolute right to remain silent if he did not wish to answer any questions, and that anything he said could be used in court against his interests.

In other words, the rights guaranteed by the Fifth and Sixth Amendments arose at the moment certain physical circumstances were present. As in Escobedo, the most important circumstance is "custody"—that is, at the point where the suspect is deprived of his freedom of action in any significant way.

The formula the court created—"focus plus custody plus interrogation" equals Fifth and Sixth Amendment protections because: "It is at this point that our adversary system of criminal proceedings commences, distinguishing itself at the outset from the inquisitorial system recognized in some countries."

And since an adversary system presupposes a certain parity of opponents, the incommunicado interrogation of suspects becomes constitutionally forbidden unless, of course, the suspect waives his constitutional rights and makes his confession with complete voluntariness. But, the court is quick to point out, any such waiver must be made voluntarily, knowingly, and intelligently. Further, proof of such waiver is the burden of the prosecution and will never be presumed from a "silent record."

The court in Miranda is telling us, in essence, that in order to have the constitutional safeguards of the Fifth Amendment mean anything, they must be operative at every stage of criminal proceeding not just when the accused is facing judge and jury in the courtroom.

The Miranda decision is worth examining in detail because it—as much as any decision of the court during the era of Law Revolution—illustrates the way the court pronouncements reach out to affect the lives of every one of us.

CHAPTER FIVE

A Trial Is Not a Happening ("Miranda—not Mirable!")

The defendant was a twenty-year-old of approximately eighth grade education, with a mental age of twelve. He was arrested by the Phoenix police on rape charges, held incommunicado for about two days, and questioned extensively during that time by police inspectors. Ultimately, Miranda confessed to the crime. He was not tortured or given the third degree, merely questioned over long periods of time in a standard police interrogation procedure.

No doubt, all the gimmicks in the books were used to encourage him to sign a statement or give verbal confession. He was, of course, not given the admonition that he was entitled to remain silent nor was he told that he had a right to see an attorney or that an attorney would be appointed to represent him if he could not afford to hire one.

Miranda's confession along with the victim's eyewitness identification was used at his trial and he was convicted not too surprisingly. Whatever defense he had in answer to the charges against him was rather well negated by his confession. Presumably Miranda had a court-appointed counsel or a public defender (overworked and underpaid) who did what he could. But a defendant's confession, once it gets to the jury, is mighty persuasive of guilt, even when repudiated and even when the eyewitness is not completely sure of the identity of her violator. Why the Supreme Court picked Miranda to use as a basis for changing the rules of the game is an interesting question, but that is the name now on the books and that is now a name that ranks with the most important in criminology. It's a *cause celebre* appellation like the Dred Scott case or the Dartmouth College case.

Please note that Miranda was retried by the state of Arizona and found guilty a second time, but without the use of the tainted confession. He is presumably doing a long jolt in some Arizona prison, probably unaware that his name is one of the two or three most important in American constitutional history and the administration of criminal justice. Does the thought make his incarceration any more bearable? Probably not.

A further note on Miranda—the admonition as to constitutional rights must be put into evidence by the prosecution as part of the foundation before *any* statement of the defendant can be used. The burden is on the prosecutor. A knowing waiver of the rights cannot be presumed from a silent record. The upshot of all this is that it is the rare case today in which the defendant makes any incriminating statement which can be introduced. In the old days (according to unofficial estimates) one-half to three-fourths of the cases could be relied upon to produce some sort of statement which was indicative of the defendant's guilt. The time has come to change sides!

Like all other cases in which decisions are rendered by the United States Supreme Court, the Miranda case had to rest upon the citation of authority and precedent. Or at least it had to appear so. The appearance was given (the myth of *stare decisis* preserved, as one commentator put it) through citation of a relatively ancient case, *United States* v. *Bram,* decided in 1897.

That case, the court claimed, stood for the proposition that the Fifth Amendment applied to the use of confessions obtained prior to trial. But the case had been ignored as precedent in later federal cases. This was because of special rules relating to federal practices which were developed by the court. *United States* v. *Bram* was not useful as authority in state level cases because of the 1908 *Twining* v. *New Jersey* decision which said the protections offered in the Fifth Amendment do not apply to the states. But, as we have just seen, Twining was at last overruled in *Malloy* v. *Hogan.*

So the Bram case, slumbering peacefully on the books for all these years, was roused from its dusty niche and found to be bursting with vitality. According to Mr. Chief Justice Warren, it "elevated the privilege [against self-incrimination] to a constitutional level" and even more importantly has always been as broad a privilege as "the mischief against which it seeks to guard."

It is this last quotation which takes us to the heart of the Miranda decision. At the outset of his opinion, it was stated that the court intended to explore some "facets of the problem" which were exposed in *Escobedo* v. *Illinois.* The problem, of course, was custodial interrogation. But Escobedo had been easy. Danny Escobedo knew very well he had a right to consult with his attorney, and had in fact seen his attorney at the police station—from a distance. But he was told in effect that he could consult with the lawyer *after* he had made his statement. Such conduct was an effective denial of the "assistance of counsel" as required by the Sixth Amendment and made mandatory on the states by *Gideon* v. *Wainright,* 1963.

During the two years between Escobedo and Miranda the "problem exposed" was the subject of a number of state appellate court opinions. Most of these looked upon the Escobedo case as another in the long line of "Confession Doctrine" cases that had bothered the Supreme Court over the years.

As we have seen, the Confession Doctrine cases went off on the "totality of the circumstances" due process test. Whether or not the accused actively sought the help of an attorney was just another circumstance to be considered on review.

(It should be noted that at least one state—California—was not caught with its doctrinal pants down when it was confronted with the "meaning of Escobedo." In *People* v. *Dorado* [1964] the court had its first chance to apply Escobedo to a state proceeding. The defendant, Bobby Dorado, was a San Quentin convict who was implicated in a prison homicide of a fellow inmate. Dorado was questioned by prison authorities and by a local deputy district attorney. He never bothered to ask for a lawyer nor was he ever advised that he had a right to consult with one. His subsequent conviction, gained on the basis of statements given to his interrogators, was reversed by the California Supreme Court applying the new constitutional standards of Escobedo. The decision evoked outraged cries from law enforcement officers, largely on the basis that the Escobedo decision did not require the result reached in Dorado. The debate, if not the hue and cry, ended with the Miranda decision.)

In earlier decisions of the court, reaching back to *Boyd* v. *United States* in 1887, the Fourth and Fifth Amendments had been seen as "almost running into each other." Now, the court was discovering, the Fifth and Sixth Amendments also ran into each other. This conclusion is reached by the realization that the right to counsel is a prophylactic device needed to be certain that the Fifth Amendment guarantees are respected by the police.

"Any lawyer worth his salt will tell the suspect in no uncertain terms to make no statements to police under any circumstances." That at least was Justice Jackson's point of view in an early confession case, *Watts* v. *Indiana*, where the defendants had sought assistance of counsel and had been denied.

Aside from the legal theories and constitutional doctrines contained in Miranda, the strongest supporting argument in behalf of the decision is the Supreme Court's more recent recognition that confessions are not necessarily to be excluded from use at trials purely because of questions of reliability. *Jackson* v. *Denno* had settled that there was more involved in the use of confession than its accuracy. This additional quality—it was described as the right to be free from undue invasions of the person by the government—is not lost by virtue of being placed under arrest as a suspected law breaker. Since the Fifth Amendment privilege is an absolute one, no government instrumentality may infringe its restraints even in the cause of more effective law enforcement. The court recognized the competing interests involved in the situation it was dealing with but chose to strike the balance in favor of the individual and his right to be let alone.

It was the Miranda decision more than any other of the court which evoked the public outcry about "coddling criminals" and "handcuffing" the police in the performance of their jobs. But Chief Justice Warren, who had been by all estimates a hard-nosed public prosecutor as district attorney of Alameda County in the thirties, had the answer ready for the critics in the decision. The police, the Chief Justice said, should not be encouraged to make their case against a suspect through the device of admissions and confessions had while the suspect is being subject to a process of interrogation. A police force that relies on these techniques becomes lazy and inefficient.

But the real vice the court was seeking to reach in the Miranda decision was spelled out in an early paragraph: "Interrogation still takes place in privacy. Privacy results in secrecy and this in turn results in a gap in our knowledge as to what in fact goes on in the interrogation rooms."

Under the old "Confession Doctrine" line of cases, question of voluntariness of statements was considered and ruled upon by the judge. But this often deteriorated into a swearing match between the accused and his accusors. Judges, faced with the problem of accepting the testimony of an accused criminal or the testimony of a police officer, could resolve their doubts easily—in favor of the policeman's version. If the defendant could show some positive evidence of mistreatment while in custody, he had a chance to have his confession thrown out as coerced.

But by the time of Escobedo and Miranda, the techniques of interrogation had become far more sophisticated than in the days of the Third Degree. It was this factor, as much as any other, that led the court to lay down new guidelines for the use of confessions. The opinion in Miranda quotes liberally from various police interrogation manuals in common use across the country. All of them stressed the importance of psychology in questioning of a suspect. The more recent editions were obviously written with one eye on the Supreme Court and its most recent interpretations of the Confession Doctrine.

As the court notes: "The manuals instruct the police to display an air of confidence in the suspect's guilt and from outward appearance to maintain only an interest in confirming certain details. The guilt of the subject is to be posited as a fact. The interrogator should direct his comments toward the reasons why the subject committed the act, rather than to court failure by asking the subject whether he did it. . . . The officers are instructed to minimize the moral seriousness of the offense, to cast blame on the victim or on society."

The emphasis is on kindness, understanding, and a general atmosphere of friendliness. Of course, if this approach doesn't get the desired results, other methods can and should be employed. "Where emotional appeals and tricks are employed to no avail, he must rely on an oppressive atmosphere of dogged persistence. He must interrogate steadily and without relent, leaving the subject no prospect of surcease. He must dominate his subject and overwhelm him with his inexorable will to obtain the truth. He should interrogate for a spell of several hours pausing only for the subject's necessities, in acknowledgment of the need to avoid a charge of duress that can be technically substantiated."

Right here, it might be time to consider the complaint of some of us who are of a different philosophy and who ask, "Damn it all, man, if the crook is guilty, shouldn't the police be allowed to use artifice and device, even selling him on confession, to protect the rest of us?"

The answer: "Let ninety-nine guilty men go free so that one innocent man won't be convicted" is too glib a response. But it is a basic reason in common law (ours) jurisprudence for our protective rules. I do think we're still hung up over our historical fears that a home isn't our castle, that the king's men—now the police—can come barging in and search helter-skelter, maybe that so many of us have so much to hide, i.e., unclean consciences, that we don't want to support any law which encourages indiscriminate search or surveillance or inquiry.

I've seen strong men blanch at the thought of cross-examination. Perhaps too many strong men have too many skeletons in their closets to warrant answering up to "any questioning."

On the other hand, if we reverse our constitutional field and premise a procedure, somewhat like the French where a man is presumed guilty when arrested and the French judge sets about to determine his innocence, then there might be more reason for abandoning our present constitutional safeguards.

We have a presumption of innocence, and jurors say they follow it. Rubbish and hypocrisy. In France there's no such fiction, but there's no such need as here for a lawyer at the beginning of the accusatory stage because really there's no accusatory stage; it's an inquisitional stage with the judge "protecting," i.e., trying to determine the innocence of the defendant.

The French would laugh at the Miranda decision saying, "Monsieur, you are making of law a game!"

The paragraph (quoted in the Miranda opinion) is taken from a standard text, *Fundamentals of Criminal Investigation,* published in 1959. Other techniques are described and commented upon—the already mentioned "Mutt and Jeff" where the suspect is questioned in relays or tandem. One officer plays it tough, the other friendly. The "faked lineup"—the suspect is identified by coached witnesses or victims during a break in the questioning. When the questioning resumes the officer proceeds as though there were no longer any doubt about guilt. A variation is the "reverse lineup"—the suspect is identified by witnesses as the perpetrator of a number of other crimes than the one he is suspected of committing. In the words of the manual: "It is expected that the subject will become desperate and confess to the offense under investigation in order to escape from the false accusations."

The manuals even contain instructions on how to deal with the "con-wise" type who knows he does not have to answer questions. The investigator is told to agree with the suspect, but then warn him that a refusal to talk makes him appear that he has something to hide.

The court could anticipate no improvement in the situation in the "foreseeable future," with the result that accused defendants would continue to be the "deluded instrument of their own conviction," because "the blood of the accused is not the only hallmark of an unconstitutional inquisition." After reviewing the common law (English) origins of the privileged against self-incrimination and its historical American development, the court was able to find the prevailing practices of station house interrogation to be clearly violative of the Fifth Amendment.

How did the court apply the new doctrine to the cases

before it for decision? In *Miranda* v. *Arizona* the factual background was uncomplicated. The defendant, a twenty-three-year-old indigent, was arrested on March 13, 1963, as a suspect in the rape-kidnapping of an eighteen-year-old girl which had occurred ten days earlier. Miranda was arrested at his home by Phoenix police, taken to the police station, and placed in a lineup. The victim identified him as the attacker and he was taken into an interrogation room by two officers. Within a short time he gave a detailed oral confession and then wrote out in his own handwriting a statement admitting and describing the crime. At the top of the page on which the statement was written was a typed paragraph stating that the confession was made voluntarily, without threats or promises of immunity and with "full knowledge of my legal rights, understanding any statement I make may be used against me."

(Here is a parenthetical comment on the case of Dykes Simmons, the "Forgotten American," who went on a vacation to Monterey, Mexico, was arrested for the murder of three children, tried, and sentenced to death. Now, some eight years later, being incarcerated all this time in a Mexican jail in Monterey, under the sentence of death, Dykes Simmons is about to be released—through no help of the American consular authorities. Mexican law requires in a "lineup" that several men similarly dressed must all appear so that the accuser can't answer the leading question—"Is that the one?" —affirmatively. While the Mexican law is fair, to the disgrace of our due process of law, our consular service in Monterey gave Dykes Simmons, an American national and a resident of Texas, no protection.

I'm convinced of Dykes Simmons' innocence and I think he will be released by the Mexican authorities just about the time this book is published. He'll tell his own full story of his lack of due process by the Mexican authorities because of nonintervention by the American consular officers upon whom he depended. How most of his trial was held when he was not present, how his sentence of death was imposed upon him by the judge's clerk after he had already been incarcerated in the condemned cell, how all the evidence that could have freed him vanished, how all of the people of Monterey, including the newspaper that published the $5,000 reward for the killer believed Dykes Simmons was innocent.)

Miranda was tried by a jury and his confession, along with testimony by the officers, was admitted into evidence. He was convicted of both rape and kidnapping and sentenced to twenty to thirty years in the state prison on each count. His conviction was confirmed in due course by the Arizona Supreme Court, in a decision that was written after the United States Supreme Court's decision in the Escobedo case. The Arizona court laid heavy emphasis on the fact that Miranda had not asked to consult with an attorney.

The Supreme Court reversed the conviction, and said, in part, "It is clear that Miranda was not in any way apprised of his right to consult with an attorney and to have one present during the interrogation, nor was his right not to be compelled to incriminate himself effectively protected in any other manner. . . . The mere fact that he signed a statement which contained a typed-in clause stating that he had 'full knowledge' of his 'legal rights' does not approach the knowing and intelligent waiver required to relinquish constitutional rights."

The three other cases which were disposed in the Miranda decision demonstrated the same arrest-interrogation-confession-conviction pattern. The only case offering any departure was *Westover* v. *United States*, in which the federal government had prosecuted the defendant for the robbery of a savings and loan association (which is, like bank robbery, one of the relatively few "violent" crimes that is a federal offense).

Westover had been arrested as a suspect by the local police of Kansas City in two Kansas City robberies. He was already on a wanted felon list put out by the FBI, but was interrogated by the local police through the course of the night. Apparently he would not crack under the pressure and was turned over to the FBI about noon on the following day—still in the Kansas City police station. Another two and one-half hours of FBI questioning—about the California robberies—followed and the defendant finally signed a written confession. He was convicted in a California federal court and the conviction was affirmed by the Court of Appeals.

The great Russian novelist, Fydor Dostoevsky, relates the procedure of extracting confessions by the police by pretending, at first, not to be interested in hearing it. Finally the criminal is so frustrated and enraged at no one "being interested" in his confession that he blurts out a detailed description of the whole foul deed, much more so than he would have done initially or at all, had the police expressed their willingness to listen.

The Westover case and Dostoevsky's great understanding of human nature remind me strongly of a similar case, one in which I had some involvement.

Billy Smith was in San Quentin for robbery, but he was harboring the guilt of a greater crime. Daily he expected the warden to come to his cell and say, "Billy, we've got you now for the murder of that postal officer. Your fingerprints matched."

Billy Smith had, indeed, killed the postal officer in Sacramento, but he'd completely escaped, and no one had checked the fingerprints of the murderer (in reality Billy's prints) with the prints of Billy taken when he was processed for admission to San Quentin. How, with the automatic procedure of fingerprinting each felon in the United States and then comparing at the national bureau in Washington, Smith was not picked up within days of his arrival, I never learned. But

I did learn the rest of the tragic story from young Billy Smith.

One day the warden did come to his cell to utter the words for which Billy had been waiting. "Billy, I'm going to have to take you over to the office. The police have come for you."

When Billy got to the warden's office, it was the Beverly Hills police he saw, not the Sacramento police. They wanted Billy for a job in Beverly Hills where he had also left fingerprints and about which he had almost forgotten. He shakily went through the interview and "confessed" but when he got back to his cell, he was so unnerved at being unable to confess to the Sacramento murder for which he thought he had finally been apprehended that he broke down and "confessed" to his cell mate about the murder.

Several days later, the cell mate "stooled" to the warden. This time, the visit by the warden was for the Sacramento job. The fingerprints were finally matched. Billy Smith was brought to trial—and executed.

This was some twenty years ago so there was nothing that could be done for Smith beyond the guilty and innocent phase of his case, and it would have been most difficult to have done anything toward saving his life. But I told the prison priest that if he would just go to court with me and sit in the front row during the entire trial, saying nothing, I would try Smith's case for free. The priest didn't go, and I didn't go, and Smith was convicted and sentenced to death.

The day he was executed I received a letter from him, not sarcastic, but completely serious. It was just one line. "Dear Mr. Belli, Thank you very much for everything you did for me. Yours sincerely, Billy Smith." I'd done nothing but listen to his "confession."

He had been born twenty years too soon. Now he would never have been executed. But his letter made me ashamed that I hadn't tried even knowing, as the surgeon sometimes must, that death was inevitable.

Twenty years later in the Westover case the results were not nearly so inevitable, not with the Law Revolution. The United States government argued that Westover's confession to the FBI men had come after being advised of his constitutional rights, the required FBI procedure. Westover, however, had been in custody and subjected to questioning for fourteen hours when the federal agents began to talk to him. By this time, the court said, the impact of the continuous questioning left him vulnerable to any interrogation. In effect, he was set up for the bureau men, even if they behaved in conformity to the law and the Constitution as it was being read on June 13, 1966.

The reversal of Westover's conviction is one of the ironies of the Miranda decision. In his opinion for the majority, Chief Justice Warren gave high praise to the Federal Bureau of Investigation. It was, in fact, the bureau's own arrest and interrogation procedures that the Court was telling the states they should follow. The case contains a detailed resume of the FBI practice and carries the introductory comment that the present pattern of warnings and respect for the rights of the individual followed as a practice by the FBI is consistent with the procedure which we delineate today—that is, the series of warnings concerning constitutional rights.

The "exemplary record of effective law enforcement" compiled by the bureau over the years was sufficient to convince at least some of the justices that the new rule could be "lived with" and that no fantastic crime wave would automatically follow from imposing these requirements on the police of three thousand counties and more than sixteen thousand cities. To buttress the conclusion that police and prosecutors would have no difficulty conforming to the new standards the majority opinion notes that Los Angeles District Attorney Evelle Younger conducted a survey of cases arising within his jurisdiction following the Dorado decision (which anticipated the Miranda rules to a substantial extent) and found no appreciable difference in the police-prosecutor operation. In fact, the most efficient, good district attorney of the nation's most populous county was quoted as saying: "It begins to appear that many of these seemingly restrictive decisions are going to contribute directly to more effective, efficient, and professional level of law enforcement."

In spite of these endorsements, the Miranda decision set off another maelstrom of criticism of the court. The critics were given plenty of fodder for their cannons in the dissenting opinions filed in the case itself. Justices Clark, Harlan, White, and Stewart refused to join the majority opinion. Clark and Harlan wrote ringing dissents. Justice Clark, who had written the first of the great Law Revolution opinions, *Mapp* v. *Ohio* (1961), was a leading spokesman of the anti-revisionists in Miranda: "Nothing in the letter or the spirit of the Constitution or in the precedents squares with the heavy-handed and one-sided action that is so precipitously taken by the court in the name of fulfilling its constitutional responsibilities. The foray which the court takes today brings to mind the . . . words of Mr. Justice Jackson in *Douglas* v. *Jeannette:* 'This court is forever adding new stories to the temples of constitutional law, and the temples have a way of collapsing when one story too many is added.'"

For the most part the dissenters were concerned with the court's failure to recognize the competing interests of society in crime suppression and prevention. Unable to find that the rules laid down by the court were constitutionally required, the dissenters thought that the majority opinion was an untoward intervention into the operations of local law enforcement agencies. The new rules, Justices White and Harlan thought, were both unjustified by the Constitution and unwise in the context of a steadily rising national crime rate.

The underlying theoretical disagreement between the majority opinion of Justice Warren and the various minority dissents is an absolutist versus a relativist view of the privilege against self-incrimination. The argument here parallels the controversy which has swirled and eddied around the First Amendment's protections of speech and religion ("The congress shall make no law . . .").

But prior to Miranda the First Amendment had been regarded as occupying a preferred position in some constitutional hierarchy of values. Now, the court seems to be saying, we are elevating the Fifth Amendment into the charmed circle of particularly favored constitutional rights. As has been pointed out, above, the Miranda decision relies heavily on the *Malloy* v. *Hogan* rationale, ignoring for the most part the point that there are in reality two privileges involved here, each having distinct pedigrees and distinguishable rationalizations for their existence. These two privileges are both found in the Fifth Amendment, to be sure, but derive historically from different sources. Malloy treated with the right not to be compelled to testify against oneself; the only testimony in the Miranda case came from police officers, or in the form of signed confessions of the defendants. Is this the testimony forbidden by the Fifth Amendment, or is it (merely) the police officers' method of investigating a crime and building a case for purposes of subsequent prosecution? This question has been debated endlessly in law journals, police publications, the popular magazines, and newspaper editorials with no end in sight.

However, since the Supreme Court must, under our system, have both the first and last word on the kinds of activities which are constitutionally permissible, the debate has little meaning except as vocal exercise. It is always possible, of course, that the Miranda decision could be reversed by a later court, i.e., Chief Justice Warren resigns. "President Nixon" appoints a "conservative chief justice who will lead the court 'back.'" Governor Reagan of California, a Republican (*sic*) like Warren, is against President Johnson perpetuating a Warren-like-replacement. But historically, even "conservative" replacements have never been able to retake the number of steps backward that the liberals they replaced had taken forward.

So while the five to four majority that made Miranda the law of the land is theoretically subject to modification, whether or not such a development will occur, at least in the immediate future, is wrapped in too many variables to hazard forecast.

The best prospect is that the court will sophisticatedly extend rather than restrict the protections established by Miranda. One hint was provided by the decision in a series of cases involving police lineup or show-up techniques, the Wade case decided on the last day of the 1966 term, that is in June, 1967. Although strictly speaking, Wade was a Sixth Amendment or Right to Counsel decision its impact on police investigative procedures put it squarely in the Miranda ball park. The decision implicitly recognizes that pretrial identifications by victims of crimes made at police conducted lineups can be as crucial to a successful defense of a criminal prosecution as the exclusion of a full confession at trial.

The victim or eyewitness of a crime who picks out a defendant at a lineup will be hard put to deny that identification when called upon to do so in court. For the reasons which are inherent in the lineup procedure, the court ordained that not only does the accused have the right to have his attorney present when a lineup is being conducted, but also the police or other authorities conducting the lineup must give the lawyer notice as to the time and place and, make every effort to schedule it at a time when the lawyer can be present. Failure to conform to these rules can result in the exclusion from testimony of any lineup identification.

Yvonne Dongiers, tops of the topless and one of the first, made new constitutional law when I pleaded that Escobedo applied to her in the lineup, that she didn't have to have her picture taken until first she was advised of her constitutional rights and given the services of a lawyer. (This does not mean that a lawyer had the right to look as well as the police. It meant that the lawyer had the duty to advise his client before the police could look.) In this famous topless case, the first in the United States, Municipal Judge Leo Friedman took the case away from the jury and directed a verdict of acquittal, thereby restoring the unadorned breasts of the luscious topless dancer to selective San Francisco culture. And I have a lifetime table closest to the stage at San Francisco's bistro "Off Broadway," so that I may better see Yvonne's constitutional rights are not violated. I feel I should have a coat of arms struck, *Semper Vigilantis,* or *Semper Paratus,* as the case may be.

A. *Nunc pro Tunc,* Baby. To the layman one of the law's most bewildering aspects must be its apparent inconsistency when attempting to balance the absolutes of personal constitutional rights against the responsibilities of law enforcement to society. The decision in *Miranda* v. *Arizona*—although it was probably anticipated by a few scholars and perhaps even fewer law enforcement officials—came as an earthquake to practically everyone, including most criminal defense attorneys. The shattering effect of the earthquake was dampened considerably the following week, however, when the court announced its decision in *Johnson* v. *New Jersey.* The Johnson case had been pending at the same time as the Miranda series of decisions so that its announcement on June 20, 1966, must have come as a great relief to virtually every person connected with the machinery of criminal justice except the convicts serving time. The question that kept everyone awake nights during the week following Miranda was: how would it affect the thousands of persons residing in American prisons whose convictions had been had through the use of admissions and confessions obtained during a course of custodial interrogation?

The avenue the court took in handling this knotty problem may not represent good constitutional theory, but it did provide the most practical (or perhaps expedient) solution to the question. The new rules respecting police procedures would have application *only* to cases in which the trial began after the date of decision of Miranda, that is, June 13, 1966. The court could have handled the problem in two other ways, either of which would have created serious problems for the administration of justice. If it had followed the rules governing the application of *Gideon* v. *Wainwright* (right to have counsel at trial), chaos would have been the result. That case was given full retroactivity by the court. The second possible approach was the one used to apply *Mapp* v. *Ohio* (Fourth Amendment—unreasonable search and seizure). In *Linkletter* v. *Walker,* the court held that only those cases which were still pending on direct appeal could have the benefit of the Mapp rule. In an irony of the judicial process, the defendant Linkletter had been arrested, tried, and convicted after Miss Mapp had been so used. But the defendant Linkletter had had the bad luck to commit his crime in Louisiana where those processes move faster than they do in Ohio. As a result, when he got to the Supreme Court on a writ of *habeous corpus,* his conviction had been final for some time before the court reached its decision in Mapp. Although these variable rules seem illogical from a purist's point of view, they are obviously explainable when considered in the light of practical effect.

The full retroactivity given the Gideon decision affected seriously only five states, all in the South, where the right to have the services of appointed counsel had never been recognized. The Mapp decision presented a somewhat different situation. At the time of its announcement by the Supreme Court fully half of the states had as a part of their own local law some form of exclusionary rules of *Weeks* v. *United States*. The Weeks case had established that the Fourth Amendment to the Constitution prohibited the use of evidence unreasonably or illegally seized by law officers, but had limited the application to federal prosecutions. This was 1914. In 1949, when *Wolf* v. *Colorado* was decided, the court refused to extend the rule to the states, but did indicate in its opinion that the states were encouraged to adopt such rules on their own. Finally, in *Mapp* v. *Ohio,* Wolf was overruled but given the limited retroactive effect previously noted—only as to cases which were not "finally decided" as of the date of the Mapp decision. This is why Mr. Linkletter, down in Louisiana, lost out: Louisiana was among the twenty-five or so states which had not seen fit to accept the Supreme Court's invitation to modify their practices, and defendant Linkletter's arrest, trial, and conviction all came about *after* Miss Mapp's, but prior to her successful appearance before the United States Supreme Court.

The situation of the Miranda decision presented an entirely different aspect. So far as is known, *no* state or local police agency had rules relating to custodial interrogation as strict or "protective" as the rules announced in Miranda. Since it is obvious that one of the prosecutions most damning pieces of evidence at a criminal trial is the defendant's own "free and voluntary" admission of guilt, and since it is equally obvious that whole or partial confessions are secured in the course of criminal investigation—i.e., interrogation of suspects —the number of men languishing in prisons who have been convicted out of their own mouths must number in the tens of thousands. If Miranda had been given full retroactive effect (as Justices Douglas and Black thought proper), American prison gates would have literally been thrown wide.

It should be pointed out that there is nothing automatic about the application of the new law established by the Supreme Court. Although judges, prosecutors, and others involved in the machinery are bound to act in conformity with Supreme Court decisions, the convict who wishes to get the benefit of a new decision must initiate legal proceeding on his own behalf, usually in the form of a writ of *habeous corpus*—a legal procedure used to challenge the validity of his detention or imprisonment. But even if his effort in this direction is successful, he is still not home free. He is still subject to retrial by the state— but the trial must be free of the error of the first case. The problem that a retrial poses for the prosecutor is, of course, substantial, especially where the first trial and conviction was based largely on evidence no longer usable, or where the first trial took place some time in the distant past. In that case witnesses will have disappeared or have forgotten details of their testimony, even if available. The stated reason by the prosecution why Danny Escobedo, for example, was not retried was the disappearance after many years of the prosecution's witness.

Does this variable approach to constitutional questions make any sense? If, as the Supreme Court says, the Fifth Amendment (as applied to the states through the Fourteenth Amendment) requires the protective devises commanded by Miranda, then they were *always* constitutionally required—not merely in cases which went to trial *after* June 13, 1966.

But the variable retroactivity approach might be defended theoretically—even without getting into the continuing argument about whether the Supreme Court "makes" laws, or "discovers" it. The justification lies in the nature of the trial process—the search for truth and in the underlying rationale of the various decisions.

The Mapp decision (exclusion of evidence which was the product of an illegal search and seizure) was based upon the Supreme Court's acceptance of the theory that those who enforce the law should also not break the law. The Mapp type of case seldom raises a question concerning the reliability of the illegally obtained evidence, or the guilt of the defendant. The purpose of the decision was prevention of police misconduct even though the price of prevention is fewer criminal arrests, or prosecutions.

On the other hand, the rules announced by Miranda were not designed to curb misconduct as such. Police interrogation practices were carefully developed by men who were fully aware of the constitutional standards established by the court. The formula was formerly: interrogation plus coercion equals unreliability. Whether coercion was present was a factual issue for the trial court to resolve, within certain Supreme Court guidelines. Without coercion, confessions and admissions were considered perfectly proper evidence of guilt. Miranda changed that, of course, but the previous practices had had Supreme Court approval in principle. No real purpose would be served by unlocking prison gates across the nation for men who had been "reliably" convicted.

The third alternative—the one used in *Gideon* v. *Wainwright,* where the question was the Sixth Amendment matter of the right to have counsel appointed and paid for by the state where the defendant could not afford to pay for his own—prescribed full retroactivity without regard to time. Gideon's approach concentrates on a "fairness" standard, but it is easy to make a "reliability" argument. After all, for anyone familiar with the trial process, it is elementary that pitting a trained, experienced prosecutor against any typical criminal defendant who is representing himself (in *propria persona,* or "pro per" as it is known) has to result in a grotesque mismatch. A popular maxim holds: any man who serves as his own attorney has a fool for a client. Criminal trials are often travesties even when the defendant is represented by counsel. When the Supreme Court made Gideon fully retroactive, it was recognizing the relationship of the lack of counsel to the possibility of a fair trial, as required by the Constitution.

CHAPTER SIX

The Supreme Court Retains Counsel

The year was 1942. America was at war. In a Maryland prison, serving a term for robbery was a convict who was positive he had been "railroaded," a good legal term used by no less authority than the United States Supreme Court in *Rideau* v. *Louisiana,* but a term most offensive to the ears of Dallasites when I applied it to their Jack Ruby trial procedures. The convict's certainty took him at last before the United States Supreme Court, where his name and case became a controversial constitutional landmark for twenty-one years, finally to be obliterated in the great upheaval of the Law Revolution of the sixties.

The convict—his name was Betts—lost his appeal to the United States Supreme Court because in those troubled times, six justices of the court could not find in the language of the Sixth or Fourteenth Amendments any requirement that a defendant in a state criminal prosecution had an automatic right to have the state buy him legal services when he was unable to pay for those services himself. (Doesn't it seem to you at first blush that "fairness", i.e., due process of law, would require as the first interchange of a fair trial that the opposing parties at the beginning at least were evenly arrived—matched with lawyers?) The only times when such legal services were given a prisoner were if he had been accused of a capital offense or if he were mentally retarded.

The Sixth Amendment guarantee of the right to "have the assistance of counsel" has deep historical roots in the Anglo-American legal system. By the time the amendment was adopted (in 1791) most American states had put the concept into their own state constitutions. The federal amendment made it certain the newer United States government would not be able to deny men this right in federal prosecutions. Although it might seem basic to any orderly system of justice, the English (whose procedures we adopted in large chunks) did not permit persons accused of a felony to have a lawyer, whether he could afford one or not. This rule was not changed until an act of Parliament in 1836.

Merely stating as an abstraction that a defendant has the right to *retain* counsel to represent him does not solve the related and much stickier problem: what if he can not afford the service of a lawyer? Is justice at the outset to depend on a man's ability to afford it? Amazingly, the Republic was more than one hundred fifty years old before this exact question was handled by the Supreme Court—at that time in the context of a federal prosecution. *Johnson* v. *Zerbst* (1938) determined that the federal government was required, absent a valid waiver of the right, to provide counsel for any defendant in *federal* court.

But what was the situation in the sovereign *states*? Outside of the deep South, state governments were providing counsel for indigent defendants in one manner or other. Although as a practical matter such appointed representation might consist of little more than advice to plead guilty, there was at least a chance the defendant would get something out of his day in court. (The Buffalo [N.Y.] Bar Association appointed "distinguished counsel" to represent the mentally ill assassin of President McKinley. The attorney was an aged former bar association president. To the disgrace of the trial bar, the "defense" consisted principally of apologies for having taken the case!)

However, it took a national (and international) *cause celebre* to fasten onto the states anything like a meaningful right to counsel requirement. This case—known to a generation of left wing writers as "The Scottsboro Case"—arose out of the alleged rape of two young white girls by seven young Negroes. The crime occurred in the state of Alabama where rape is punishable by death, on a jury recommendation. The time sequence of the prosecutions is worth noting: the crime is alleged to have occurred on March 25, 1931. The defendants were arrested on the same day and made a formal court appearance on March 31. At the time the judge presiding appointed "all the members of the local bar association" to represent the seven defendants. The local prosecutor asked that the case be severed into three cases for trial purposes and the first case was heard on April 6. Each of the three trials was completed in one day. The juries voted death penalty verdicts against all seven defendants.

The Scottsboro boys were represented by counsel both at the trials and prior to them. Even so, the Supreme Court said, appointment of counsel (as required by Alabama law at the time) in this case was little more than an expansive gesture on the part of the court. In order to satisfy the requirements of due process of law, the appointment must be more than *pro forma.* The court specifically rejected the suggestion that the Sixth Amendment's guarantee of the right to counsel should be fastened as such onto the states. It severely limited its holding to the facts and peculiar circumstances of the case before it, but subsequently the case had been taken to stand for the proposition that in all capital cases state courts are required to appoint counsel—and appoint them in such a way as to assure effective pretrial assistance. An element of due process is a "fair hearing," and this can only be secured where the accused has the assistance of counsel, but with two large qualifications: if it is an accusation of a capital offense; if the defendant is feeble-minded, illiterate, or for some other reason incapable of preparing his own defense.

The foregoing became known as the "special circumstances" rule of the appointment of counsel for indigents and it was the application of this rule that caused the prisoner Betts to lose. As noted in the opinion, the "accused was not helpless, but was a man forty-three years old, of ordinary intelligence and ability to take care of his own interests. . . . He had once before been in a criminal court, and was not wholly unfamiliar with criminal procedure." His crime had been robbery and his defense was an alibi. The only question in the case was the believability of the witnesses produced by the two sides. In this "simple" situation the defendant was able to do as much for himself as a lawyer could do or would have done.

As noted, *Betts* v. *Brady* got to the Supreme Court in 1942, when civilian attorneys were in short supply. Indeed, even prosecutors were having trouble filling their staffs because of national military requirements. Had the court seen fit to accept the position Betts was urging, the burden on the civilian legal apparatus could have become intolerable.

In spite of these considerations, three justices dissented from the majority opinion. Two of the three dissenters had the satisfaction to be sitting on the court twenty-one years later when their dissenting opinion became the law. Justice Hugo Black, an Alabaman who has now had more than thirty years service on the court was the author for the court of the unanimous opinion in *Gideon* v. *Wainwright* (1963).

The saga of Clarence Earl Gideon's progress from the Bay Harbor Poolroom, Panama City, Florida to the United States Supreme Court is a true "only in America" story. It is also an "only in the era of the Law Revolution" story. While it is true that during the twenty-one years between *Betts* v. *Brady* and *Gideon* v. *Wainwright*, the court heard and decided dozens of right to counsel cases—each time refining the "special circumstances" doctrine so that circumstances got progressively less special—the Betts case stood fast for the principle that there is no constitutional right to have the services of an appointed attorney. The standard was still one of "fairness" as established by the Scottsboro case (*Powell* v. *Alabama*, 1932).

But Gideon, a poorly educated drifter who had spent a fair portion of his adult life in one prison or another, knew that this was wrong. In effect, he proclaimed, a man cannot get a "fair" trial representing himself, regardless of the circumstances. He had told this to the judge presiding at his trial for the offense of burglary, thereby "saving" the question for an appellate proceeding. The judge had not agreed, and advised Gideon that Florida law did not require the appointment of counsel except in capital and other special cases. There was nothing special about Gideon's case—it was merely another routine burglary. The complaint alleged that Gideon had, on or about a certain date in 1961 "feloniously entered the property of another with intent to commit a misdemeanor therein, to wit, petty larceny."

After trial to a six man jury Gideon was convicted and shortly thereafter sentenced to the maximum term: five years in the Florida state penitentiary at Raiford. It was from Raiford that Gideon pressed his appeals: first to the Florida Supreme Court, which turned him down without bothering to write an opinion, and finally to the United States Supreme Court. His became one of the hundreds of so-called *forma pauperis* appeals which are received in the course of each year by the court. They are treated by the court as petitions for *certiorari* and the usual formal requirements are dispensed. The great majority of these are disposed by the court with little more than a notation of denial among the memorandum decisions.

For once in his heretofore unfortunate life, Gideon was in the right place at the right time. During previous terms the court had been uniformly reversing convictions in cases where the right to counsel had been denied (many originating from the same prison where Gideon was confined), but on the basis that the special circumstances rules of *Betts* v. *Brady* required such a result. Perhaps the court was tiring of having its docket crowded with these kinds of cases. Each case required a full-dress review of the entire record of the trial proceedings in order to justify a reversal under existing law. Or perhaps the retirement (in 1961) of Justice Frankfurter (a supposed "liberal" in his early years who became increasingly, cantankerously, conservative), the last member of the six man majority of the Betts case to leave the court, indicated the time was ripe for a reappraisal. A further factor had to be the practical problem that the special circumstances rules themselves created. In each of the cases decided (and reversed) new "factors" were coming to light to give rise to the doctrine. By the time Gideon's petition was received, a careful reading of the previous opinions could isolate almost two dozen of these factors. It was a rare case which could not marshall at least a handful of these for purposes of appeal, on both sides of the controversy.

Gideon, down in Raiford, was certainly unaware of these developments. But his handwritten, *pro per* petition had not alleged any "special circumstances" in his trial and conviction —merely that he had been denied the assistance of counsel because he had been unable to afford an attorney. In effect, his only special circumstance was poverty.

But, for once it was enough. A case the court had decided only five years before carried a lot of theoretical weight for Gideon. In *Griffin* v. *Illinois* (1956), two men had been convicted of armed robbery in Chicago. When they attempted to appeal the conviction, they discovered that Illinois law did not entitle them to a free transcript of the trial proceedings. Without the transcript they could not satisfy Illinois appellate procedural requirements, thereby effectively preventing the possibility of an appeal. The Supreme Court held: the equal protection clause of the Fourteenth Amendment makes it a mandatory duty of the states to provide a transcript where such is necessary to perfect an appeal. Penalizing one man for being poor is contrary to all American theories of equal justice under law.

Somewhat later the court had reversed a conviction where the defendant had ample funds to hire an attorney but had been forced to go to trial without the services of the particular attorney he had retained. In that case the court was able to state the right of a defendant in a state criminal case to be heard through his own attorney was "unqualified." In the words of Justice Douglas (a dissenter in *Betts* v. *Brady*): "This [situation] draws a line between rich and poor that is repugnant to due process. The need of counsel is the same, whatever the economic status of the accused. If due process requires that a rich man who wants a lawyer be allowed the opportunity to obtain one before he is tried, why should not due process give the same protection to the accused who is indigent? Even penniless vagrants are at times caught in a tangle of laws that only an astute lawyer can resolve, as our own decisions show."

Justice Douglas advanced these ideas in a 1961 case (*McNeal* v. *Culver*) in which the Supreme Court reversed the conviction of a Florida defendant. In his concurring opinion (joined by Justice Brennan) Douglas revived his criticism of *Betts* v. *Brady* ("I cannot believe that a majority of the court would agree to *Betts* v. *Brady* were it here [again].") and added a question which may have seemed rhetorical at the time but proved prophetic: "Are we to wait to overrule it [Betts] until a case arises where the indigent is unable to make a convincing demonstration that the absence of counsel prejudiced him?"

Justice Douglas might have had Clarence Gideon in mind, when he asked this question because Gideon's petition relied almost entirely on the fact that his only disagreement with his trial was the failure to appoint counsel.

When the Supreme Court grants "cert," i.e., a writ of *certiorari,* agrees to hear a case, it may advise the contending parties to prepare briefs on particular points of law which the case has raised. This is one of the methods the court employs to give notice to members of the legal profession that an important change in the law may be imminent. In Gideon's case the warning was explicit. The parties were advised to research and brief the question: should *Betts* v. *Brady* be overruled?

Clarence Gideon may never have heard of *Betts* v. *Brady,* but that didn't make any difference because when a petition is granted by the Supreme Court the petitioner gets the benefit of the Supreme Court's own "right to counsel" rules. In Gideon's case the rules obtained the services of an attorney—and a firm—of national prestige. Abe Fortas, of Arnold, Fortas, and Porter of Washington, D.C., would himself take his place among the nine members of the court not long after arguing the case on behalf of Gideon.

The appointment of Fortas to represent Gideon in his appeal is another aspect of the "only in America" nature of Gideon's story. Unable to obtain the services of the least competent court house hanger-on for his trial, Gideon drew one of America's most competent constitutional lawyers and advocates after finding his way to the Supreme Court.

When the decision in *Gideon* v. *Wainright* finally came (on March 18, 1963, two months after it had been heard in oral argument) there was little surprise. The court—through

Justice Black—corrected an error of twenty-one years standing. *Betts* v. *Brady* was overruled. (Was Betts still in a Maryland prison? Probably not). The court noted that the factual situations presented by Betts and by Gideon were indistinguishable, and as such, the overruling of the prior case was mandatory. Black listened to the first of the counsel cases—the Scottsboro Boys—where the court had ordained that the right to have counsel is of a "fundamental character." The experience of thirty years had shown the truth of that premise. ". . . reason and reflection requires us to recognize that in our adversary system of criminal justice, any person hauled into court, who is too poor to hire a lawyer, cannot be assured a fair trial unless counsel is provided for him."

Few defendants charged with a crime fail to hire the best lawyers they can get to prepare and present their defenses. Lawyers in criminal courts are necessities, not luxuries.

The only unexpected aspect of the decision was its unanimity. All nine justices agreed that the Betts decision was dead, although for somewhat different reasons. The concurring opinions exposed the spectrum of philosophies represented in the court: Justice Douglas felt the decision should flatly be based on the theory of incorporation of the Bill of Rights into the Fourteenth Amendment, a position which he acknowledged in the opinion "has never commanded a court." Conservative Justice Harlan agreed on the result because the truth was that Betts had been overruled anyway by the series of cases revolving around the special circumstances doctrine. Sometimes conservative Justice Clark went along because the distinction between a capital and non-capital case is more artificial than real, at least where the assistance of counsel is concerned. From a practical point of view defending against a murder charge is apt to be less complicated than defending against a forgery accusation.

One other aspect of *Gideon* v. *Wainwright* bears noting.

Twenty-five state governments—through their attorneys general—appeared (that is, filed briefs) in the case, in addition to the state of Florida. But of these twenty-five, only two supported Florida's position; the remaining twenty-three agreed with Gideon that the Betts case should be overruled. (As previously noted, only four other states beside Florida had no provision for the appointment of counsel in non-capital felony prosecutions prior to the decision in Gideon.)

Several related issues were not considered by the Gideon case, but have been dealt with either by the Supreme Court or the lower federal courts. The first of these is retroactivity, and the basis for applying the *Gideon* rule to full retroactive status, without regard to time, arises from the court's view of the importance to the fact-finding process of a trial of representation by counsel. Convictions obtained where the accused was denied counsel are suspect.

The second problem area opened by Gideon is the reach of the decision. Must the state provide counsel for defendants in misdemeanor prosecutions? In traffic court? Before administrative bodies which have the power to revoke licenses or impose other sanctions? These are still open questions, but my guess is that the state must, in all cases, provide counsel.

A third area that may require court decision to clarify concerns the standards the state imposes for eligibility for court appointed defense counsel. Must a defendant be absolutely destitute before he can qualify? What if he is employable but is voluntraily unemployed? Could a state constitutionally adopt some sort of part-pay, part-free plan for representation?

The problems of the representation of indigent defendants were not solved entirely by *Gideon* v. *Wainwright* although the case made a healthy start toward the solution.

A. *Who* Must Allow One Phone Call? The laws of many states in the past provided—even required—that *one* (but only one) phone call could, had to be made by or for one just now jailed. Who was to make the call, how? ("For free?") (What if the line was busy?) Whether he got his "party" was a question that reached the Supreme Court and will still be reaching it for additional refinements.

Let's see how one criminally charged goes about getting a lawyer to whom he's "entitled" by phone call, direct mail, Western Union, or the old smoke signal means of communication.

In *Gideon* v. *Wainwright,* the Supreme Court decided that every defendant, regardless of his education and personal circumstances, was entitled to be represented by counsel at trial. Lack of such representation, the court said, often reduced the trial to the level of a farce and a sham. Few attorneys or judges would disagree with this conclusion. No one who has sat in a criminal court and watched a defendant proceeding in *pro per* (the courtroom shorthand for the Latin *in properia persona* or self representation) can be in doubt about the crucial need. This is not to say that in certain exceptional cases an individual can not represent himself adequately. Every courthouse hanger-on can recall anecdotes about individual defendants who were able to beat the system while acting as their own attorney. And of course no one is *required* to have a lawyer. This right, like all constitutionally guaranteed rights, may be waived. And if the waiver is made intelligently, with full knowledge of the consequences, the defendant will not later be permitted to challenge the proceeding on the ground of lack of representation.

But, given the fact that the individual has the right to have a lawyer, the next logical question becomes: *when* does this right arise? In the United States, the lawyer may refuse a criminal case; not so in England. Of course, if a judge ordered a lawyer to take on a criminal client, I suppose the lawyer could not refuse the judge this side of contempt of court, even in this country.

Wrapped up in the answer to this question is a fair amount of complicated constitutional theory and litigation. For the affluent defendant the problem has never been acute. Anyone who is arrested will arrange for the services of an attorney by telephone from the jail as soon as the "booking" process is complete.

I suppose a surgeon's and lawyer's delights are the bedside telephone and the midnight phone calls. I believe doctors do it with better grace than lawyers, a hasty drive to the operating room, the scrubbing, and the all-night surgery. But then, it's easier to do something with one's hands when sleep is at a premium than to sit silently, and quietly, and advise as the lawyer has to do.

And usually for the lawyer there's a third person present, on these midnight calls, which even the Constitution can't refuse—"Mr. Jim Beam."

And the later the call, the more "constitutional" becomes the question, at least to the incarcerated. In the hard light of the morning and black coffee, most defendants are willing to start at least in Superior Court rather than, as loudly announced the night before, at the International Court of Justice, or at least the United States Supreme Court.

But these midnight calls are not without their tragedies too. The bailable boy is taken home to his family and the lawyer is the buffer in the first punishment and chastisement between parent and child. The lawyer must sit and listen to the reproachment of self, the castigation of others, the repeated "You're a lawyer, do something about this!" when the man in front of him has already done it all.

Then there's the delightful drunk with money (which makes him even more delightful) who called me one evening with a dreadful tale that sped me, half-dressed, to the jail. There he was, looking at his watch and announcing to the jailer, "I owe you fifty bucks—he got here ten minutes faster than I bet you he could."

But the calls aren't limited to my own city of San Francisco, they can and do come in from all over the United States and Greenwich time is not necessarily a common denominator. Every prisoner has one telephone call, at least under California law, and most states must have the same law because I've had calls from New England in the middle of the night, from the lock-up no less, asking me to hop on over and right now!

All of this goes to prove that we haven't changed much in national character from the time there was a state flag with a rattlesnake painted on it and the legend, "Don't tread on me." We know our rights and we're rapidly learning more of them. And we want them protected, every one of them, for twenty-four hours a day. We're also learning that these rights aren't self-executing and even though the Constitution "guarantees" so many delightful endowments, only a lawyer—on a twenty-four-hour basis—can enforce these guarantees.

But the indigent defendant presents a different question. Most states, by statute, require a defendant to be arraigned (that is taken before a judge and informed of the charge against him) within a specified period of time, usually two days or thereabouts. The purpose of the pre-arraignment detention used to be the opportunity it afforded the police to "talk" things over with the suspect, often resulting in voluntary confessions of guilt. The Supreme Court changed that particular aspect of police procedure in 1964 in *Escobedo* v. *Illinois*. The defendant, Danny Escobedo, was in custody on suspicion of homicide. His family had contacted an attorney who had gone to the police station where the defendant was being held (and interrogated). The lawyer saw his client as he was being moved from one part of the jail to the other—but at a distance. *No* contact was made, even though the defendant had asked to talk to the attorney.

Escobedo knew he had a right to talk to an attorney, even though he had not retained one, but nothing in Illinois' law at the time required the police to permit him to do so. Incriminating statements made by him during the period of detention were used by the prosecution at his trial and he was convicted. The reversal by the Supreme Court was a logical extension of the Gideon theory: the right to counsel attaches at every stage of a criminal proceeding, not merely at the trial. Any other holding would make no sense given the realities of the criminal law and the prosecutorial process. To limit the right to counsel to the end stage of the criminal process, the trial itself, would be like telling a mountain climber he could only use ropes during the last one hundred feet of the ascent of a ten thousand foot mountain.

Of course, Danny Escobedo (or his family) had retained counsel. For this reason, the Escobedo case is properly a Sixth Amendment decision, although it had Fifth Amendment overtones. These overtones were not fully developed until *Miranda* v. *Arizona,* decided two years later.

But what of the indigent defendant who has no lawyer and is without funds to retain one? Under the formula required by the Miranda decision, the arresting agency must tell the prisoner not only that he has the right to hire a lawyer, but that if he is without funds, a lawyer will be appointed by the court. (Note that the police are NOT actually required to give the arrestee this information—only in cases where they desire to interrogate concerning the crime, and then only if they asked to testify concerning what the accused said while being questioned.)

However, when the accused is arraigned he must be advised of his right to have counsel and must be given a reasonable time to retain and consult with one, as well as being told the nature of the charges against him. After consulting with counsel—either retained or appointed—a plea is entered. If the charge is a felony (that is, a crime which is punishable by imprisonment in a state prison) the case is routinely set for preliminary examination. In some cases the preliminary examination is by-passed by the use of a grand jury indictment—a specific requirement of the Fifth Amendment. ("No person shall be held to answer for a capital, or otherwise infamous crime, unless on a presentment or indictment of a grand jury. . . .") But notwithstanding the clear language of the Constitution, it is still the law that the grand jury is not a requirement of a state criminal proceeding—even though the Fifth Amendment has been held to apply to the states through the due process clause of the Fourteenth.

This apparent inconsistency is explainable by the due process clause itself: if the state procedure meets the basic requirement of due process of law the Constitution is satisfied. The California procedure, which involves the proceeding on an "information" which is filed by the district attorney of the county in which the offense was committed, after a preliminary examination, satisfies the due process compulsion. (In fact, it is more due process, i.e., fairer to the defendant that the district attorney proceeding by grand jury because in this instance, the defendant has no right to be present, to cross-examine prosecution witnesses, or have a lawyer before the grand jury, as he does at a "preliminary examination." In some states, grand jury proceedings are completely secret and not even a transcript is made of their activities.) This point was raised in one of the earliest challenges to a state criminal practice ever taken to the Supreme Court. The case was *Hurtado* v. *California* and was decided by the court in 1884. Although Hurtado lost his appeal, the court, through Justice Mathews, put everyone on notice that the due process clause of the Fourteenth Amendment did contain within its words the potential for protecting individual rights against the operations of the laws of state governments.

His message to the states was, for its time, surprisingly modern. It anticipated by three-fourths of a century the doctrines which inform the court's contemporary decisions.

"Arbitrary power," Justice Mathews wrote, "enforcing its edicts to the injury of persons and property of its subjects, is not law, whether manifested as the decree of a personal monarch or of an impersonal multitude. And the limitations imposed by our constitutional law upon the action of the governments, both state and national, are essential to the preservation of public and private rights, notwithstanding the representative character of our political institutions. The enforcement of these limitations by judicial process is the device of self-governing communities to protect the rights of individuals and minorities, as well as against the power of numbers, as against the violence of public agents transcending the limits of lawful authority, even when acting in the name and wielding the force of the government."

In short, even if the people of a state, by popular vote or through their legislatures, want to deprive themselves of certain elements of due process of law, the Supreme Court will not permit it. Of course, if two-thirds of the Congress and three-fourths of the states agree to such a change, that is beyond the power of the court to affect. This agreement has been reached only about a dozen times in the one hundred seventy-five years of the nation's existence—the amendments to the Constitution excluding the Bill of Rights itself, which was really part of the original constitutional package.

Suppose Congress passed a "crime bill" which overruled the Supreme Court's overruling of a theretofore congressional act. The Supreme Court could hold the second congressional act—the "crime bill"—unconstitutional, too. That is the doctrine of judicial review: there are three branches of our government—legislative, executive, and judicial. Judges judge what is constitutional. They are supreme in this area, and can "overrule the will of the people," i.e., the legislatures, as governors such as Ronald Reagan of California, who do not understand or will not understand the doctrine, contend. The Supreme Court, too, is the will of the people—the highest will.

With stops along the way, the warning in Hurtado quoted above, has become the *modus operandi* of the "new" Supreme Court in the age of revolution of the law.

The defendant's right "to have the assistance of counsel for his defense" can be read literally to mean only at the trial of his case. But if all courts could (or should) do is read the constitution literally, there would be no need for courts. Thus, the "assistance of counsel for his defense" language of the Sixth Amendment comprehends the entire criminal process—from the moment the need for counsel arises. And that need arises the moment the accusation of a crime is made—when the person is arrested or otherwise restrained of his liberty.

If this "reading" of the Constitution was implicit in *Escobedo* v. *Illinois,* it became explicit in *Miranda* v. *Arizona* two years later, although as noted, the decision in the case was bottomed on Fifth Amendment self-incrimination theory. The point of these cases however is not a search for an appropriate constitutional pigeonhole in which to file the "discovered" constitutionally-guaranteed right. This is a favorite activity of certain legal scholars who have compartmentalized minds. The real point of the Law Revolution decisions of the sixties is the approach to the operation of law as an interconnected process which must be viewed in the context of what actually happens to a man who is placed under arrest, interrogated by the police, brought to trial and convicted of his crime. This is why it may be said that with the words "due process" of law as the touchstone, the courts have been able to peer deeply into the totality of circumstances surrounding the accusatorial-prosecutorial machinery and institute basic reforms from on high.

The criminal law divides itself neatly enough into three

distinct phases: the investigatory or accusatory stage, the adversary or trial stage, and the appellate or post-conviction stage. Each of these phases involve the talents and services (with a certain degree of overlap) of different arms of the state: police and/or district attorney; district attorney and trial courts; and finally attorney-general and the appellate courts. The Law Revolution has touched and affected the operations of all these instruments of society's control mechanisms. Some states have been more profoundly affected than others by the changes which the Supreme Court has ordered. For example, prior to the decision in *Gideon* v. *Wainwright*, only five states did not provide counsel in all felony prosecutions of indigent defendants. In contrast, however, probably only a handful of local police jurisdictions adhered to the pre-interrogation procedures that are now required by *Miranda* v. *Arizona* (although, as the court was pleased to point out in its opinion in Miranda, the federal government's own law enforcement arm, the Federal Bureau of Investigation, used a similar formula before interrogating arrestees—with no apparent detriment to their effectiveness). In states having foreign-language-speaking minority populations, the warning card is printed and readily available in the foreign language.

But whatever the prior practice may have been, when the United States Supreme Court has spoken, new law is made (or discovered, if you prefer) and the sworn officers of the law—from rookie police officers to state supreme court justices—are bound on their oaths to adhere to the rules, regardless of their personal feelings or preferences.

As a unifying thread running through all the Supreme Court's decisions modifying the administration of criminal justice in our country is the underlying concept of the basic nature of the legal system in the United States. We are committed to the adversary system in both our civil and our criminal courts. In the civil courts this concept has never been in question or danger, but the criminal courts have presented a different situation. The adversary system, to be meaningful requires that the parties be of roughly equal status, tactically and strategically.

The focus of this concern has been the trial itself as the place where truth is found. But pretrial procedures have been scrutinized and post-trial activities of the states have received a share of attention. But the search for a "fair" trial is at or near the heart of the whole revolution.

A defendant does not get a "fair" trial when the judge and the prosecutor may comment on the fact that the accused did not offer himself as a witness and deny under oath that he committed the crime charged (*Griffin* v. *California*, 1965).

An accused does not get a "fair" trial when he is denied the opportunity to confront the witnesses against him (*Pointer* v. *Texas*).

A defendant does not get a "fair" trial if he is not represented by counsel (*Gideon* v. *Wainwright*, 1963).

And an accused does not get a fair trial when the local news media turn the proceedings into a "Roman carnival," when jurors become local celebrities, or when the television camera invades the courtroom (*Shepherd* v. *Maxwell*, 1966; *Estes* v. *Texas*, 1965).

The Shepherd and Estes cases demand more extensive consideration because of their implications for all cases where the crime or charge involved is one which arouses the public's interest. Most crime makes "news" only at the time it occurs or when the suspected criminals are apprehended. But the actual process of the adjudication of guilt or innocence ordinarily is ignored. This is not out of any special considerations of self-restraint on the part of the news media but merely because the trial process is not normally susceptible to reporting as hard news. Much of the actual trial is tedious for those not personally involved. Perry Mason to the contrary notwithstanding, most trials are humdrum affairs with neither side able to surprise the other with any dramatic "surprise" witness or great revelation.

Nevertheless, an occasional crime does catch on—either because the people involved are celebrities at the outset, or because the circumstances of the crime are bizarre and improbable, or the lawyer is "interesting."

The trial of Jack Ruby is, of course, in a category all its own. The assassination of President Kennedy and the killing of the accused assassin by Jack Ruby in the televised view of forty or fifty million persons created a factual situation which can never recur.

But Jack Ruby's trial took place prior to the Supreme Court's decisions in the Shepherd and Estes cases. And those cases established that the constitutional right to a "speedy and public trial" (Sixth Amendment) can be infringed when the trial gets too public.

Billie Sol Estes' conviction for swindling gave the court an opportunity to expound on the question of how public is too public in an atmosphere free from the usual emotional context of a crime of violence. In the usual case where prejudicial publicity is claimed to have infected the trial process the defendant has been accused of the commission of crimes of violence—the kind of offenses that create "juicy" copy for the news media. The more gory the crime, normally, the more extensive and detailed the publicity. As a result, when an appellate court reverses such a conviction on the basis that news coverage denied the defendant the right to a fair trial, the accompanying publicity and adverse editorial comment is apt to be severe. For example, the court had, in 1963, reversed a Louisiana conviction where the defendant had confessed to his crime in front of television cameras. This was *Rideau* v. *Louisiana,* and the showing of the confession on local television—to be seen by all potential jurors—so prejudiced the defendant, the court said, as to be an inherent denial of due process of law. The case had to be removed to a jurisdiction in which prospective jurors had not seen the TV. (Could that have been done with Jack Ruby?)

But Billie Sol Estes was no ordinary smash-and-grab type criminal. He was a Texas wheeler-dealer who had constructed a formidable financial empire before being arrested as a species of con man. He was as "regular" as Billy Graham and black-eyed peas, or so he seemed.

The Estes case was "covered," with some restrictions by live television, a practice permitted by the Texas rules of court. In reversing Billie Sol's conviction, the court was primarily concerned with the distracting influence on judge and jury that television must inevitably have. The juror's psychological awareness of the "telltale red lights" on the television cameras which were in use in the courtroom during parts of the proceedings must have had their effect. In the words of the opinion, "It is the awareness of the fact of telecasting that is felt by the juror throughout the trial." The opinion then ventured a conclusion for which no authority could be cited: "We are all self-conscious and uneasy when being televised. Human nature being what it is, not only a juror's eyes but his mind will often be on that fact rather than on the witness stand."

As an afterthought, the court considered the effect on a potential retrial that televising of a trial could have. Television viewers who "participate" in a trial through the magic of electronics are not apt to be completely open-minded about the defendant's guilt or innocence if they happen to be called as veniremen on any retrial of the matter.

As secondary and tertiary matters, the court was concerned with the effect of television on witnesses and on the trial judge. As to witnesses, "the quality of testimony in criminal trials will often be impaired." The judge on the other hand, in the view of the Supreme Court, has all he can do to supervise the conduct of the trial, without also assuming the role of assistant producer ("When television comes into the courtroom, he must supervise it").

Finally, and perhaps most importantly, the court considered the effect of the tube on the defendant himself. The presence of television in the courtroom is a "form of mental—if not physical harassment, resembling a police lineup or third degree—a defendant on trial for a specific crime is entitled to his day in court, not in a stadium, or citywide or nationwide arena!" Moreover, the presence of the television camera could work a deprivation to the accused of the right to counsel. The court viewed it this way:

The distractions, intrusions into confidential attorney-client relationships, and the temptation offered by television to play to the public audience might often have a direct effect not only upon the lawyers, but the judge, the jury, and the witnesses.

In short, according to Justice Clark from Texas and the five man majority, the introduction of television cameras into the proceedings worked an effective denial of the right to a "fair" trial—an implicit requirement of the Fourteenth Amendment's due process of law clause. Or did the opinion say that? The question may have been made moot by the Estes case, since the reservation announced by the "swing" vote in this case—that of Justice Harlan—was to the effect that because this was a "heavily publicized and highly sensational affair, the use of television had a prejudicial effect." Thus, only four of the justices subscribed to the view that the introduction of television into the criminal trial process is per se grounds for reversal of a conviction.

But as a practical matter, it will only be the sensational and highly publicized cases which the television broadcasters will find worthy of their time and effort. The routine criminal trial—of the kind which is conducted every day in the courthouses of the United States—would be ignored by the media much as they have always been, even if "live" or filmed broadcasting of the proceedings were permitted by the trial judge and the local court rules. (Note too, that only a few states [six] permit any photographing or televising of the activities during the trial.)

For the dissenters in *Estes* v. *Texas,* the case posed a question of the conflicting claims created between the First Amendment's freedom of the press and the Sixth Amendment's implicit right to a fair trial for the individual. As Mr. Justice Stewart put it: "It is important to remember that we move in an area touching the realm of free communication, and for that reason, if for no other, I would be wary of imposing any per se rule which, in the light of future technology, might serve to stifle or abridge true First Amendment rights."

Thus, although all the members of the court agreed that television *could* result in deprivation of due process through its effect on the trial process in a given situation, only four of the nine justices condemned the practice outright. In some ways, of course, the Estes decision can be criticized as "antirevolutionary." The majority opinion fails to note the tremendous educational possibilities that could flow from the televising of the judicial process. The rapidly accelerating "state of the art" of television recording and transmission certainly should overcome objections to the obtrusiveness of the media as such. Since a courtroom is a public place, by express constitutional command, merely making it "more public" through the application of electronics does not change the substantial nature of the process.

The most effective argument in support of the majority opinion in the Estes case relates to the possible effect on potential jurors should the case being televised end in a mistrial.

"Hung" juries are not uncommon in the criminal law where the vote of a single juror can frustrate the conclusion of the case. In other cases a conviction may be reversed on appeal and remanded (sent back) for retrial. In any such case a person who has seen the prior trial via television is unlikely to have a completely open mind about the guilt or innocence of the defendant. This problem might seem to be only one of finding jurors who don't watch television, or who didn't watch the particular trial on its first run, but the majority of the justices in the Estes case saw it as precluding the possibility of a fair trial the second time around.

The Billy Sol Estes case gave the Supreme Court an opportunity to cope with a type of legal problem which is among the knottiest in the entire panorama of the law: the head-on clash of two distinct constitutional principles. By definition this sort of case is difficult to resolve and inevitably creates a deep division of the court. The multiple opinions which accompanied the decision gave an indication of the nature of the conflict. Dissenting and concurring opinions fell like snowflakes in a blizzard of constitutional arguments. The court's normally solid liberal coalition of justices fell apart on this occasion and the conservative former Justice Clark delivered the opinion of the court while Justices Warren, Douglas, and Goldberg felt it was necessary to add special concurring opinions. Justice Douglas' normal ally in free speech situations, Justice Black, dissented along with the normally conservative Justices Harlan and Stewart.

However, during the year following, the court's unanimity was restored in a case which presented essentially the same legal-theoretical problem, a conflict between the First Amendment's absolute limitation on the power of government to control free speech and the free press and an accused defendant's right to a fair trial in an atmosphere unpoisoned by publicity.

The case—*Shepherd* v. *Maxwell, Warden*—arose out of one of the most celebrated murders, and murder trials, of the decade. The accused was the Cleveland osteopath, Dr. Sam Shepherd and the victim was his attractive, pregnant wife Marilyn.

Now murder, particularly husband-wife murders, is no rarity in United States criminal law. (Statistically speaking you have a far better chance to be killed by someone you are related or married to than to be killed by a total stranger.) What was there about the Shepherd murder case that turned it into a nationally and internationally celebrated crime? Prior to July 4, 1954, Sam Shepherd was no better known than millions of his fellow citizens. Moderately affluent, a pleasant home, an attractive, ordinary couple whose lives were indistinguishable from the other Americans of comparable social and economic status. But somehow the discovery of Marilyn Shepherd's bludgeoned body in her bedroom in the family home in the Cleveland suburb triggered an incredible reaction in newspapers, radio, and television serving the Cleveland area. "Dr. Sam" as he quickly became known to the larger public, was tried, found guilty, and sentenced to die in the city rooms of the Cleveland newspapers even before he was formally arrested and charged with the crime. Shepherd's defense—that a bushy-haired intruder had committed the deed—was found to be patently ridiculous by the press. Prior to Shepherd's arrest, one newspaper wondered editorially why the osteopath wasn't taken into custody and "given the third degree, just as any other suspect would be treated." (An interesting comment on the Cleveland police practices of the time, if the editorial was accurate.) There were hints that the Shepherd family, well-placed in the Cleveland social hierarchy, was using undue influence to block the murder investigation and shield the doctor. When a prestigious member of the local bar—a noted criminal defense attorney—was retained as counsel for Dr. Shepherd it became clear to the news media that guilt was established. After all, ran the theory, if he were innocent any lawyer would do, or perhaps no lawyer at all. Everyone knows that if you are innocent you have nothing to fear from the police or prosecutors.

Every detail of the case became front-page news—a fact which was amply documented when Dr. Shepherd's conviction was finally reversed by the United States Supreme Court: the appellant's brief had annexed to it five large volumes of newspaper clippings culled from the Cleveland newspapers printed during the period between the discovery of the crime and Shepherd's conviction by the jury. Coverage of the case was comparable in both radio and television, and the actual trial brought forth a covey of nationally and internationally famed reporters. With all this journalistic talent on hand it was inevitable that everyone connected with the proceedings would become an overnight celebrity. Witnesses were interviewed in advance of their testifying; police officers issued statements; and perhaps most importantly, the potential jurors themselves acquired notoriety. Their names and addresses were printed in the newspapers and the twelve who finally sat in the box were as much a part of the publicity surrounding the case as the defendant and the attorneys.

Although no "live" television or radio coverage of the trial was permitted, each day's testimony was printed in the newspapers of the following day. As the trial progressed interviews with participants and nonparticipants continued. Necessarily the source of most of the information reaching the public was the prosecution side of the case. But all this might not have mattered once the jury was impaneled and the case began—if the jurors had been in any way insulated from the barrage. That simple expedient was not thought necessary by the trial judge, who merely "suggested" to the jurors that they not read the newspaper accounts of the trial during its progress. That this suggestion was ignored was proved when, during the course of the trial, a particularly damaging fact concerning Dr. Shepherd's prior behavior was broadcast by a national news commentator. Several jurors, under questioning, admitted to having heard the particular broadcast, but the defense motion for a mistrial was denied because the court felt that they could ignore the information they had learned while deliberating on the defendant's guilt or innocence.

Shepherd was, of course, convicted of the crime and thereafter began his arduous twelve-year-long fight for life and freedom. After two state appellate courts affirmed the trial result the United States Supreme Court, on direct appeal, denied his petition for *certeriori* in 1956. Then years later, represented by a new attorney, and after considerable advances in the level of judicial awareness concerning the relationship between newspaper publicity and the trial process, the Supreme Court again had Dr. Shepherd on its docket. This time however, it was *Shepherd* v. *Maxwell, Warden,* and the case had worked its way through the federal court system. Dr. Shepherd had won his freedom briefly in the interim when a federal district court had ordered the case retried. This order was reversed—on a divided vote—by a three judge Court of Appeals, when the state had appealed.

Shepherd's new champion in his federal court proceedings was a young Boston attorney who was gaining a reputation as one of the best criminal defense attorneys in the country. F. Lee Bailey was still in law school when Shepherd was first tried, but this fact didn't inhibit his efforts to free Dr. Shepherd on the theory that the 1954 trial was made unfair by the activities of the Cleveland news media. I can remember seeing Lee Bailey in the airport in Chicago during the appeal. The way he fervently "argued" his case to me as we waited for our planes, I knew Lee would not be turned down when he had the chance to present his case in court. And he wasn't.

On the second opportunity to review the conviction and with *Estes* v. *Texas* and a number of other cases on the books as reliable precedent, the Supreme Court was able to concur. In an opinion which was joined by eight members of the court (without so much as a concurring opinion) the court reversed the decision of the three-judge federal appellate court and remanded (sent back) the case to be either retried within a reasonable time or dismissed. Sam Shepherd's trial for his life in the "Roman Carnival" atmosphere of Cleveland in 1954 had been grossly unfair.

But when does such unfairness achieve constitutional dimensions, thereby requiring a reversal on the purely constitutional ground which was being urged at this stage of the Shepherd case? In other words, what happened in the Shepherd trial that impelled the Supreme Court to, in effect, reverse his conviction and lay down a new set of rules which henceforth will govern the conduct of criminal trials in every court in the United States?

The outstanding vice of the Shepherd trial was the presentation in the press of a great deal of information about the case and about Shepherd personally, which was never heard from the witness stand. For example: Shepherd had impeded the murder investigation and must be guilty because he had hired a prominent criminal lawyer; he had sexual relations with numerous women; his dead wife had characterized him as a "Jekyll and Hyde"; he was a "bare-faced liar" because of his testimony as to police treatment; a woman convict claimed to be the mother of his illegitimate child.

And as the Supreme Court noted: "Nor is there doubt that this deluge of publicity reached at least some of the jury." Dorothy Kilgallen told me the circuit judge told her in almost the same language that Judge Thayer had used prior to the

Sacco-Vanzetti case: "They're guilty as hell, but I'm going to give them a fair trial." The circuit judge said, "Shepherd is guilty as hell, but I'm going to give him a fair trial."

This "fundamental" error was compounded by the trial court's erroneous belief that it lacked power to control the publicity about the trial. Even so, the court could have done a better job of controlling the carnival atmosphere of the trial, "since the courtroom and courthouse premises are subject to the control of the court." Even though the trial judge believed that "freedom of the press" guaranteed the reporters carte blanche to write anything about the case that they chose, it was well within the court's power to limit the activities of the newsmen in the court itself—a measure the court never felt it could employ. Beyond this, the Supreme Court said, the trial court could have and should have found some way to insulate the case witnesses from daily interviews and press conferences. Although non-testifying witnesses were excluded from the courtroom (a standard defense tactic), witnesses told reporters in advance everything they expected to testify about—and more. In addition, the actual trial testimony was reported verbatim in the daily coverage of the case. Persons who had not testified were, of course, free to read these accounts under the laissez faire rules of the Shepherd trial.

Lastly, the court made no effort to control the activities of the trial participants in their relations with the press, although this constraint was clearly available to it without argument.

Twelve years after the commission of the crime, Dr. Sam was retried by the Cuyahoga County authorities for the murder of his wife. But in conformity to the new trial rules which his case had fastened onto the courts of the nation, the retrial of Sam Shepherd was a far different affair. Had it been any other case the Cleveland authorities might well have let it drop, but the decision to try again for a conviction was made, probably as a matter of pride or honor for the local district attorney's office. With F. Lee Bailey in charge of his defense —the attorney who had won the right to the retrial in the United States Supreme Court for Shepherd—the proceedings were marked by extreme caution, and probably somewhat less enthusiasm by the media. During the intervening twelve years everyone had learned a little. And this time around, the twelve citizens who sat in the jury box could find that there was indeed a "reasonable doubt" that Dr. Shepherd had done in his pregnant wife on that long-gone holiday weekend.

Although the Shepherd type of case is a rarity in American criminal law, the right to the atmosphere of judicial serenity is now secured to every defendant. Judges are now on notice that they may constitutionally restrain newspaper coverage of trials at least indirectly through their jurisdiction over the activities of trial participants and witnesses. The contempt power may be employed where conduct does not conform to the court's specific ground rules and the threat of this authority should insure responsible reporting. The era of the "trial by newspaper" is ended, just as the era of trial by battle or trial by ordeal was concluded with the adoption of disinterested juries. In all probability, everyone connected with the criminal law, with insignificant exceptions, is pleased that the Supreme Court has given its ultimatum.

However, the real grounds for reversal of the holding were that it was the fault of the court in not controlling the press. Thus, there wasn't a clear-cut decision on free press retrial.

CHAPTER SEVEN

How Free Is Free Speech?

"Congress shall make no law . . . abridging the freedom of speech." United States Constitution, First Amendment.

Do these words mean what they say, or do they mean something different? Taken literally, of course, they would eliminate a substantial body of work of the Supreme Court—not to mention the other courts of the American legal system. If Congress (and by logical extension, the state legislatures) in fact had no power to write laws "abridging the freedom of speech" the only question the courts would have to answer in a given case is whether the material in issue is "speech." Once this determination has been made, the case becomes simple.

To one without a knowledge of the history of the American Constitution, the flat prohibitory language of the First Amendment should not require interpretation. But it was a mere eight years after this limitation was added that the federal Congress enacted the Alien and Sedition Acts of 1798. These laws made criminal the writing or publishing of "any false, scandalous, and malicious" comments about the government of the United States or its elected officials. Punishment for a violation of the law could be a $2000 fine and two years in prison. By its terms, however, the law expired in 1801 and no prosecution brought under the acts was ever reviewed by the Supreme Court. The federal government was happy to see the laws die and no comparable experiment was attempted until the Smith Act, one hundred and fifty years later.

However, before the Smith Act appeared on the scene, the Congress did attempt legislation designed to cope with the problem of internal subversion and the protection of military secrets. This law—the Espionage Act of 1917—gave the Supreme Court its first series of cases in the modern era in which the dimensions of First Amendment protections of speech freedom could be probed.

One of the sections of the Espionage Act related to a curiously present-day phenomenon: activities (primarily speech) which tended to obstruct or inhibit the recruiting efforts of the military services of the United States. Support for "Mr. Wilson's War" was far from unanimous, particularly after the collapse of Russia and the replacement of the Czarist government by the Bolshevik in 1917. American Socialists worked hard at convincing American draftees that they were the "lackeys of Wall Street imperialism" and that they should refuse to allow themselves to be sent to foreign lands to kill.

Such a person was the defendant, Schenck, who admitted he had tried to influence draftees to avoid induction into the armed forces. His federal court conviction was affirmed by a unanimous Supreme Court in an opinion by Associate Justice Oliver Wendell Holmes which has since become one of the classics of the legal literature. Its language is worth quoting: "We admit that in many places and in ordinary times the defendants in saying all that was said in the circular would have been within their constitutional rights. But the character of every act depends upon the circumstances in which it is done. The most stringent protection of free speech would not protect a man falsely shouting fire in a theatre and causing a panic. It does not even protect a man from an injunction against uttering words that may have all the effect of force. The question in every case is whether the words used are used in such circumstances and are of such a nature as to create a clear and present danger that they will bring about the substantive evils that Congress has a right to prevent. It is a question of proximity and degree. When a nation is at war many things that might be said in time of peace are such a hindrance to the effort that their utterance will not be endured so long as men fight and that no court would regard them as protected by any constitutional right."

These words of Justice Holmes—one of the most revered men ever to sit on the American Supreme Court—have established the parameters of First Amendment litigation for the past fifty years. The idea has been refined and the language has been made more gaudy by successive generations of Supreme Court justices, but the doctrine has hardly been altered. The differing applications of the standard which have been elaborated in differing contexts have merely represented various judicial views of the "clarity" or "presentness" of the danger which the state has sought to prevent by restraint. In illustration of Justice Holmes' thesis; sometimes the shout of "fire" has been too feeble to be heard—nothing prevents one from whispering "fire" if no one hears the whisper; or sometimes the audience is so sophisticated that they don't believe the cry; or sometimes the theater isn't crowded at all, in which case the shout of "fire" presents no actual danger.

Subsequent developments concerning the First Amendment and its protection of speech illustrate a number of aspects of the judicial artistry. In the same term of court in which he wrote the unanimous opinion in the Schenck case, Justice Holmes was moved to dissent in the matter of *Abrams v. United States,* also a prosecution under the Espionage Acts. Here, however, the Justice found that the defendants were being punished for expressing opinions and, in effect, criticizing the operations of the government. The dangers which he perceived in these cases were neither clear nor present, but merely advocacy of "unpopular" ideas. This was too close to the kind of conduct which the Alien and Sedition Acts of 1798 had proscribed and which Justice Holmes thought the United States had "repented" of enacting. (Justice Holmes' dissent in Abrams came to be accepted by the Supreme Court as the court's "prevailing attitude"—but this occurred considerably later.)

Six years later the first great advance in American Constitutional theory since *Barron* v. *Baltimore* (decided in 1833) was scored when the court allowed the idea that the First Amendment to the Constitution applied with equal force to the respective states of the union via the "due process" clause of the Fourteenth Amendment. It was a back door entry—the defendant's conviction of violation of a New York "criminal anarchy" law was affirmed—but the wall that had been erected between the Bill of Rights and the states by the Slaughter House cases of 1878 finally began to crumble. *Gitlow* v. *New York* was in the nature of a postwar "red hunt" prosecution, although the particular law in question had been enacted in 1902 in the wake of President McKinley's assassination in New York State. Again, Justices Holmes and Brandeis dissented—on the argument that the mere advocacy of ideas cannot create criminal liability. So far as Justice Holmes could determine, the defendant Gitlow had merely urged the "workers of the world to unite" in classic socialist jargon. In answer to the charge that the document in question, a "left wing manifesto" was more than an idea—it was also an "incitement" the learned justice pointed out that ". . . Every idea is an incitement. It offers itself for belief, and, if believed, it is acted on unless some other belief outweighs it, or some failure of energy stifles the movement at its birth. The only difference between the expression of any opinion and an incitement in the narrower sense is the speaker's enthusiasm for the result. Eloquence may set fire to reason . . ."

Then in a sentence that was truly "radical"—but close to expressing the core meaning of the First Amendment—Justice Holmes offered this comment: "If, in the long run, the beliefs expressed in proletarian dictatorship are destined to be accepted by the dominant forces in the community, the only meaning of free speech is that they should be given their chance and have their way."

Justice Holmes (with his colleague in dissent, Justice Brandeis) was espousing the "free market of ideas" with as few customs barriers as possible. Through such a free interchange, "truth" will always emerge; and the essence of freedom is the search for truth, wherever it carries one.

This theme was expanded and elaborated with great eloquence by Justice Brandeis in his concurring opinion in *Whitney* v. *California,* decided in 1927. Mrs. Whitney had been convicted under the relevant state laws prohibiting criminal syndicalism, an activity which was defined by the law as: ". . . advocating, teaching, or aiding, or abetting the commission of a crime . . . or unlawful acts of force and violence . . . as a means of accomplishing a change in industrial ownership or control, or effecting any political change."

Further, membership in any organization advocating criminal syndicalism, as defined, was a felony. Mrs. Whitney's offense was assisting the formation of the Oakland Chapter of the Communist Labor Party of America, a splinter group of the regular Communist Party. Mrs. Whitney attended a convention at which the CLP adopted an activist resolution, and she and a number of others were prosecuted by the Alameda County district attorney (whose staff then included a promising young lawyer by the name of Earl Warren—really more plodding than brilliant.)

The Supreme Court examined the Criminal Syndicalism Law and found it fully consistent with the due process of law and the First Amendment. Justice Brandeis' concurring opinion warned against the dangers inherent in repression of speech and ideas of this kind, without first establishing the immediacy of the harm or danger threatened. "Fear of serious injury cannot alone justify suppression of free speech and assembly. Men feared witches and burned women. It is the function of speech to free men from the bondage of irrational fears."

To Justice Brandeis the whole (and only) question to be answered when reviewing legislation which makes advocacy of ideas a crime is: what is the probability or imminence of the threatened danger? He summed it up this way. "Even advocacy of violation, however reprehensible morally, is not justification for denying free speech where the advocacy falls short of incitement and there is nothing to indicate the advocacy would be immediately acted on."

The Justice then threw in an offhand comment of the role of the Supreme Court in cases in which constitutional freedoms were alleged to have been violated: "The legislative declaration, like the fact that the statute was passed and was sustained by the highest court of the state, creates merely a rebuttable presumption that these conditions have been satisfied."

In other words the Supreme Court is not "bound" by the legislative finding or the state court's determination that constitutional standards have been met, in the same way that it is "bound" when the question is one of commercial regulation or ordinary exercise of the police power.

In this deceptively innocent statement we find the seedling of the next major advance in First Amendment theory. This advance was the so-called preferred position of the First Amendment whereby legislative restrictions on freedom of speech do not enjoy the same presumption of constitutionality that limitations on purely economic activities might. This germinal concept was not picked up by the court for ten years after Whitney was decided and in the interim a further gloss of significance was added. This was the consideration by the court of how far a state might go in putting out of business a publisher who printed defamatory material. The case, *Near* v. *Minnesota,* concerned the publisher of a small weekly journal of opinion whose content, charitably, could be called trash. A state law permitted the abatement, as a public nuisance, of such publications. The Supreme Court found this law to represent the "essence of censorship" and struck it down. Even though the defendant may have in fact published libelous material, the remedy permitted could only be through post-publication actions, not outright suppression. Near established the principle that although one could be prosecuted for his words, one still had the right to say or publish the words.

Things remained relatively quiet on the free speech front for several years. But then, in 1937, the Supreme Court was confronted with *Herndon* v. *Lowry,* a case in which the defendant Herndon had drawn a twenty year sentence for possessing a booklet called *The Communist Position on the Negro Question.* The defendant could have gotten the death penalty for the offense, a violation of the pre-Civil War laws relating to the incitement of insurrection by slaves. After the Thirteenth Amendment had been adopted, the law had deleted references to slaves, but otherwise was the same. Herndon's jury had gone easy on him, recommending only twenty years on the chain gang. By the barest of margins (five to four) the court reversed the conviction when the case finally was given a hearing on a *habeas corpus* petition.

Now the Supreme Court in 1937 was not overrun by men who would today be characterized as "liberals." A year later

Franklin Roosevelt would castigate them as the "nine old men" who had torpedoed his ship of social reform, and attempt to dilute their constrictive effect by enlarging the membership of the court. Even so, the treatment of Angelo Herndon, Negro and Communist, by the Georgia law enforcement authorities raised hackles on the necks of a majority of these ancient nine.

But the problem that the majority had was to find a justifiable basis for intervening in a state criminal proceeding, with all of its "presumptions of validity." The peg the court found to hang its judicial hat on was the elaboration of Justice Brandeis' opinion in Whitney: "The power of a state to abridge freedom of speech and of assembly is the exception rather than the rule and the penalizing of utterances of a defined character must find its justification in a reasonable apprehension of danger to organized government."

The law was bad, Justice Roberts said, for the majority because it was vague and did not establish an ascertainable standard of guilt. There was no evidence that Herndon had in fact distributed any materials or had *done* anything except talk about relief and public welfare. The Georgia Supreme Court said it didn't matter that he hadn't done anything: he was intending to do something, and that was enough to satisfy the statutory prohibition. His intention to stir up trouble was all the "clear and present danger" necessary to justify invoking the Georgia law.

Still, the preferred position of the First Amendment was not firm constitutional doctrine. The Herndon case had merely put on the state the onus of showing the "reasonable apprehension of danger." But, in a *footnote* in an opinion the following year (*United States* v. *Carolene Products,* a commercial regulation case) the majority opinion clearly distinguished between the presumption of validity which attends an economic regulatory statute and one which restricts the operation of the political processes which can be expected to bring about repeal of undesirable legislation.

In the Carolene Products case, the problem was a violation of a federal law prohibiting the shipment, in interstate commerce, of products which appear to be milk but which do not contain dairy fats. In the course of deciding that the federal statute was not unconstitutional on its face (that is, as written) the court threw in some important constitutional doctrine in which it differentiated between economic regulations and regulations which have an effect on the exercise of First Amendment rights. The words of the court (in what at the time seemed an inconsequential footnote) have since bulked large in constitutional litigation. The essence of the footnote was an admission that laws which inhibit the operation of the political processes should be subject to "more searching judicial inquiry" than those which merely affect commercial practices.

The "preferred position" of the First Amendment was solidified in subsequent Supreme Court decisions so that by 1942—after a series of cases in which Brandeis' concurring opinion in the Whitney case became the accepted basis for deciding First Amendment problems—the decision in *Chaplinsky* v. *New Hampshire* must have come as something of a surprise to constitutional theorists.

The defendant, Chaplinsky, was something of a troublemaker. A member of the Jehovah's Witnesses, he had violated a New Hampshire "breach of peace" statute by calling a city police officer a "racketeer" and a "fascist."

Affirming his conviction, the court majority engrafted onto the whole area of free speech a "two-level" theory which has plagued the courts and litigants ever since. This new doctrine was defined as follows: "There are certain well-defined and narrowly limited classes of speech, the prevention and punishment of which have never been thought to raise any constitutional problem. These include the lewd and obscene, the profane, the libelous and the insulting or 'fighting' words—those which by their very utterance inflict injury or tend to incite an immediate breach of the peace. It has been well observed that such utterances are no essential part of any exposition of ideas and are of such slight social value as a step to truth that any benefit that may be derived from them is clearly outweighed by the social interest in order and morality."

These few sentences took out of the First Amendment (and its protections) several large chunks of human activity. The "clear and present danger" test which had previously been thought to limit the federal government and the states in their restriction of communications just had no application when the words in question could be said to fall within one of the several broad categories announced by the court. As can be noted, these several categories might encompass a multitude of sins—or speeches. Subsequent Supreme Court decisions did establish how broad a sweep was comprehended within this paragraph. The process of group libel (*Beauharnias* v. *Illinois,* 1952) and obscenity (*Roth* v. *United States,* 1957) were not deserving of First Amendment protection. (Of course, merely saying that something called "obscenity" is not within the protection doesn't really solve anything. The question remains: what is obscenity?)

Having established "clear and present danger" as the magic verbal formula to treat one class of cases and then glossed that test with the "two-level" of speech approach, the court might have called it a dogma and left the subject alone. But somehow, the court found itself called upon to cope with situations which did not lend themselves to either of these approaches. These were cases in which the state could show a clear interest in preventing (or punishing) the speech in question but in which the "danger" of the speech was at most a matter of speculation, and the speaker could show some social utility in his expression.

Cases involving defamation and political commentary often seemed to raise this kind of problem and the court adopted what came to be called an "*ad hoc* balancing" approach to deciding them. "Balancing" as a method of resolving constitutional questions pleased few critics—especially those who were looking for absolutes in First Amendment litigation.

The "balancing act" in free expression cases related largely to the control of communism and communist influences in government and labor unions. The "clear and present danger" test wouldn't work in this context because the various loyalty oaths and "non-communist affidavits" required, for example, of union officials bore a relation only to what was presumed to be the likely future conduct of communist union officials. The balance to be struck was between the governmental interest in its own security and the citizens' interest in holding a job, getting a passport or refusing to answer questions before a congressional committee concerning past political associations.

A great many such cases came to the court during the decade of the fifties and early sixties and the balance was struck first one way, then the other as the personnel of the court changed and shifting political winds and international developments apparently affected the weight to be given the government's interests. The theory was stated succinctly in a case of the early sixties: "While the Constitution protects against the invasions of individual rights, it is not a suicide pact."

Nevertheless, as the court moved into an era of greater political sophistication it began to shift the balance generally in favor of the individual, requiring more stringent standards on the part of states (and the Congress) in their declarations that members of certain organizations or holders of certain political beliefs could have basic constitutional rights limited. As the so-called liberal majority on the court has solidified around Chief Justice Warren and Justices Black and Douglas, a liberal majority was far easier to obtain than during the middle and later fifties. One catalyst which added greatly to the court's work load and required the justices to rethink their First Amendment theory was a by-product of the Civil Rights Revolution in America—a revolution which the court itself had started in 1954 with the School Desegregation decisions. Those cases held that "separate but equal" in school facilities for white and Negroes was a violation of the Fourteenth Amendment's equal protection clause. As this principle was extended—through litigation—to all aspects of public facilities and government services, the civil rights movement gathered steam. Legal counsel for many civil rights cases was provided by the National Association for the Advancement of Colored People and other such organizations.

Many southern states unwilling to comply with the Supreme Court's ruling in the race relations area, sought to counter the effect of the ruling by the enactment of laws designed to strike at the organizations which were leading the integration battle. A series of cases reached the court in which the opposing parties presented conflicting claims of states' rights versus individual liberties. One of these, *NAACP* v. *Button,* arose from a Virginia statute which was part of the Old Dominion's program of "massive resistance" to school integration. The state sought to prohibit certain conduct with relation to the seeking of legal advise—parents of school age youngsters were directed to NAACP attorneys for advice on ways to challenge local school boards. The court held the prohibitory statute unconstitutional as too broad a limitation on free expression. Similar cases, usually involving disclosure of membership names of civil rights groups, produced similar results.

During this same period, however, other defendants (generally "political" defendants who refused to answer questions posed by legislative investigating committees) fared less well. During these years the court was sharply and narrowly divided, but in general struck its balance in favor of the governmental interest in getting information and to the detriment of the individual's First Amendment rights.

The other "free expression" cases which have troubled the judicial waters during the most recent years have been concerned with the "breach of peace" problems arising out of efforts at direct action by Southerners—primarily Negroes—who have taken their cause into the streets. As long ago as 1941, in *Thornhill* v. *Alabama,* the court had extended First Amendment protections to physical expressions such as picketing (Thornhill arose in the context of a labor dispute)—again with limitations relating to public convenience and safety. When the earliest "sit in" cases reached the court it was inclined to extend the rationale of the picketing cases to cover the protests of Negroes and their allies who were challenging various Southern anti-integration laws, or nonspecific disturbing the peace or trespass violations.

Although the Supreme Court uniformly held that convictions of this kind arising out of attempts to integrate various public facilities were constitutionally unsound, no case which dealt directly with First Amendment rights in the context of the civil rights movement was presented directly to the court until 1964. However, in that year the court was required to confront—head-on—just such a problem. And in a true "Law Revolution" kind of decision, it wrote an opinion whose reverberations may still be audible fifty or one hundred years from today—if the Supreme Courts of the years to come are willing to apply the broad concepts and sweeping principles of the decision in analogous litigation.

The case in question—*New York Times* v. *Sullivan*—arose as a result of an advertisement which was printed in the *New York Times* newspaper. The advertisement was highly critical of the actions of the police of Montgomery, Alabama, in the course of putting down a civil rights protest which was held in that city. The police commissioner, Sullivan, sued a variety of persons who were identified as the sponsors of the advertisement—and the publishing newspaper, the *New York Times*.

Sullivan, as the aggrieved party, brought a defamation suit against an assortment of defendants. As publisher, the newspaper was joined as a defendant—the only defendant incidentally in a position to pay any large judgment which might be returned. The case was tried before a jury of Alabamans and resulted in a plaintiff's verdict of a cool half-million dollars. In view of the fact that only thirty-five copies of the offending publication had been circulated in the plaintiff's home county, there might have been some serious question as to the reality of the damage to his reputation, especially since the accusation was that Sullivan, as police commissioner, had been somewhat overzealous in his repression of civil rights activities—conduct which has not been known to lose many votes in the South during recent years. The jury's verdict however found that the plaintiff was entitled to "punitive" as well as actual damages, since under prevailing Alabama law the showing of "implied malice" on the part of the publisher gave rise to the inference of malice. The verdict failed to differentiate actual and punitive damages, but merely required the losing defendants to shell out $500,000 as balm to Commissioner Sullivan.

This was not the extent of the potential cost to the New

York newspaper: other suits based upon the same or similar advertisements were on file in the Alabama courts in which an additional two and one-half million dollars was being demanded. If the verdict in the Sullivan case were allowed to stand, every publication in the United States would be on notice that it would be assuming a substantial risk merely through the reportage of civil rights activities. (The advertisement did contain several factual errors, thereby precluding the defendant, the *Times,* from asserting the defense of "truth," the traditional and classic defense in libel actions in the United States.)

At the outset, the court was faced with the premise that this type of litigation—defamation—presents no basis for its jurisdiction. Indeed, few tort cases have reached the Supreme Court to make new law—that's been done in state supreme courts—with the exception of railroad and maritime cases. The Supreme Court has really "swung" in these two classes of cases.

Libel, as a civil action between two nongovernmental entities, exhibits no apparent federal question or constitutional issue—the two principal concepts which will cause the Supreme Court to grant *certeriori* in a given case. Further, this was a state court decision which had been reviewed and affirmed by the highest state tribunal. Beyond this, the plaintiff could argue that the Supreme Court itself had said that "libel" was beneath the protections of the First Amendment, as speech which played no important part in the communication of socially important ideas. This had been the holding of *Chaplinsky* v. *New Hampshire*—and it had never been overruled. The principal had in fact been reaffirmed in the many cases relating to pornography and obscenity which had been before the court during the intervening years.

The answer to all this came in a few brief words which can be taken as overruling the "two level" theory of speech.

"Libel," the court said, "can claim no talismanic immunity from constitutional limitations. It must be measured by standards that satisfy the First Amendment." The court then harked back to the concurring opinion (of Justice Brandeis) in the forty-year-old Whitney case for the general proposition that "freedom of expression on public issues is secured by the First Amendment." With this quick maneuver the court took the case out of the general law of libel and moved it into the more sacred precincts of public discussion of important social issues. Debate on these issues, the court felt, should be "uninhibited, robust, and wide open." With unobtrusive (to some) sleight of hand, the opinion took judicial notice of the context of the litigation before it; the advertisement at issue was "an expression of grievance and protest on one of the major public issues of our time." As such it was deserving of more than superficial scrutiny. Having decided that it could look behind the facade of the litigation to determine what the effect of such a judgment would be in the context of the civil rights movement, it found itself faced with the need to rewrite the libel laws of more than one-half of the states. It did this in effect by extending to publications (as well as private citizens) a much broader defense to libel actions than the classic one of "truth." The *New York Times* decision said in effect that the "malice" element needed to support an award of punitive damages could not be presumed. That it became the burden of the plaintiff to show an actual malicious intent, or a reckless disregard for truth.

The court reached this position through an analysis of the competing interests involved in such litigation. It found that the fear of having to satisfy a libel judgment because of a reporter or commentator's erroneous statement about the conduct of a public official would have a "chilling effect," on the free public discussion that is prized so highly in an open, democratic society. The reporter, at least when he is talking about public officials in the performance of public duties, should have the breathing room to be wrong. In this analysis the interest that the public official has in his own reputation is of less importance than the right of his critics to be wrong in their assessment of his activities. It was Harry Truman's warning to politicians and those in public life, "If you can't stand the heat, stay out of the kitchen." Of course, the competing philosophy is that an open season on defamation of public officials would cause many good men to stay out of public life with the answer, "Who needs that!"

To Justice Brennan, the author of the *New York Times* case opinion, the question to be answered was the same as the one that the court had to answer in the Roth (obscenity) case: does the speech in question have any redeeming social value? Does it contribute anything to socially useful goals? If it does, it should have First Amendment protection. In Roth, Justice Brennan found that "hard core pornography" plays no part in advancing the social order. Similarly, libelous falsehoods do not qualify for this protection. The distinction was summed up by the court in a case involving the stormy petrel, District Attorney of New Orleans Parish, Jim Garrison. Garrison had been held in contempt by a judge of the state for certain out of court comments on the judge's conduct. The Supreme Court reversed the contempt conviction by in effect extending the rationale of the *New York Times* case decision to include judges as the kind of public officials whose conduct should be open to criticism—so long as the comment was something other than a "calculated falsehood." The knowingly false statement, made with reckless disregard of the truth, does not enjoy constitutional protection.

The long range effect of the *New York Times* case in "free expression" litigation is not certain. Some things are clear from the opinion, however. If the person about whom the comments are made is in some way a "public" person, a different standard will be applied by the courts to determine whether he has been actionably defamed. Further, comments about public officials, at least in the discharge of their public duties, will be accorded the broadest possible latitude without sanction or interference. The "chilling effect" of a possible libel judgment will not be permitted to inhibit the free expression of public issues so long as certain minimum standards of honesty and good faith are met. The burden is placed on the plaintiff to show that the defendant uttered a "knowing falsehood" rather than on the defendant to prove the "truth" of his charges. Although this may seem a minor shift in emphasis, as a practical matter it will make a substantial change in the probability that a plaintiff will be able to get his case to a jury.

This aspect of the case aside, it seems that *New York Times* rewrote a fair amount of free speech constitutional doctrine, in that the traditional "tests" applied in First Amendment litigation were either ignored or passed over lightly as inappropriate to the decision. Whether these doctrinal yardsticks will resurface in future cases remains to be seen. Clear-and-present-danger, balancing and two-levels-of-speech theories were all ignored by Justice Brennan in reaching his conclusion about the need for open and robust debate on public issues. However, to the advocates of free and open discussion, the *New York Times* decision was the most hopeful and encouraging sign to come from the Supreme Court since *Gitlow* v. *New York* in 1925.

CHAPTER EIGHT

The Words on the Barroom Door: a Judicial Disaster Area

Supreme courts are not "dirty old men" because they've recently seemingly opened the floodgates to "dirty" plays, literature, and performances. They're trying to be careful old men with modern ideas protecting the right of individual expression. The Law Revolution is particularly pertinent here in the protection of the individual's right of unique expression. Stifle a novel expression, we may smother an "Ode to a Grecian Urn."

There has been considerable case development during the past few years, particularly in decisions of the United States Supreme Court, with respect to obscenity. This development culminated in *Ginzburg* v. *United States* (1966). (Had Ginzburg not made "the bucket" now, he'd have made it sooner or later. This is not my criticism; this is my evaluation.)

The defendants in Ginzburg were an individual and three corporations who used the mail for distributing allegedly obscene literature. This included the magazine *Eros*, containing articles and photo essays on love and sex, a bi-weekly newsletter, dedicated to "keeping sex an art and preventing it from becoming a science," and *The Housewife's Handbook of Promiscuity*. The trial court convicted defendants on charges of having violated the Federal Obscenity Statute. Court of Appeals (Third Circuit) affirmed.

The United States Supreme Court affirmed in an opinion by five members of the court, in which it was held that even if the material involved was not obscene in the abstract, the trial judge's conclusion that the mailing of these publications offended the statute was supported by evidence showing that defendants engaged in the sordid business of pandering—that is, the business of purveying textual and graphic material openly advertised to appeal to the erotic interests of defendants' customers.

The court pointed out that in all the obscenity cases cited by the Supreme Court since *Roth* v. *United States* (1957), the landmark case, the court had regarded the materials involved in obscenity cases as sufficient in themselves for the determination of the question of obscenity. In Ginzburg, the court for the first time held that although the publications standing by themselves may not be obscene, consideration must be given to the setting in which the publications were presented as an aid in determining the question of obscenity. Court then went on to find that in that respect the record supported the decision of the trial judge in finding that the mailing of the three publications offended the statute. The court held that: "where the purveyor's sole emphasis is on the sexually provocative aspects of the publications, that fact may be decisive in the determination of obscenity."

There were four separate dissents in Ginzburg. Justice Black dissented on the grounds that the federal government is without power under the federal Constitution to put any type of burden on the speech and expression of ideas of any kind as distinguished from conduct and that the Federal Obscenity Statute, as applied, was invalid. This is in accordance with Justice Black's view that the First Amendment rights are in absolutes.

Justice Douglas dissented on the ground that the First

Amendment allowed all ideas to be expressed, even those which are offbeat or repulsive; and further on the ground that, looking at the advertising techniques as the majority did, was violative of the First Amendment and an unwarranted approach.

Justice Harlan dissented: the federal government is constitutionally restricted from banning from the mails only "hard core pornography"; that the material did not fall within that class.

Justice Stewart dissented: there was no federal statute which made the conduct of the defendants a criminal offense and any such statute would be unconstitutionally vague, that the court had no right or power to deny the defendants their First Amendment protections because it disapproved of their sordid business, i.e., commercializing sex.

The Supreme Court has evaded clarifying its obscenity standards in three 1967 cases: *Redrup* v. *New York*, involved the conviction of a bookseller; *Gent* v. *Arkansas*, concerned that state's attempt to suppress and destroy various girlie magazines such as *Gent* and *Bachelor; Landau* v. *Fording*, involved the conviction of a distributor for showing Jean Genet's film *Un Chant d'Amour*. In the first two cases, convictions were unanimously overturned on the ground that none of the publications was obscene, the court setting no new guidelines for determination. A five to four vote with no comment affirmed the California court's determination that the Genet film was obscene, despite unanimous testimony of all witnesses and experts of its social and artistic value.

Before Ginzburg, the test of obscenity seemed to be whether the communication raised a present prurient desire and that, taken as a whole, had no redeeming social value. Roth indicated a present collective social community standard.

Here we have the problem of definition; are words yardsticks or changeable? What is obscenity? The writing of "fuck," "shit" on a wall at the University of California? Of course, these words may be in bad taste, but bad taste is more the subject of parental chastisement than it is governmental jailings.

The application of constitutional standards of obscenity, i.e., contemporary community standards, appealing primarily to prurient interests, etc., raise obvious problems of who is to judge these. Ultimately it will be the appeals court. But in the first instance, that is, at the trial level, who is qualified to testify on these questions?

A rather novel solution was attempted in *State* v. *Watson* (Ore., 1966), prosecution for disseminating obscene matter. The prosecution presented as its star witness the district attorney (who coincidentally was the complainant), testifying that in his opinion the book in question satisfied all statutory requirements for obscenity within the bounds set by the United States Supreme Court.

On cross-examination the witness revealed that he knew little of relevant contemporary community standards and virtually nothing of contemporary literature. Since 1939 or 1940, he admitted he had read no books outside his professional field, and only the *Readers Digest,* religious papers, and the first two chapters of the book in question.

The Supreme Court of Oregon reversed the conviction on the ground that the trial court had committed error in permitting a witness with no special qualification so to testify, to tell the jury that in his opinion a crime had been committed. (I'd personally revel in such a golden opportunity to cross-examine some prosecutors we met, all the way up from police court prosecutors to and including Mr. J. Edgar Hoover, on their reading habits!)

I think Lenny Bruce (who, unfortunately for his memory, is remembered principally for having made of "mother" a hyphenated word) summed it up rather nicely. He came on the stage to shock and uttered the words "mother-fucker." He looked about and then said, "There are two of San Francisco's finest policemen standing at the back wall. They will now rush up to arrest me for 'obscenity.' If they do, I want all of you to note that the chief of police, under the United States Supreme Court decisions, should send them to a psychiatrist rather than me to jail because if the uttering of the word 'mother-fucker' raises in them a 'present prurient desire,' makes them 'horny,' *they* should be examined!"

In this area we find, once again, the caveat to be careful in determining what at first blush may seem to be the least of our liberties, that constitutional restraints do not extend to the greater of our liberties. The careful recognition here is that law is a whole body, and that infection of one area, no matter how small, can infect all of it. One's right to worship as he may please, in a place of his choosing, just may depend upon a Lenny Bruce's right to do his "thing," have his "bag."

A. "Read any Good Books Lately?" One of the unique attributes of the United States Supreme Court is that it nearly always decides "hard" cases—in the lawyer's sense of the word. An opinion of the court which is the unanimous holding of all nine of the justices is a rarity indeed; a case which does not draw at least two dissenting votes, if not full-dress opinions by the dissenting justices, is exceptional. This quality has been especially noteworthy during the years of the Law Revolution as cases have found their way onto the Supreme Court docket which in previous years would never have surfaced for decision. (There's the old adage, "hard cases make hard law.")

But if any area of the law has fragmented the court more than any other, it must be those cases in which the court has sought to deal with the problem of allegedly obscene expression. One of the most recent confrontations with obscenity, for example, involved three cases, decided the same day, which produced fourteen separate opinions all attempting to cope with the same question: when is a published expression a species of obscenity and therefore properly subject to the various state or federal laws which make dissemination of such material a criminal offense?

The court said: there is no answer. All fourteen opinions tell us something about the current attitude of the highest court in the land about sex and its expression in books and periodicals in twentieth century America—but they do not tell us what is or is not criminally punishable obscenity.

I'm puzzled whether the words "shit," and "fuck," the now garden variety of four-letter words which, since time immemorial, have been chalked on board fences about vacant buildings, on cement walks, subway walls, and toilet stalls—I wonder if these words are in such category of bruised bodies, broken bones, forged checks, and drunken driving so that the malefactor uttering these words should be imprisoned or punished. Just what are they? Of course, to someone speaking Congolese, they are as intelligible as "ugh," "gibu," and "zibranda." They are obscenity? Why and how? They are "dirty"? Just what is "dirty"? They may be "smart" and "shocking," but when does fecal matter turn into "excretia," into "shit" so that one of these is criminally punishable? And why? I don't even essay an excursion into whether these four-letter words are in "bad taste" because "bad taste" is such an amorphous concept and as changeable as fashions that there could hardly be predictability of any charging law.

I remember when my friend, the famed San Francisco criminal lawyer Jake (The Master) Ehrlich, defended a nudie tenderloin show with the observation, "This is poor man's art—if you went to the De Yound Museum and paid five bucks for champagne, you could see statuary just as bald-ass naked as anything we have here on the stage."

The three cases—a book named *John Cleland's Memoirs of a Woman of Pleasure* v. *Attorney General of the Common-*

wealth of Massachusetts (Memoirs v. *Massachusetts), Ginzburg* v. *United States,* and *Mishkin* v. *New York*—were decided on March 21, 1966, having been argued orally in the court four months previously. The result in the three cases pleased no one, in all probability. The Supreme Court reversed the Supreme Court of Massachusetts which had declared the book in question—better known as *Fanny Hill*—obscene and therefore not saleable. But it also affirmed two convictions, one federal and one state, for disseminating obscene matter.

The reversal of the *Fanny Hill* decision no doubt distressed members of the Boston Watch & Ward Society, the Thursday Chowder Clatch, and other proper Bostonians; but the affirmance of the convictions of Mishkin and Ginzburg sent shock waves through the literary community, as well as the legal. To many lawyers the Supreme Court had changed the rules in midstream in order to affirm the convictions of Mishkin and Ginzburg, as basic a denial of due process of law as could be imagined.

But in order to appreciate the peculiar nature of the decisions in these three cases it is necessary to go back to the relatively unsophisticated days of 1957 when the Supreme Court first found itself involved with questions of pornography, obscenity, and the First Amendment.

Prior to 1957, the specter of sex had not reared its head in the august chambers of the court. But in that year, perhaps in response to the then recently published studies concerning human sexuality, written by Dr. Kinsey at putatively staid and just as putatively unsexy Indiana University, the court began to look at state and federal court prosecutions of authors and booksellers for allegedly purveying obscene material to a (1) defenseless, (2) avid public, as the case might be.

At this time—as today—there were federal anti-obscenity statutes, as well as state laws. The federal laws were primarily concerned with interstate mailings of obscene materials. (*Esquire* magazine had been involved in a prosecution some years earlier which had finally reached the Supreme Court. The magazine won.) But some state laws were really Alice-in-Wonderland kind of enactments. One hundred years ago an English court had established a formula for determining what is or is not obscene; some states had merely adopted the language of this mid-Victorian decision as its own standard, and applied it to every member of the reading public, regardless of age or maturity. The case was *Regina* v. *Hicklin* and the test of obscenity announced by it was about as follows: . . . whether the tendency of the matter charged as obscenity is to deprave and corrupt those whose minds are open to such immoral influences, and into whose hands a publication of this sort may fall. Now with regard to this work, it is quite certain that it would suggest to the minds of the young of either sex, or even to persons of more advanced years, thoughts of a most impure and libidinous character.

Here was the standard which was largely guiding the decisions of judges in mid-twentieth century America. Thus in *Butler* v. *Michigan* the court threw out (unanimously) a statute of the state of Michigan which reduced the legally available material to those which would not tend to incite or corrupt youthful morals.

"The incidence of this enactment is to reduce the adult population of Michigan to reading only what is fit for children," Justice Frankfurter noted in his opinion for the court. But Butler was the last "easy" case the court was to decide in this prickly area for many years to come. In the same term it confronted two additional "obscenity" cases which it apparently hoped would create new, workable constitutional standards for sexual expression while at the same time holding the line against "hard core" pornography, whatever that is.

To start with, obscenity is not constitutionally protected free speech, because it is utterly without redeeming social importance, whatever *that* is. In this view the "clear and present danger" test that is traditional in First Amendment cases has no application. Thus, whether the challenged material presents a "clear and present danger" to the instigation of anti-social conduct is irrelevant to a determination concerning its protectibility under the First Amendment. But, these are after all, First Amendment problems that the court is looking at, so some standard must be applied. The result—out of the two 1957 cases in question, *United States* v. *Roth* and *Alberts* v. *California*—was the Brennan test of obscenity: whether to the average person, applying contemporary community standards, the dominant theme of the material taken as a whole appeals to prurient interest.

This test, often quoted, contains several mares' nests of definitional problems. Who is the average person? How do you define the community? Who decided what its standards are? Who decides whether the dominant theme of the material appeals to the prurient interest? And just what *is* prurient interest?

About all that may be said in defense of the Brennan test is that it is an improvement on the 1868 English test then popular in the United States.

The most obvious problem however is the highly subjective nature of the test. As it has been remarked, one man's pornography is merely another man's boredom.

But once the Supreme Court's front door was opened to the question, cases began arriving with monotonous regularity to the only body of men equipped to decide whether a given work was within the definition, thus the court was put in the unwelcome position of national censor, a role many of its members deplored strongly.

The question of the average person came before the court

in 1962 when the Post Office prosecuted the disseminators of several magazines whose appeal could only be to homosexuals (*Manual Enterprises* v. *Day*). These cases added a gloss to the Roth-Brennan test which for want of a better phrase became known as the "patent offensiveness" test. This approach was needed because to hold the publications involved here to be obscene would *ipso facto* determine that any representations of the undraped male figure (e.g., a photograph of Michelangelo's magnificent "David") was an obscenity. To so hold would impute to congress a "quixotic and deadening purpose" which would raise constitutional problems.

The next case which offered the court an opportunity to "redefine" obscenity was *Jacobellis* v. *Ohio,* a motion picture censorship problem. The film in question, a French import called *Les Amants (The Lovers),* contained some explicit scenes of sexual behavior and a suburban Cleveland motion picture exhibitor (Jacobellis) had been prosecuted for showing it.

The Jacobellis case is a good illustration of the difficulty the Supreme Court has had in reaching any conclusions in this area. Five of the justices wrote opinions. The prevailing opinion, again by Justice Brennan, won the concurrence of only Justice Goldberg. Black and Douglas concurred in one opinion; Stewart concurred on a different ground. White concurred, but without an opinion. Chief Justice Warren with Justice Clark dissented, and Justice Harlan dissented but on a different ground.

Since he wrote the prevailing opinion, the words of Justice Brennan are of the most interest. As the author of the basic Supreme Court test (Roth and Alberts), he apparently felt it was time to elaborate the verbal formula for the guidance of police, prosecutors, and lower court judges. This he did by again calling attention to the language of Roth and

Alberts in which he had said that the reason obscenity is excluded from constitutional protection is because it is "utterly without redeeming social importance" but that the portrayal of sex, as such, is not of itself sufficient reason to deny material the constitutional protection of freedom of speech and press.

The remainder of the court's prevailing opinion was concerned with the problem of defining and applying the word "community" in the context of obscenity prosecutions. In this field as in others respecting constitutional rights, the standard to be applied is a "national" not local one. And, weighing heavily in favor of the defendant, the fact that the film in question had been shown in one hundred other cities (presumably without any trouble from the law) indicated to the court that Mr. Jacobellis had encountered a largely local problem. "It is, after all, a national constitution we are expounding," Justice Brennan said.

The prevailing opinion also felt it incumbent to rebut the criticisms of two of the dissenters, Chief Justice Warren and Justice Clark. The Chief Justice was in basic disagreement with Justice Brennan about what Brennan meant in the Roth case opinion concerning national versus local community standards of pornography. The national community standard is something beyond definition and therefore an abstraction which can be ignored. He further took issue with the theory advanced by Justice Stewart (concurring) that only "hard-core pornography" is properly proscribable under the First Amendment. This position still leaves the problem of defining that elusive concept ("I know it when I see it," Justice Stewart had said) and ultimately leaving the question up to some super board of censorship somewhere. The nature of the American legal system inevitably made that super board the nine justices of the Supreme Court.

Where did the Jacobellis case leave the question of censorship and obscenity? For one thing, the forces of censorship had had a dismal record in the Supreme Court since the Roth-Alberts decision. Convictions which had been pursued to that forum was uniformly reversed without opinion—merely a citation to Roth-Alberts. By the Jacobellis decision, the court was putting states and local government units on notice that a book (or motion picture or whatever) had to be something more than merely dirty in order to get past a finding of obscenity. The significance of "redeeming social importance" by its reemphasis in Jacobellis made it seem that any expression with any claim to literary or artistic pretentions, no matter how slight, would save a publication from the censor's scourge.

Although the problems of obscenity and the First Amendment were far from solved by the various decisions and the various opinions within the decisions, the motto of many publishers could have been taken from a popular song of the thirties—"Anything Goes." One by one the barriers fell; classics of pornography that had been available only as smuggled goods were suddenly as easy to obtain as *Time* magazine, which surveyed the scene and decided that "just about anything is printable in the United States today." Free publication of such famous underground books as Henry Miller's *Rosy Crucifixion* trilogy (*Sexus, Nexus, Plexus*) went along with the pulpiest of trash—and no man could legally distinguish the two.

Where would it end? Or would it end? Across the nation they were unleashed on the public in the wake of the Roth-Jacobellis decisions by the so-called Warren Court. Citizens groups were formed to combat local distribution of "obscenity"; law enforcement agencies despaired of attempting prosecutions and state legislatures struggled with the challenge of writing anti-obscenity law which would satisfy Supreme Court standards while still offering protection against smut.

The lower courts attempted conscientously to apply the tripartite Supreme Court test—and found themselves approving for distribution materials which a generation earlier could only have been peddled as the grossest kind of contraband.

In the welter of opinions which the Supreme Court had authorized was there any hope of damming the tide? Well, it seems that after all, there was. It was contained in a little-noticed concurring opinion offered by the Chief Justice himself in the case which had started the whole problem—Roth-Alberts. In that opinion Chief Justice Warren had expressed himself as concerned about not so much the materials themselves as about the motive and activities of the purveyor of the materials. The sordid business of pandering to the baser human instincts: the exploitation of sex for purely commercial motives had seemed to the Chief Justice relevant to the determination of obscenity. Thus, one who circulated the long suppressed courtesan's autobiography *Fanny Hill* out of historical interest in Georgian England's literary styles was acting with constitutional protection. But if the book were being sold because it contained remarkable detailed accounts of the young lady's sexual awakening and coming of age—that was something else.

The opportunity to apply this new approach to the problem of obscenity and the First Amendment was offered by a young and enterprising New York publisher, Ralph Ginzburg. Mr. Ginzburg (or his lawyers) had obviously been keeping up with the Supreme Court decisions because he launched several publishing ventures which were the product of a new era of sexual candor in his own evaluation of the times.

In brief review, Mr. Ginzburg was prosecuted by the federal government in a Philadelphia district court for violating the basic federal statutes on the use of the mails for the distribution of obscene materials. At his trial the court purported to apply the Roth-Alberts tripartite test sanctioned by the Supreme Court and was able to find the material obscene within the language and meaning of those cases. The Court of Appeals affirmed the convictions—which carried stiff fines and a five year prison term.

Naturally, Ginzburg appealed to the Supreme Court, anticipating that the court would reverse his conviction as it had dozens of those since the Roth-Alberts cases were decided. After all, his publications—an expensive, hard cover quarterly called *Eros,* a short autobiographical work called *The Housewife's Handbook on Selective Promiscuity,* and a newsletter called *Liaison*—seemed no more offensive than such gems as *Sin Island* or hundreds of other sexy potboilers having even less claim to "redeeming social importance."

But Ginzburg had sent his material from Blue Balls, Pa., and thus he became a classic illustration of being in the wrong place at the wrong time. Even though the Law Revolution was in full cry (see *Miranda* v. *Arizona,* decided only three months later) a five-member majority of the court—including Chief Justice Warren—held that Mr. Ginzburg had indeed violated the federal obscenity statute, but in a way that had not occurred to (1) the government prosecutor; (2) the trial judge; (3) the Court of Appeals; and, most of all, (4) Ginzburg's attorney.

What was the defendant's crime? Not necessarily obscenity, but *pandering.* But when did sexual pandering (engaging in the sordid business of purveying textual and graphic matters openly advertised to appeal to the erotic interest of his customers) become a crime?

The answer was simple: 1940, when the Court of Appeals for the Second Circuit (New York) had decided the virtually forgotten obscenity case of *United States* v. *Rebhuhn,* where it became the settled law that the "mode of distribution may be a significant part in the determination of the obscenity of the material involved."

Little matter that Rebhuhn was not mentioned in any prior Supreme Court decision in an obscenity case, including Roth-Alberts—or that the case was not mentioned, cited, or relied upon in any of Ginzburg's lower court proceedings. This fact, taken with the court's own admission that the materials in question, "viewed in the abstract," are not obscene within the definition of Roth, leads inescapably to the conclusion that:

1. the court rewrote the statute which Ginzburg was accused of violating, *or*
2. rewrote the federal indictment under which he had been prosecuted, and then
3. found him guilty of the crime which it had created.

In reviewing the decision it becomes clear that Ginzburg's real problem was his honesty. He never made any bones about his intention to exploit the new era of sexual candor that the court itself had made possible by its decisions for the most American of reasons—the profit motive. Ginzburg was a capitalist of sex ("one of the great human weaknesses," according to Justice Clark) and his attempt to earn dividends without hypocrisy was his undoing. His advertising matter, his promotional material was introduced against him at his trial (probably to satisfy the court's earlier added requirement of scienter—i.e., knowledge of the arguable obscene nature of the materials), but this material revealed, in the hands of the five-man majority, the "leer of the sensualist." Five years in the federal lock-up for indulging oneself in a leer seems unduly harsh.

But on the day it decided Ginzburg, the court also handed down two other obscenity decisions which in their various majority, concurring, and dissenting opinions revealed how far the court is from articulation of any rational standard in this area. Altogether, the three cases decided on March 21, 1966, produced fourteen separate opinions. In two of the cases (*Ginzburg and Mishkin* v. *New York*) convictions were affirmed. In the third case, which involved the eighteenth century classic of pornography, *Fanny Hill,* the state of Massachusetts had attempted to suppress the distribution of the book. The Supreme Court reversed the supreme judicial court of the state in a six to three opinion which applied the Ginzburg-Mishkin "pandering" test—and found this element lacking.

The Mishkin case added only one element to the Ginzburg opinion: the defendant here was a sexual specialist in that his publications catered to the whims and interests of the boots and whips crowd. Straight man-woman sex, missionary style (i.e., face-to-face in the dark) did not engage his or his readers' interests.

To buttress its contention that Mr. Mishkin purveyed obscenity, the court drew upon a variety of authorities, including of all people D. H. Lawrence whose own *Lady Chatterly's Lover* had had its share of censorship problems prior to the new era. Again the record showed the "leer of the sensualist" in defendant's instructions to his stable of authors and illustrators. That was enough for six of the nine justices, although Justice Harlan concurred on the special ground that since this was a state prosecution, different standards to support a conviction should be applied. For the most part it was a replay of the Ginzburg opinion, as refined by the Kraft-Ebbing *Psycopathia Sexualis.*

But *Fanny Hill* was something else. The nominal defendant here was the long dead English author John Cleland and his presumably mythical heroine of the aggravated id, Fanny Hill. The "real party in interest," however, was a publisher, the prestigious firm of G. P. Putnam's Sons. The *Fanny Hill* case (in lawyer's shorthand reference it is known as "*Memoirs,*" after the more formal title *Memoirs of a Woman of Pleasure*) is intriguing for a number of reasons, not the least of these the fact that it is, by consensus, pornographic.

But merely because something is pornographic, the majority of the court found, it is not *ipso facto* obscene—i.e., suppressible. This is because even pornography is not necessarily "utterly without redeeming social importance" and this is where the Supreme Judicial Court of Massachusetts had run afoul of the United States Supreme Court's standards. There was in the book some "minimal literary value," according to the state court, but this was not enough to rescue it from the slag heap of obscenity. Not so, said the United States court. This is a misunderstanding and misapplication of the Roth-Alberts test. The crucial fact distinguishing *Memoirs* from Mishkin-Ginzburg was the absence, in the lower court record, of the pandering element, in spite of specific legislation which makes evidence of such activity relevant in an obscenity prosecution.

The author of the prevailing opinion in *Memoirs* was, again, Justice Brennan—the court's obscenity specialist. He was in particularly good position to speak for the court on the meaning of the Roth-Alberts decisions. And according to Justice Brennan, the "utterly without redeeming social importance" test was an explicit requirement of Roth-Alberts. But, it has been pointed out, Mr. Ginzburg's publications could hardly be said to be "utterly without redeeming social value." *Housewives Handbook* for example had been previously distributed to an audience of doctors, psychiatrists, and marriage counselors—some of whom presumably found something of value in the autobiography. So how do we distinguish Mr. Ginzburg from G. P. Putnam's Sons, purveyors of an item which is pornographic almost by judicial notice?

Easy, the court found. We are not in the business of figuratively buring books. That practice is offensive. What we are concerned with is conduct—the conduct of the disseminator. Thus, where the material in question meets the social value test, but is within the other standards of the Roth-

Alberts test, then evidence that pandering or exploitation was part of the distribution process will make the defendant punishable, even if his materials are not. This approach of course makes a great leaping assumption: that conduct in the promotion of constitutionally protected material is not itself constitutionally protected. Since the "conduct" in question most often consists of the printed word—paid advertising, brochures, and the like—the distinction created seems to make little sense. To First Amendment scholars writing in the country's law reviews, it makes no sense at all.

The answer here is that the court has arrived at something which Chief Justice Warren advocated a decade ago: contextual obscenity, as opposed to definitional obscenity—which was the standard of the majority in Roth-Alberts.

The answer to the riddle of the Ginzburg-Mishkin *Memoirs* trilogy lies in the unsatisfactory nature of the Roth-Alberts definition. The censors do not like the test because it permits far too much; the libertarians dislike it because it does not go far enough. After ten years the "moral election returns" seem to be in. Those voices raised in favor of the censors seem to reflect the wishes of the majority, which unfortunately seem to favor hypocrisy in matters of sexual expression. Henceforth the same material will be disseminated, (perhaps even "rougher" stuff will become available) but it will be more subtly merchandised. This will satisfy those whose knowledge of the kinds of sexually frank materials available is limited to overt newsstand displays and general circulation advertising, especially for such products as motion pictures.

A secondary result will probably be a rush by state legislators to add a "pandering" dimension to state anti-obscenity laws. Previously the question of pandering was only considered relevant to the issue of scienter or foreknowledge of the pornographic nature of the materials—the actions themselves were not considered an offense.

Where do we stand now on the question of pornography and the First Amendment? Two decisions of the Supreme Court during 1967 shed little light on the subject. These reversed, *per curiam* (without opinion), two lower federal court decisions holding certain magazines which were nominally of interest to the "nudist way of life" to be obscene. These publications consisted primarily of photographs of nude men and women focusing on the genitalia. The promotion and the accompanying textual material was bland to the point of insipidness. No "leer of the sensualist" there. No evidence concerning merchandising or promotion was available in the record. The Supreme Court could only follow its own precedents involving similar publications devoted to nudism and reverse the convictions.

Not enough time has elapsed since the Ginzburg-Mishkin decisions for lower court prosecutions to reach the Supreme Court for review. But the problems of the so-called contextual approach to obscenity will be no less simple to resolve than the ones which arose when the court was using the "definitional" standard. For one thing there was hardly anything like a clear majority of the court which could agree on any one approach and the Ginzburg pandering test seems clearly the result of an internal compromise. One member of the five justice majority in that case had already left the court. The fair and able, but probably the most blue-nosed and hard-pantsed, Justice Clark had been replaced by the former Solicitor General, Thurgood Marshall, whose views on the subject are not yet known.

In *Bantam Books* v. *Sullivan*, the problem arose after the Rhode Island legislature had created the Rhode Island Commission to Encourage Morality in Youth. The commission members wrote to booksellers suggesting books which they, the commission, had decided were obscene or objectionable. Following the sending of the letter, a policeman called on the bookseller and rather than "face the possibility of some sort of court action against ourselves, as well as the people that we supply" the bookseller "cooperated."

The Supreme Court held this was an effective intimidation. It is true that appellants' books have not been seized or banned by the state, and that no one has been prosecuted for their possession or sale. But though the commission is limited to informal sanction—the threat of invoking legal sanctions and other means of coercion, persuasion, and intimidation—the record amply demonstrates that the commission deliberately set about to achieve the suppression of publications deemed "objectionable" and succeeded in its aim. We are not the first court to look through forms to the substance and recognize that informal censorship may sufficiently inhibit the circulation of publications to warrant injunctive relief.

Not ones to mince matters, the justices used language which gave proponents of free speech great encouragement. Although the matter involved questions of defamation, the analogy to other "free expression" situations—including pornography—was quite clear.

Herein lies the vice of the system. The commission's operation is a form of effective state regulation superimposed upon the state's criminal regulation of obscenity and making such regulation largely unnecessary. In thus obviating the need to employ criminal sanctions, the state has at the same time eliminated the safeguards of the criminal process. Criminal sanctions may be applied only after a determination of obscenity has been made in a criminal trial hedged about with the procedural safeguards of the criminal process. The commission's practice is in striking contrast, in that it provides no safeguards whatever against the suppression of non-obscene, and therefore constitutionally protected, matter. It is a form of regulation that creates hazards to protected freedoms markedly greater than those that attend reliance upon the criminal law.

The Ginzburg decision, however, was a clear about-face from the possibilities opened up here. But this is a matter, I think, of the tide being temporarily out. Make no mistake about it, the tide will be back in, and this important area in the Law Revolution will be pounded into shape by an inevitable force of time.

CHAPTER NINE

Obey the Law—What Law?

The incongruity of our law is that we don't want our officials to follow it. That is, we don't want them to follow it 100 per cent, or to "the letter of the law." We want our officials to be lenient, to hand out a little "armchair equity," or "fireside justice." This is, supposedly, good politics.

I once represented a zealous young district attorney in Santa Cruz County, California, just graduated from Stanford Law School. He was incited for the infrequently charged crime of "obstructing justice." The gist of the complaints against him was not that he was violating the law, but that he was guilty of a too rigorous enforcement of it, particularly in his naive attempt to close all of the whorehouses in Watsonville, clearly illegal ventures, against the wishes of a practical chamber of commerce which felt that such houses of pleasure were a community necessity for the fun-loving Philippino and Latin community of the county. (He resigned and became a Catholic priest.)

Then there is a "lady assessor" (so characterized by the press, who, when aberrant activities present, seem to delight in attributing them to the innate traits of femininity) recently elected in Sacramento, on a program of "cleaning up hanky-panky in assessors' offices." The electorate took her at her word and elected her on her reform ticket.

Reciprocally she took them at their word and started to assess under the constitution of California, the ancient, 1869, obsolescent, and wildly disregarded organic law of the state whereby all property should be assessed at "full cash value."

In an editorial in the *San Francisco Examiner* it was desperately noted of this good and law-abiding assessor that if she did not mend her ways and violate the law there would be chaos in the state's financial machinery: "It readily appears that if the vast machinery of taxation is not to be brought grinding to a halt, the lady assessor of Sacramento must somehow be induced and persuaded to rise above constitutional principle and return to doing business by the well-worn guidelines established by those members of the assessing fraternity who are not currently in jail."

The "lady assessor" (*County of Sacramento* v. *Hickman*) on Monday, January 16, 1967, announced that taxable property in Sacramento County would be assessed at 100 per cent of "full cash value" for the 1967–68 fiscal year. Petitioners filed for a writ of mandate to compel respondent to reduce the assessed valuations to 20 to 25 per cent.

The Supreme Court said, "There can be no doubt that respondent's duty to assess in accordance with law for violation of which she may be civilly or criminally liable, is . . . mandatory."

The "lady assessor" pointed to Article 11, Section 12 of the California constitution, which declares in relevant portion that "all property subject to taxation shall be assessed at its full cash value."

But the Supreme Court of California and the twenty page opinion held that the "full cash value" did not mean full cash value and furthermore, "there was a long standing administrative practice of assessment at a fraction of full cash values sanctioned by the State Board of Equalization," etc.

Concluded the California Supreme Court, "from the foregoing seventeen pages of legal arguments and history, it is obvious that neither the assessing authorities nor the legislature, nor the courts believed that the addition of the full cash value provision to the constitution in 1933 had been intended to effect any change in the lawfulness of the assessment practice under the prior statutory law. Indeed, it seems clear that 'full cash value' are accepted words of art in the field of taxation."

So, sometimes one can get just as much in trouble obeying the law as breaking it, particularly when some apparently mandatory words in a law are not that at all, but are "words of art."

With such examples as those above, it is difficult for those attempting rehabilitation behind prison bars to know just which way morality lies. Or perhaps, more properly put, they are more than ever impressed that law and "morality" are not necessarily either constant or consonant. While there must be less of "yielding" in academic morality there must be more of practicality in expedient law!

A. The People Get a Break (Certainty of Accusing Law). One of the most interesting of the Law Revolution areas is the holding unconstitutional of old, and many times heretofore court-tested statutes, because of their newly determined "uncertainty."

The constitutional requirement of certainty of charging language in statutes has been more abused than honored. Very few are the statutes which have not heretofore been challenged that they were uncertain, vague, or not "in plain English," sufficiently intelligible to warn a defendant adequately of that which he had been charged. The revolution has brought a new look to some of these statutes and, again, we find that the new decisions indicate a zealousness to protect the individual in his idiosyncratic activities so that he may specifically know with what he is being criminally charged, and, before that, be forewarned.

A well-considered opinion replete with early common law history and English decisions is *in re* Davis (June, 1966). This is a "topless" case.

I have heretofore represented topless waitresses and entertainers (bare bosomed), at the Off Broadway night club in San Francisco, and in the first case to come before the courts, I had successfully contended that Escobedo should be extended to include the taking of pictures as well as taking of statements.

Judge Leo Friedman, of the Municipal Court, San Francisco, held that unless a defendant at the accusatory stage was warned that she did not have to submit to "topless pictures" taken of her in the "lineup" and that she had the availability of a lawyer's advice, the pictures could not be admitted into evidence. Judge Friedman, one of our best criminal lawyers before taking the bench, extending Escobedo to such pictures, was the first judge in this country so to act to my knowledge.

Following on the heels of the trial court decision in the Off Broadway cases, a "topless" entertainer was arrested and convicted in Los Angeles under a statute, California Penal Code 650-1/2 which prohibited a person from "willfully and wrongfully committing any act which openly outrages public decency." It was held on *habeas corpus* in the Davis case that this statute, heretofore many times tested, was unconstitutional because it has no guidelines of any kind concerning its intended application and because it was too vague.

Court cites a number of cases from other jurisdictions showing the trend holding constitutionally vague statutes which "outrage public decency," are "against the health, morals, and welfare," etc.

Said the court of a New York case: "The kind of blank

check from the legislature of which the New York court speaks, not only poses problems of due process because of vagueness, but raises very serious questions concerning the principle of separation of powers. This, of course, is primarily a question under our state constitution."

Compare a German law, signed by Adolph Hitler on June 28, 1935, which, in translation, reads in part as follows: "Whoever commits an act which the law declares to be punishable or which deserves punishment according to the fundamental concepts of the penal law and sound popular feeling, is punishable. If there is no penal law which directly applies to such deed, it shall be punished according to the law, the basic concept of which is most applicable."

An old Chinese statute quoted in *Chicago & N.Y. Ry. Co.* v. *Dey* is said to have read: "Whoever is guilty of improper conduct, and of such as is contrary to the spirit of the laws, though not a breach of any specific part of it, shall be punished at least forty blows; and when the impropriety is of a serious nature, with eighty blows."

Interesting is the historical comment of the California court on the old English cases, that they were not applicable since in the English courts a residuum of legislative power was reposed. The California court indicated that the separation of powers so basic to the common law in the United States does not fully pertain in England under the English common law.

Another quote from the United States Supreme Court: "When a statute on its face is narrow and precise, however, it lulls the potential defendant into a false sense of security, giving him no reason even to suspect that conduct clearly outside the scope of the statute as written will be retroactively brought within it by an act of judicial construction. If the Fourteenth Amendment is violated when a person is required to speculate as to the meaning of penal statutes . . . or to guess at [the statute's] meaning and differ as to its application . . . the violation is that much greater when, because the uncertainty as to the statute's meaning is itself not revealed until the court's decision, a person is not even afforded an opportunity to engage in such speculation before committing the act in question."

And as another interesting aspect of the courts as they deal with this type of uncertainty, a Nebraska statute prohibiting operation of any vehicle upon any highway in such manner as to endanger the safety of others or to cause immoderate wear or damage to the highway has been stricken as unconstitutional. Pointing out that the mere operation of a vehicle endangers the safety of others to some extent, the Nebraska Supreme Court held that the measure failed to prescribe an ascertainable standard of guilt, and that it was accordingly void for vagueness. This was *State* v. *Adams*, and it came as recently as 1966.

B. "I'm Sitting This One Out, Officer!" It was held in *State* v. *Koonce*, a 1965 New Jersey case, that force cannot be used to resist an illegal arrest by a police officer. One must submit to arrest and seek later his remedy.

Does such holding show a trend against unlicensed individualism, i.e., picketing, etc.?

Resisting arrest—the common law rule, unlawful arrest. Two policemen, not in uniform, broke into defendant's room and, after a violent struggle, subdued him and arrested him for possession of narcotics. Later, at the trial, the prosecution advanced the event of the struggle as evidence of defendant's guilty mind. The defense asked for, and was refused, an instruction that an individual has the right to resist an unlawful arrest. Appellate court reversed, sustaining defendant's argument.

The arrest here was unlawful. The officers had neither a warrant, nor cause to believe that defendant had committed an offense. They were not wearing uniforms and did not identify themselves. Although every citizen must submit to a lawful arrest, reasonable resistance to an unlawful one may rightfully be made either by the person sought to be arrested or by third persons acting in his aid. The reason for the rule is that false arrest is a public offense, and a person, about to become the victim of such an offense has the right to resist it.

One of the great American authorities of law is the work *Prosser on Torts*. Written by a noted jurist and legal educator, this work says of false arrest: "If the arrest is unlawful, it may be resisted by reasonable force. But here again, the harm which is likely to be inflicted by unlawful imprisonment is not sufficiently important to justify the infliction of serious injury, and the use of deadly force is not reasonable, where the personal safety of the one resisting is not in danger."

Along these lines the common law rule has been statutorily changed in some states. For instance, California's Penal Code, Section 834a, says: "If a person has knowledge, or by the exercise of reasonable care, should have knowledge, that he is being arrested by a peace officer, it is the duty of such person to refrain from using force or any weapon to resist such arrest."

Does this apply to an unlawful arrest? Yes. This was tested in a 1953 case, *People* v. *Spinoza,* where the defendant was convicted of resisting arrest. He claimed that his arrest was unlawful, and therefore he had a right to resist. Not so. The appellate court, interpreting the then recent addition to the penal code, *supra,* sustained the conviction. The former rule inevitably led to riots and violence by fostering a belief on the part of many people that they were the sole judges as to whether their arrest was or was not proper. Those persons who were inclined to resist or escape found a ready excuse in stating that the resistance or escape was because of a belief in the unlawfulness of the arrest.

It should be noted that the new section does not eliminate the right of a person improperly arrested to pursue his lawful remedies against the peace officer. It merely eliminates his right to the use of force at the time of the arrest and requires him to seek his redress by resort to the courts, rather than by resort to violence.

Still another aspect of resisting arrest behavior is found in *People* v. *Burns,* where a group of defendants were convicted of resisting arrest by "going limp" at an outdoor demonstration when told that they were under arrest. The court held that obstructing an arrest in any manner constituted the offense of resisting arrest.

"This court wishes to make abundantly clear that abuse of the police in situations such as here described is disgraceful conduct, violative of the obligations and duties of citizenship. The claim of police brutality which has been given prominence in the press is utterly without foundation. Breach of the peace with its concurrent infringement upon the rights of fellow citizens cannot acquire immunity because the prior inception of the activity was a proper exercise of the right of assembly and freedom of speech. Assault upon or conduct which has a moral tendency to incite others to assault and to interfere with the exercise of police duties by police officers likewise can acquire no immunity because of a correctly initiated constitutional activity." (The court here was referring to a demonstration which began as a lawful "ban the bob" meeting in a park on a Sunday afternoon, and turned into a near riot.)

If Ghandi were alive and well in America today, his passive resistance approach to social change might get comparatively short shrift. Those who contemplate acts of civil disobedience should properly do so expecting to be punished. Indicative of this is the now famous "sit-in" cases in the administration building of the University of California at Berkeley in 1964, where the defendants were arrested. These student defendants were convicted of, among other things, resisting arrest. Specifically the acts constituting the charge "going limp" when informed that they were under arrest. Thus necessitating the arresting officers carrying them out of the building.

The Court of Appeals affirmed the conviction, holding that the passive tactic of "going limp" constituted resistance to arrest. Where the arrest is lawful, the offense of resisting an officer can be committed without the employment of actual violence or direct force. A person who is arrested by a peace officer may not use passive resistance or interpose any obstacles which in any manner impede, hinder, interrupt, prevent, or delay such arrest. "We hold, therefore, that a person who goes limp and thereby requires the arresting officer to drag or bodily lift and carry him in order to effect his arrest causes such a delay and obstruction to a lawful arrest as to constitute the offense of resisting an officer . . ."

As an aside, I once defended Mario Savio in a Berkeley "sit-in" case. His co-defendants in civil disobedience were models of courtesy and cooperation. Mr. Savio was the most undeserving and arrogant "world-owes-me-a-living" defendant I have ever represented.

C. Abortion. The layman has criticized abortion laws as being archaic, not in keeping with modern society.

The old California penal admonition against abortion was contained in California Penal Code, Section 274. Every person who provides, supplies, or administers to any woman, or procures any woman to take any medicine, drug, or substance, or uses or employs any instrument or other means whatever, with intent thereby to procure the miscarriage of such woman, unless the same is necessary to preserve her life, is punishable by imprisonment in the state prison not less than two nor more than five years."

It should be a matter of pride to Californians that their state was among the very first to adopt statutorily a more modern approach to the timeworn problem of abortion.

In June, 1967, the California legislature enacted the Therapeutic Abortion Act, following the course previously taken by Colorado and North Carolina.

Under Section 25951 of the California act, a licensed physician is authorized to perform an abortion where there is "(1) substantial risk that continuance of the pregnancy would gravely impair the physical or mental health of the mother, (or) (2) the pregnancy resulted from rape or incest."

Unfortunately a provision was rejected which would have permitted a therapeutic abortion when "there is substantial risk that the child would be born with grave physical or mental defect."

Despite such forward-looking changes such as we have seen in California, Colorado, and North Carolina, at least forty states still retain laws essentially the same as California's outmoded pre-1967 statute—abortion remains illegal except to preserve the life of the mother.

How are these laws archaic? The pertinent answer is not to that question but to another, "What do we want the abortion laws to proscribe?"

It would serve us little here to engage in a policy discussion on the divergent medical opinions held about abortions except to note that this is a question of policy.

The Thalidomide cases (defendant manufacturers recently charged with manslaughter in Germany), caused considerable lay controversy. One of the users of that drug had to leave this country in order to have her abortion abroad. Her fears impelling the abortion were justified, the child was born deformed, the effects of Thalidomide. Being involved in these cases, I had the opportunity of seeing to what lengths the German pharmaceutical makers, like their American cousins, go to escape liability to the users of their products—products which are deleterious and unwholesome.

Probably no other subject this side of capital punishment raises such controversy as abortion. Church, educators, parent-teacher associations, doctors, and psychiatrists all engage. But the law has been most implacable in this area. Little consideration has been given the expression "necessary to preserve her life" in extending that to a consideration of psychiatric damage, etc.

The conflict between two clergymen of different faiths and the right of lawyers to speak out on controversial matters was sharply focused recently. Bishop James A. Pike, a member of the California bar and Chairman of the California Advisory Committee, United States Civil Rights Commission, challenged Francis Cardinal McIntyre's criticism of the Conference of Barristers (lawyers of age thirty-six or under) which recommended an abortion law change. Cardinal McIntyre had condemned the lawyers' action at the conference as "scandalous" and had branded abortions as "tantamount to murder." He said further that the barristers' action was ". . . further evidence of increasing disrespect and irreverence for basic law and divine moral principles."

Bishop Pike defended the right of lawyers to assume "responsibility" as community leaders in taking positions on issues such as the abortion question. He said: "The legal profession at its best is not only concerned with the practice of the law but with the reform of the law better to meet human needs. The passage of this act would line the law up with sound morality. Cardinal McIntyre has charged that abortion under such circumstances is 'tantamount to murder.' In this inflammatory labeling His Eminence overlooks two things: (1) Roman Catholic authorities, such as St. Thomas Aquinas and Popes Innocent III and Gregory XIV do not regard the foetus as being a person before the time of 'quickening.' (2) Even if the Cardinal, rather than St. Thomas Aquinas, is right in regarding such earlier abortion as the taking of a human life, there are other situations in which for the real or supposed greater good we take human life: through capital punishment, in war, and in the present non-war in Vietnam, where, for example, innocent children are killed with American napalm bombs. The Cardinal has not cried 'murder' in regard to these takings of life.

"I agree with the Cardinal that the amendment of the law would 'free' the courageous physicians who, with the consent of the therapeutic abortion boards of their respective hospitals, have engaged in civil disobedience against an evil law as conscientious duty."

In any event, I hardly think there will be the "judicial legislation" that there has been, for example, in determining the philosophical question of compensation in utero injuries. In that area the courts have pretty well changed the law. They are not likely to do so in the abortion cases, and what's the pity, the layman doesn't appreciate that the status quo law in abortions and the changed law in utero injuries is exemplary that *policy* questions are with the legislature—not the courts.

D. Military Orders—and Others. Whose order should the military man follow, what law should he observe? Can a soldier have an individual conscience?

I've always found it difficult to rationalize how the chaplain in the armed services can counsel a soldier to "perform his duty." A soldier's duty in combat is killing. A chaplain's duty is "thou shalt not kill." To me the function of a chaplain in the military is a hypocrisy, a great one.

Then the soldier doctor: should army doctors follow medical ethics or military orders when they conflict? Perhaps primarily it is hypocrisy first to shoot the enemy human being, trying to kill him, then have a medical corp patch him up and save him. Not only are the two purposes inconsistent, but much military time and money is spent in the patching up, which could go for more killing. So we have a medical corp to save those we didn't kill. (Couldn't *all* lethal bullets be "outlawed" for tranquilizers instead? Or don't the military, and the police, and true-blue patriotic home defenders want to take prisoners?)

But suppose the commanding officer directs his subordinate military doctor to "not save that man." What law should the military doctor obey?

First, is there a conflict with his own conscience; secondly, is there conflict with his ethics as a medical man? And is there a conflict when he took his military oath with his medical ethics?

One of the defenses of Captain Howard Levy on disloyalty charges and refusal to teach medicine to United States Special Forces medics bound for Vietnam was that this violated his medical ethics. Five doctors, including baby specialist Benjamin Spock, testified that serious problems in medical ethics would be raised by an order to teach medicine to men whose primary mission is to kill. And Spock said he didn't get his view as a result of his opposition to the United States military effort in Vietnam. He said he got it because he is a doctor.

But Captain Peter Bourne, an army psychiatrist who spent a year in Vietnam, said army doctors traditionally have been permitted to choose ethics over regulations when they conflicted. "I would never suggest that a physician disobey an order involving purely a military matter," Bourne said, "but where there is an order involving his medical ethics, he should be permitted to make the decision, otherwise the quality of medical care in the army would be considerably downgraded." But Captain Bourne begged the question. Levy was convicted.

E. The New Anatomy. The sexual laws (on homosexuality, masquerading, transvesting) and the whole penal code pertaining to the sexual "abnormalities" may have to be revised even as the surgeon has learned to revise the human body. In my own practice I have had clients who wanted to be female and were female in every respect except anatomically. They were not perverse in their "abnormal drive." I think they were impelled physiologically beyond their own capacity to control.

And at least Johns Hopkins Hospital must agree with this. It has established a "gender identity clinic" staffed by a special committee of psychiatrists, surgeons, and other specialists to screen applications for the operation to change sex by surgery.

Although the controversial surgery has been performed in many European countries in the last fifteen years and by a few surgeons in this country, Johns Hopkins is the first American hospital to give it official support.

In the male to female operation which takes three and a half to four hours, the external genitals are removed and a vaginal passage created.

F. The New Court Form. On the last opinion day of the spring 1967 term of the United States Supreme Court, a number of opinions were handed down which occasioned almost a full page of reporting in the *San Francisco Chronicle*. There was the General Edwin Walker libel case, the New York Eavesdropping law, the Martin Luther King decision, and the obscenity decision of the Chant of Love.

All four decisions were five to four.

The court adjourned with a heavy caseload undecided. Among the issues awaiting settlement are state laws forbidding Negroes and whites to marry, the authority of state judges to permit police to carry on electronic "bugging," the right of the Associated Press to report events during the Oxford, Mississippi riot in 1962, the constitutionality of federal laws requiring gamblers to pay occupational and excise taxes and to register with the government, and a number of other substantive questions.

As the court closed, the question was presented because of several late decisions, "have the courts swung to the right?"

No doubt political philosophy had swung to the right, many of the far right concepts of John Birch were being propositioned under different banner and while he was not principally responsible, Governor Ronald Reagan in California "returned government to 'conservative probity.' "

Whether the conservatives are the "good guys" and the liberals are the "bad guys," many lawyers pointed out that the United States Supreme Court generally turned itself into the times and current political thought.

I can't agree this is necessarily so. Certainly the court didn't go along with many of President Roosevelt's New Deal plans. President Lincoln had to "pack" the court in order to get his decisions. Obviously there's a lag in a new administration with court appointees of the old administration. But nevertheless, when the United States Supreme Court came down against California's Proposition Fourteen (the Rumford Fair-Housing Act), by a narrow five to four margin (the California Supreme Court had voted five to two against it), the "liberal" position was weakened. The Supreme Court barometer readers also saw a trend toward conservatism in the ruling giving police greater authority to seize evidence in a criminal suspect's home.

But a clear analysis of all of these cases, a clear reading of the position of the dissents, indicates they are not clear-cut decisions of a turn to the right at all.

CHAPTER TEN

"Outlawed!"

A. I'm Still a Citizen. In times past, a felon, on his first offense, had a T burned in the palm of his hand. A man pronounced "outlaw" could be hunted down like a wild beast (unless he took refuge in the "sanctuary chair" of the church). Now we punish our malefactors with more sophistication; we deny them the right to vote, positions of honor, certain property rights, and other real punishments in an age when man, fortunately, is increasingly more concerned about what others think of him.

A convicted felon under the laws of most states still is a "citizen." But without any of the rights, privileges, and immunities of a citizen. He is "civilly dead." Once released from prison he can no longer vote, serve upon a jury, or have most of the prerogatives, social and political, which were granted him upon his arrival on this continent—some by naturalization, a few more by birth. What's more, if he comes out of prison on parole or he is on probation, he still is regarded as being in "constructive possession" of prison authorities. Then many of the new rules protecting the citizen, i.e., search and seizure, do not apply to him.

Whether it's because of this inhospitable return to civil life, or because of his stay in prison, or because he's "innately bad," he reverts. Former tough convict, now brilliant humanitarian Bill Sands, author of the best-selling *My Shadow Ran Fast,* quotes ominous statistics which prove that it is of little consequence what felony sentence a convicted defendant is given, "one year" or "life," because 8 per cent of those who serve time in a prison (the distinguishing element between felony and misdemeanor) are recidivists—return to prison!

Some innocent men do go to prison. Some innocent men suffer capital punishment, although this is difficult of proof; and, indeed, Borchard in his *Convicting the Innocent* showed one hundred cases of condemned prisoners, sentenced to capital punishment, who were later proved innocent and pardoned. But even he couldn't show an actual case of an innocent man executed.

I suppose this is the same tenor as proof of the "perfect crime." To prove the "perfect crime" one would have to show it was committed, and in this proof, the culprit would be found out. Therefore the proof of the act must carry its own built-in negation, its disproof.

So it is with capital punishment. I've heard Erle Stanley Gardner say as the principal argument against capital punishment, "It's too final!" This isn't as trite an argument as at first blush it appears, because, once executed, proof and disproof from the principal actor is, for all eternity, dispelled by the most percipient witness!

Most jurists today are against capital punishment. And the text above is their most compelling argument. Now they admit the capacity presently of law to err. But rather than this being derogatory of modern law, it's probably the most cogent argument that is modern, for it acknowledges its humanity: "to err is human."

Most states now have statutes providing statutory relief for those innocently convicted. Every now and then a newspaper acknowledges the reality, but not the economics, of such statutes by announcing the awarding of some $15,000 or so to a prisoner "wrongfully" convicted and having served "twenty-nine years of bad times." While these statutes are a new acknowledgment of the capacity to err on the part of our courts, recognized by our legislatures, their quantum is still as inadequate as are most of our workmen's compensation laws.

The Law Revolution has extended, at least in New York, to allow compensatory damages for false imprisonment when a trial court lost jurisdiction through an inordinately long delay in sentencing a man over whom the committing court did not have jurisdiction. Damages were based on his probable earnings while incarcerated (*Harty* v. *State,* 1966).

An editorial in the *San Quentin News* states, "Times have changed. Prisons are no longer tiny islands of darkness cut off from the sights and sounds of a society. The public is now interested in what is happening inside their prisons. They want to know more about their prisoners. Much of this interest has been generated by the inmates themselves, through such functions as the annual Arts and Crafts Show and the Inmate Vocational Trades Fair. Most who have come to see what is happening inside the prisons have been impressed. We have been successful . . . society is interested."

In a 1965 Colorado case, *Gomez* v. *United States,* it was held that even though compensation coverage may be available to federal inmates under the prison industry's fund, this does not bar Federal Torts Claims Act suit by an inmate injured due to the government's negligence.

But in California the state has statutorily denied any liability for injury to prisoners (California Government Code 446). However this did not prevent the widow and children of a prisoner, who died as a result of the dangerous condition of prison property, from recovery for wrongful death, and such action was held to be an original and distinct cause of action belonging to heirs and representatives of the deceased and is not derivative from the rights of the deceased.

One of the first prison injury recovery suits was a federal case I brought for a client, "Mickey" Cohen, brutally beaten by a fellow inmate while in the Atlanta, Georgia federal prison. A federal judge sitting without a jury—no juries are used in suits against the government—allowed my client $110,000 in judgment, and an additional $15,000 for attorney fees. But the appellate court took the $110,000 back along with the attorney fees saying "We'll apply this on the money Mickey owes us for back income taxes—that's why he's in prison anyhow!" And Cohen is still in prison, badly paralyzed from the effects of the beating.

The personal manner in which the then United States Attorney General Robert Kennedy rebuffed me when I pleaded clemency for Mickey was, I felt, particularly in keeping with the ruthless image held by the late senator.

In the past, heaping injury upon injury—barbarous prison conditions leading to the felon's injury—the convict was regarded as civilly dead. And he was corporally so treated in many prisons. Now the Law Revolution has extended to him in one of its most exemplary pronouncements. The prisoner, injured in prison, has been given redress against his government, either in workmen's compensation or common law tort or tort claim.

In *United States* v. *Muniz,* it was held that under the Federal Tort Claims Act inmates injured while in federal penal institutions (one by negligence in the diagnosis and treatment of a benign brain tumor and the other by negligent supervision permitting an assault on him by twelve fellow inmates) could recover. Opinion by the then Chief Justice Warren. In a New York Court of Claims decision, *Lincoln* v. *State* (1959), a $2000 award for the loss of a prisoner's finger was affirmed. In the unique *Hungerford* v. *United States* (1961), a pending case of ours, criminality involves a brain lesion incised by a surgeon's scalpel, a "far out" case that would please any Sunday supplement editor. The suit is against Uncle Sam. The prisoner was injured as a result of defendant's negligence while working on a military reservation. Since he was not injured while working *in* a penal institution, he was not entitled to compensation from the prison industry fund.

In *Fleishour* v. *United States* (1965), it was held that the placing of newly transferred prisoners together by federal prison officials, in an unsupervised dormitory, did not constitute negligence rendering the United States liable in the Federal Tort Claims Act suit brought by one of the prisoners. The plaintiff was injured by a fellow prisoner who used a fire extinguisher available in the room to severely injure him. The court held that all aspects of prison promoting rehabilitation with responsible conduct by prisoners inevitably involved calculated risk. This case, on its facts, was close to the Cohen decision, but a close ball game can still be won, perhaps two to one, and cases sometimes five to four.

B. Compensation to Criminal Victims. A corollary to the new trend in recognition of prisoners' rights, both in courts in their suits and in prisons in their treatments, is the legislation being proposed in many states to award the victims of a criminal act compensation. Under these statutes generally, one, for example, suffering a beating in a robbery receives compensation from the state in money as well as payment of hospital and doctor bills, etc.

While this, too, is recognition of individual rights, the theory is based on ancient law, that the community is responsible for the individual. The theory behind these new acts was that which made "The Hundred," a workable entity in medieval England and the rationale behind the law of the "Riot Act." Under the latter and in many cases under the former, "The Hundred," a sheriff would appear before a mob and read the "Riot Act" three times (this is the origin of the expression "reading the Riot Act") ordering the rioters to disperse. If they did not disperse, and did subsequent damage, then everyone within the jurisdiction was assessed to pay the damage done by the rioters. The VJ Day riots in San Francisco resulted in suits by hotel owners against the city of San Francisco on this principle.

Of course, the California legislature, politically inspired in an election year, sought to pass a riot act, "as an aid to preventing riots in the race-riot city of Watts." Such legislation is not necessary. But here again we see a legislature trying to inundate the growth of the common law.

Even in early and communal communities such as Chinese villages we see prevalent community responsibility in that everyone in the community responds for some act done in the community by one of the community ("The Hundred") against an individual.

Dr. Joseph Satten of the Meninger Foundation tells us that "more and more we psychiatrists are moving away from the philosophical discussions within the courtroom . . . we are moving into the hospitals, into the diagnostic centers, into the correctional institutions, and working with parole and probation officers, where we'll be able to deliver the goods in a way that eventually the community can see that certain people can be rehabilitated at a very economical level, and others may not be able to be rehabilitated but can be identified as dangerous."

And Dr. Bernard Diamond: "It makes more sense to focus reform efforts directly upon the total system of administration of criminal justice, and thus attempt to cope with the bulk of antisocial deviation in constructive, humane, and effective ways. From such a viewpoint, the solution is not to make new laws that will displace large portions of the prison population in the mental hospitals, which then become prisons in disguise. Rather, it would be better to transform correctional systems in prison institutions into fit places to which mentally ill persons may be sent for treatment, rehabilitation, and eventual restoration to a normal life in their families and communities."

It is these above concepts of the modern administration of criminal justice which prompted the Council of Judges of the National Council on Crime and Delinquency to promulgate a Model Sentencing Act.

The Council of Judges is a group of fifty judges from all levels of the judiciary, state and federal, and from all parts of the country. Functioning as an adjunct of the National Council on Crime and Delinquency, it has promulgated guides for sentencing, guides for juvenile court judges, procedures and evidence in juvenile courts, and more recently it has done a work entitled *The Law of Criminal Correction.*

These judges have worked together to provide the Model Sentencing Act, based upon their experience and study of the problems in sentencing.

The basic purpose of the Model Sentencing Act is to provide a diagnostic center for the detection of the dangerous offender, and to insure his incapacity, where the court finds that the accused is "suffering from a severe personality disorder indicating a propensity toward criminal activity." (Model Sentencing Act, Section 5.) This definition of the dangerous offender follows closely the Durham philosophy, at the point of disposition. In some instances, the Model Sentencing Act would empower the court to formulate a sentence to fit the offender. If found to be dangerous, he may be permanently incapacitated. If found to be rehabilitable, either by supervised probation or suitable institutionalization, the sentence may be patterned accordingly.

This above comes pretty close to the modern penal philosophy in the Russian prisons to which the offender is sentenced "until cured."

C. Religious Rights of Prisoners. Convict William Howard, thirty-nine, asked the chaplain at Virginia State Prison back in 1962 (as he told it) if he and any of his fellow prisoners who were Black Muslims could hold their own religious services. Howard's request eventually came to the prison superintendent who responded by demanding the names of the other Black Muslims. When Howard refused to give them, he was packed off to maximum security, a restricted privilege ward. He unsuccessfully petitioned the state court, then the United States District Court, the latter unavailingly also, on the ground that Howard refused to name his group not because he wanted religious services.

Judge Sobeloff of the United States Court of Appeals for a unanimous court held that Howard was being arbitrarily punished "for making a reasonable attempt to exercise his religion." He was ordered back to the main prison for "as long as his conduct conforms to proper prison regulations."

The attorney general then petitioned a rehearing saying that the case was "of major importance." The court said Button (attorney general) has "now substituted its judgment for that of experienced penal administrators."

We have so far extended the right of all citizens (even those deprived of "citizenship") that now those "citizens" in prison can petition for redress of grievances. In *Holiday* v. *McGinnis* (1963) the Appellate Division of New York ruled that prison guards may not discriminate against any adherent of the Black Muslim sect because of the peculiar name he bears in connection with his beliefs. The prisoner informed the sentencing judge that he had always been known as Wallace Muhammad—though he had committed "several felonies" under the alias of Lamont Holliday.

The judges in the latter case ordered the prison administrator to cease intimidating "Wallace Muhammad" and denying him the equal protection of the law because of his name and commitment to Black Muslimism. Most courts seem to be leaning toward the view espoused by Disney F. Wheeler in the *Georgia Bar Journal* of May, 1962: "The state is completely powerless and incompetent to define the metes and bounds of a relief dealing with the inscrutable relationship to the supernatural power of God."

A California case, *in re Ferguson* (1961), held that the confiscation of a religious scrapbook of Black Muslim teachings in a state penitentiary did not run afoul of constitutionally protected freedoms inherent in the First and Fourteenth Amendments to the Constitution. Said the court: "Nor does it appear that petitioners may rely on federal constitutional guarantees since, of necessity, inmates of state prisons may not be allowed to assert the usual federal constitutional rights guaranteed to nonincarcerated citizens."

A New Jersey court had to determine whether a "recalcitrant and incorrigible" prisoner named McBride assigned to the segregation wing of the state prison, could be barred from participating in the regular Mass on Sundays and holidays. Catholic chaplains were permitted to administer the sacraments to McBride and other inmates in the segregation wing. McBride refused to accept the ministrations of his priest and demanded access to the regular service. The court held that order and discipline in the prison justified denying McBride his wish.

In *Price* v. *Johnson* (1948) the United States Supreme Court said, "Lawful incarceration brings about the necessary withdrawal of many rights and privileges, a retraction justified by our penal system." But courts also have upheld that the inmate has "residual civil rights which he does not relinquish when he is in prison." Said the United States Court of Appeals: "It has never been held that upon entering a prison one is entirely bereft of all his civil rights and forfeits every protection of the law."

D. Sentencing, Rehabilitation, Prisoner Therapy. The revolution has also extended to a more intelligent (and benign?) treatment of prisoners in prisons. But perhaps today the Russian concept of prison is still the best: a man is sentenced to prison in Russia, practically, until "cured."

There are almost as many psychiatrists in the Russian prisons as prisoners. A prisoner is allowed cohabitation rights with his wife and family on weekends and a cottage on the prison grounds (accord consortium in Mississippi and most South American prisons). He is paid a wage and, more importantly, when he is returned to his community as "cured," he is not derided by neighbors or by the community as an "ex-felon." The rate of recidivism in the Soviet Union, though statistics are almost impossible to obtain because of the manner in which they are kept for political propaganda is, comparable to us, minimal. I was tremendously impressed with the curative character of the penology when I visited the Russian prisons.

In the United States the most brutal and primitive prisons seem to be in the Midwest, such states as Kansas and Missouri. Property rights there seem to predominate over personal rights.

Perhaps the most enlightened prison in the United States is the Men's Medical Facility at Vacaville, California. Earl Warren, when governor, looked forward to the establishment of a prison that had a "back door" as well as a "front door."

In California now a prisoner standing before the judge upon arraignment may, before trial, be sent to Vacaville for a work-up and portfolio, a some months stay to determine really what makes him act. After conviction, if the accused hasn't availed himself of the preconviction procedure, every prisoner sentenced to prison, with exception of death-penalty cases, goes to Vacaville for a full work-up before he is assigned to his prison of detention. His examination enables prison authorities as well as the prisoner to get the most out of each towards rehabilitation. (We're beginning to appreciate that's what prison is for—if we subscribe that there is a "back door" to every prison for every prisoner, excepting death-penalty cases. As to "rehabilitation" of a prisoner sentenced to death, see Louis Nizer's report of the commutation of Paul Crump in his *The Jury Returns.*)

The Law Revolution here has made more progress with the assistance of medicine and has become more consonant with psychiatric capacities than in any other field of human relations, except in the divorce cases, where we have done little to avail ourselves of modern medicine. Reversing the trend of expanding rights of persons is a United States court decision which held that a prisoner becomes a public figure by virtue of his crime and subsequent trial. Thus, no actionable invasion of privacy occurred when two hidden TV cameras recorded the parole hearing of a former Connecticut state prison inmate. "Care was taken to keep his identity secret." (*Travens* v. *Broadcast Plaza, Inc.*, 1967.)

E. Moral Turpitude. World War II selective service registrants classified as conscientious objectors, who pleaded guilty to violation of the Selective Service Act and served prison terms, cannot be denied the right to vote in California as persons convicted of "infamous crime."

Basically, denial of suffrage is premised on the fact that a person committing a crime has evidenced his moral corruption and ought not to be allowed to defile the purity of the ballot box. Avoidance of such a danger, when present, is an adequately compelling state interest to justify an appropriate restriction.

However, on reviewing the history and purpose of this ground of voter disqualification, the court concluded that to preserve its constitutionality it must be limited to conviction of crimes involving "moral corruption" and "dishonesty," thereby branding their perpetrators as a threat to the integrity of the elective process.

Dissent. The inquiry must focus on the nature of the crime itself, and determine whether the elements of the crime are such that he who has committed it may reasonably be deemed to constitute a threat to the integrity of the elective process.

Neither the registrar of voters nor the courts ought to be expected to attempt a determination of whether a convicted felon should be permitted to vote until he has first exhausted the administrative remedies made available (*Otsuka* v. *Hite,* 1966).

A recent cover of *Esquire* magazine carried a picture of the "average American male" rouging his lips. The point was obvious: the war in Vietnam is disliked by many of us. Many of us have taken many ways to avoid military service even to the point of answering the initial questionnaire that we are "homosexuals." This disentitles us to serve our country, or, put another way, we are willing to take this stigma to avoid the draft.

But in our complex ideological society there's another side to this coin, there have been petitions circulated by avowed homosexuals that they have the "right" to serve in the armed forces, and they feel that they are being discriminated against and are not being accorded "equal protection of the laws" in denial to them of the privilege of fighting and if necessary dying for their country.

It should be remembered that it's not the simple cases that reach the United States Supreme Court. It's only those cases that have been shot at, pummeled and mauled and anesthetized and resuscitated and sniped at and loop-holized by lawyers at the level of justice of peace, trial court, state appellate court, circuit court, before they get to the United States Supreme Court.

The layman forgets, and we lawyers have been derelict in not pointing out, that the United States Supreme Court doesn't get the simple cases. If they were simple, they would have been decided unanimously and "properly" below.

Again, the fact that the decisions are "five to four" shows that the United States Supreme Court, rather than being an "arbitrary court" is an individual court protecting the individual. It's also a human court and has a built-in capacity of errancy. It's not an IBM machine. If it were, its decisions would protect mechanization and uniformity rather than individuality and humanity (and thereby perpetrate errancy).

A unanimous New York Court of Appeals reversed a determination of the Superintendent of Insurance which denied the applicant an insurance broker's license on the ground that he was shown to be "untrustworthy" by reason of a conviction of violating the Selective Service Act. The applicant's claim to conscientious objector classification had been rejected by the Selective Service Board, and the appellate court reasoned: "If it is determined upon evidence that the Selective Service Board believed petitioner to be a sincere person, but one whose beliefs did not entitle him to conscientious objector status under the congressional act, then denial of his application for a license where this is the only evidence of his untrustworthiness would be arbitrary and capricious."

Changing concepts of morality have made it increasingly

difficult to define "moral turpitude." Does violation of a law per se constitute moral turpitude or must a court look further into the *nature* of the offense? With the increasing recognition of civil disobedience as, in some instances, a legitimate means to a legitimate end, certainly the courts must look into the character of the offense. From Tweed, Segal and Packer, *Civil Rights and Disobedience to Law: A Lawyer's View*, 1964: "Disobedience to law is always prima facie unjustifiable. It can be justified, as we have shown, particularly in situations in which obeying the law defeats the enjoyment of constitutionally guaranteed civil liberties. But the burden is always on the person who claims that his violation of law is legally justifiable."

And what of conduct which, although not always in violation of the law, is generally considered to be "antisocial"?

The California Supreme Court was recently called upon to examine the consequence of both types of conduct in reviewing a refusal by the state bar to admit a learned applicant to practice law. In *Hallinan* v. *Committee of Bar Examiners* (1966) petitioner was, after lengthy investigation by the Committee of Bar Examiners, refused admission to the bar on the grounds that he did not possess good "moral character." The committee reached its conclusion on the basis of petitioner's activities in connection with civil disobedience "including three arrests," and because of testimony that the petitioner manifested a further disregard for the law through a propensity for violence.

Speaking on the question of petitioner's civil rights activities, the court pointed out that violation of the law per se is not grounds for excluding an individual from membership in the legal profession. In determining whether a person's character is satisfactory for bar admission the nature of the offense which he has committed must be taken into account. After pointing out that the petitioner explicitly repudiated violent civil disobedience, and that all the demonstrations in which he engaged were peaceful, the court said: "To the extent that acts of civil disobedience involve violations of the law it is altogether necessary and proper that the violators be punished. But criminal prosecution, not exclusion from the bar, is the appropriate means of punishing such offenders. The purposes of investigation by the bar into an applicant's moral character should be limited to assurance that, if admitted, he will not obstruct the administration of justice or otherwise act unscrupulously in his capacity as an officer of the court. We do not believe that a petitioner's participation in the civil disobedience here shown can be characterized as involving moral turpitude. If we were to deny every person who has engaged in a 'sit-in' or other form of non-violent civil disobedience, and who has been convicted therefore, the right to enter a licensed profession, we would deprive the community of the services of many highly qualified persons of the highest moral courage. This should not be done."

In addition to petitioner's civil right activities, the state bar introduced evidence of nine fist fights in which the petitioner was involved during the period from 1953 to 1964 which, it was contended, tended to establish the petitioner's alleged disregard for the law and his propensity for violence. After summarizing many of these incidents, the court held that they did not constitute sufficient grounds for exclusion from the bar. Most of the fights in which petitioner had engaged, the court pointed out, occurred when he was "much younger and much less mature." There was also the testimony of the family doctor indicating that a thyroid deficiency contributed in a large extent to the petitioner's pugnacious attitude. "After an independent examination of the record, we are in agreement with the apparent belief of the members of the sub-committee that the evidence of petitioner's intemperate resort to fisticuffs, however censurable, does not support the conclusion that he lacks the good moral character requisite to admission. The question is not whether petitioner's conduct can be condoned. It cannot. The question is whether such conduct demonstrates that he does not presently possess the character to be entitled to practice law. We think that it does not."

Do civil rights demonstrations and arrests evidence sufficient bad moral character to prevent an applicant admission to the bar?

Across the land there is dispute. In a judicial system largely limited to deciding an actual "case or controversy," lawyers must be cognizant that most of the landmark decisions defining constitutional rights and liberties involved cases of those who have intentionally violated the law they felt to be unjust. The court in *Repouille* v. *United States* (1947) said: "Many people—probably most people—do not make it a final ethical test of conduct that it shall not violate law; few of us exact of ourselves or of others the unflinching obedience of a Socrates. There being no lawful means of accomplishing an end, which they believe to be righteous in itself, they have always been conscientious persons who feel no scruple in acting in defiance of the law which is repugnant to their personal convictions, and who even regard as martyrs those who suffer by doing so. In our own history it is only necessary to recall the Abolitionists."

Mr. Justice Douglas, *in re Anastaplo* (1961): "To force the bar to become a group of thoroughly orthodox, time-saving, government-fearing individuals is to humiliate and degrade it. But that is the present trend, not only in the legal profession but in almost every walk of life. Too many men are being driven to become government-fearing and time-serving because the government is being permitted to strike out at those who are fearless enough to think as they please and say what they think."

In *West Virginia State Board of Education* v. *Barnette* (1943), the court said: "If there is any fixed star in our constitutional constellation, it is that no official, high or petty, can prescribe what shall be orthodox in politics, nationalism, religion, or other matters of opinion or force citizens to confess by words or act their faith therein. If there are any circumstances which permit an exception, they do not now occur to us."

CHAPTER ELEVEN

The Godless but Effective Juries

On "charter days," Fourths of July and other red-blood rousing anniversaries, heady—too often in voice only—American orators, from councilmen to congressmen, declaim the virtues of American constitutions guaranteeing trial by jury.

But they were and still are wrong: the Law Revolution still hasn't extended a full trial by jury to the states. Although every state constitution provides for the ancient "XII" (trial by jury), the guarantees in the federal Constitution still have not been applied to the states. In some cases jury trial is constitutionally denied. In some, less than twelve jurors can constitute a valid jury.

Paldo v. Connecticut (1937) determined that a citizen of a state did not have a right to trial by jury in all cases. And still the federal Constitution doesn't guarantee to citizens of the states trial by jury in all civil and criminal cases.

Justice Cardozo speaking for the court in Palko said: ". . . Immunities that are valid as against the federal government by force of the specific pledges of particular amendments have been found to be implicit in the concept of ordered liberty, and thus, through the Fourteenth Amendment, become valid as against the state. The line of division may seem to be wavering and broken if there is a hasty catalog of the cases on the one side and the other. Reflection and analysis will induce a different view. There emerges the perception of a rationalizing principle which gives to discreet instances a proper order and coherence. The right to trial by jury and the immunity from prosecution except as the result of an indictment may have value and importance. Even so, they are not of the very essence of a scheme of ordered liberty. To abolish them is not to violate a principle of justice so rooted in the traditions and conscience of our people as to be ranked as fundamental."

We know also that trial by jury is only preserved, even federal-wise, in the types of cases which were accorded jury trial at the time of the Constitution; thus juvenile court cases and even some drug addiction and mental aberration cases can be tried without a jury since they were not "customarily tried" by juries at the time the founding fathers struck off the Great Instrument.

So, though we have jury trials guaranteed by the states to their citizens, there still remains a disparity between the states with respect to the size of the jury and its availability.

Expediency, as in England, would dictate a "six man jury" or a "waiver of jury." Here there is a tugging between a return to the old concept of the full twelve man jury for "all cases" or the more expedient trial by jury waiver or a smaller number of jurors. Ultimately, I believe, expediency will prevail, that there are going to be more and more inroads into the jury trial with smaller numbers of jurors, more waivers of juries, all in the interest of making more efficacious the judicial process. I am willing to waive jury trial now in most of my civil cases principally because civil jurors have been so propagandized by insurance companies that when they do vote the adequate award they measure it with President McKinley's dollar. (However, the zealousness with which jury trial is protected is made brutally clear to me in a civil case,

Collins v. *Virgin Islands* [1966], in which the government of the Virgin Islands was "guaranteed trial by jury" with all the fervor, at least by the United States Circuit Court, of one accused of first degree murder.)

A. Do All Criminals Have Peers? Most Americans take for granted that they have some sort of basic, inalienable right to a trial "by a jury of their peers" if they are accused of committing a crime. And this idea has been correct, both as to the federal government's prosecutions and in the states. Every state constitution grants the accused criminal this right, but not in every kind of case. Crimes denominated "petty" offenses may be tried by a court or judge alone in some states. One such is Louisiana with its strong heritage from the French-European legal system where the jury is not used. The Louisiana constitution provides that in cases where the maximum sentence is neither death nor imprisonment at hard labor, the accused must be tried without a jury. Gary Duncan, a youthful Negro resident of Plaquemines Parish, was accused of "simple battery" upon the person of a young white man—a crime for which he could have received a maximum sentence of "only" two years in jail (but not at hard labor) and a fine of $300. (The same Louisiana constitutional provision that denied young Duncan any jury also provided that where the possible punishment was hard labor, it was only necessary to convince three-fourths of a jury of twelve of the accused's guilt. Where life is at stake the jury must be unanimous.)

As it worked out in Duncan's case, the sentence handed down was sixty days and a fine of $150. But in 1966, when this conviction was imposed, the Law Revolution was in full cry (see, for example, *Miranda* v. *Arizona*) and it appeared to someone in Louisiana that the time was ripe for some new law in the area. The forecast was accurate as, in June of

1968, the Supreme Court by a seven to two majority voided the defendant's conviction and remanded his case for retrial —this time before a jury of his peers.

Duncan v. *Louisiana* did not answer all the questions or put to rest all the doubts and confusions about the use of jury systems. For example, the practice of requiring less than a unanimous verdict or the practice of permitting conviction for serious crimes by a jury smaller than the ancient and venerated twelve. However the case did accomplish—if only by indirection—a line-drawing process that may or may not prove satisfactory. It undertook to distinguish "serious" from "petty" offenses by considering the punishment maximum to be meted out: one year incarceration. In some states the one year term is the distinguishing line between felony and misdemeanor—a jail term is seldom permitted for longer than one year. Any crime more severely punishable must be handled by the state prison system.

The Duncan case is a Law Revolution decision in its adoption of another of the guarantees of the Bill of Rights —that of trial by jury by the Supreme Court and made applicable to the states through the due process clause of the Fourteenth Amendment. Previous Law Revolution decisions have fastened onto the state criminal proceedings many other of the specific guarantees of the Bill of Rights. With the Duncan case the advocates of the "incorporation" theory— that the men who wrote the Fourteenth Amendment intended these rights to be fastened onto the states—seem to have carried the day, although the prevailing opinion of the court by Justice White would not go so far. His view of the case and the problem focused on the factors of fundamental fairness and the prevailing standards in the overall administration of criminal justice. The prevailing opinion—in which only five justices concurred—indicated that a state *could* permissively do away with the jury system, providing it substituted for it some other system of adjudicating criminal guilt which met the fairness criteria. The court did not presume to advise the state of Louisiana just what form this alternative system might take—but the implication was clear that if a state recognizes that a jury has a place in the administration of criminal justice, it must be available to all defendants accused of "serious" as opposed to "petty" offenses. For purposes of demarking a dividing line the court seemed to approve the New York City practice of permitting jury trials only in cases where the maximum penalty was more than one year. Most states, the opinion notes, provide for jury trials in all matters which carry more than a six month sentence.

The "great debate" which enlivened many Supreme Court decisions of recent years between Justices Harlan and Black concerning the "incorporation" theory of the Fourteenth Amendment will still go on—at least as long as the principal protagonist and antagonist are sitting on the court. Justice Black, in a concurring opinion, used the Duncan case to restate his incorporation theory and to reassert his belief that the proper theory to govern these questions was spelled out by him in *Adamson* v. *California,* decided in 1947. In that case the defendant had challenged the California constitutional provision which permits the prosecutor and judge to comment on the failure of the defendant to testify in his trial. The Supreme Court upheld the practice and the California law and Justice Black's dissenting opinion (concurred in by three other justices) was finally vindicated in 1968 in *Griffin* v. *California* which overruled the Adamson case. The court, like a reluctant swimmer, has ventured very close to the waters of the incorporation theory—the Duncan case is actually logically explainable on no other ground—but has never taken the full incorporation plunge. Whether this is important now since the specific rights of the first eight amendments with very minor exception have been incorporated via specific case by case adjudication is not clear.

By an irony of history the only remaining substantive right within the first eight which is not now incorporated is the Fifth Amendment's provision that "no person shall be held to answer for a capital or otherwise infamous crime, unless on a presentment or indictment of a grand jury." This procedure, designed to act as a check on over eager public prosecutors is not used by many states where a criminal proceeding is commenced by means of a complaint and a district attorney's "information." The system of proceeding by "information" was attacked in the very early case of *Hurtado* v. *California* (1884)—the defendant urging in effect that his constitutional rights had been abridged because the prosecutor had bypassed the grand jury in a capital case. The court rejected the claim, but noted in passing that the court had jurisdiction to examine all state proceedings in the light of a fundamental fairness test.

The language of the court in Hurtado contained the seeds of the entire Law Revolution, come to fruition almost one hundred years later when a former district attorney from Alameda County moved into the chair of chief justice of the United States. And it has been this same chief justice, largely unconcerned with doctrine (sometimes described as asking how many lawbooks can be balanced on a pinhead) who has moved the court into the position of asking: is it fair and not, is it in the Bill of Rights? Thus, the "information" method of commencing a criminal action is, to the present court, fair—and therefore defensible. By a further irony of history, the court may shortly be asked to void a grand jury indictment—because the method of grand jury selection is alleged to have been improper in the first instance. It may be that the court will find itself coming full circle on itself—but with the underlying notion that what is required in the American process of criminal justice and the administration of the laws is nothing more or less than the unsophisticated question: is it fair?

As this book was sent to press, it has now been determined by the United States Supreme Court that trial by jury in state courts is a requirement of due process of law.

B. Belief in God; Jurors' Oaths Held Unconstitutional. In *State* v. *Madison* (1965), it was held that Maryland's requirements that prospective grand and petit jurors expressed belief in the existence of God, invalidates indictments against believers as well as indictments against nonbelievers. However, in *Schowgurow* v. *State* (1965), it was held the new rule does not apply retroactively except for convictions that have not yet become final.

In *Hernandez* v. *State of Texas* (1954), the United States Supreme Court said: "Throughout our history differences in race and color have defined easily identifiable groups which at times required the aid of the courts in securing equal treatment under the laws. But community prejudices are not static, and from time to time other differences from the community norm may define other groups which need the same protection."

C. Peremptory Challenge of Negroes Valid; All-Male Jury Valid. In *Swain* v. *Alabama* (1965), the United States Supreme Court upheld the peremptory challenge of Negro jurors. Court held the striking of Negroes in a particular case is not a denial of equal protection of law, for in a quest for an impartial and qualified jury, Negro and white, Protestant and Catholic are all subject to being challenged without cause. To rule otherwise might very well deny individual rights and guarantee a minority jury.

In *State* v. *Hall* (1966), Mississippi's total exclusion of women from jury service does not deny equal protection of law to women indicted for murder by all-male jury: ". . . the fixing of qualification for juries is a legislative matter and . . . if it is necessary to resort to classification, such by sex is reasonable."

D. Waiver of Jury Trial. In *Singer* v. *United States* (1965), the Supreme Court upheld the validity of Rule 23(a) of the Federal Rules of Criminal Procedure, which requires the consent of the court and prosecutor before allowing defendant to waive trial by jury in a federal criminal case. (Most civil jury trials in personal injury cases are demanded by defendants nowadays. But it's the old and still modern adage that the revolution hasn't supplanted with either logic or slogan: "where evidence of guilt is great—to the jury; where it's innocence that overwhelms—to the judge.")

See also *Collins* v. *Virgin Islands* (1966), where a $550,000 personal injury judgment was reversed because jury trial demanded by defendant government was held not waived.

An issue which is collateral to the waiver of a jury trial is the waiver of the right to be tried by a complete jury. In *Williams* v. *United States* (1964), (1965), after the jury was impaneled, the attorney for the defendant and government counsel orally agreed to continue the trial with less than twelve jurors in the event of the illness of not more than two members of the jury. One of the jurors became ill and was excused, and the remaining jurors found the defendant guilty.

The circuit court did not agree with the defendant that he was denied his right to trial by twelve jurors, "because the oral stipulation was not raised and again agreed to by both counsel and by (the defendant) at the time when the juror actually took sick and had to withdraw." Since the defendant was present when the oral stipulation was made and was also present when the agreement in regard to proceedings with less than twelve jurors was put into effect, there was not error in proceeding with the trial before eleven jurors.

On a related issue, a federal court held that the defendant in a criminal matter was not deprived of due process of law when the selection of the jury was conducted in the absence of the trial judge. The court ruled that by failing to object to the judge's absence, the defendant waived the presence of the judge; and that where a defendant so waives, and no prejudice is alleged or shown to have resulted from the judge's absence, such absence is not ground for vacating defendant's sentence (*Haith* v. *United States,* 1964).

E. Fifth Amendment Does Not Require Indictment. *State* v. *Kanistanaux* (1966) held Fifth Amendment does not require that Washington defendants charged with manslaughter be indicted by grand jury.

The trial court appears to have been of the opinion that the Hurtado decision was impliedly overruled in *Mapp* v. *Ohio. Hurtado* v. *People of State of California,* was not mentioned (in Mapp), and the court did not hold that all of the provisions of the Fifth Amendment apply to the states. The court in the Hurtado case had held that a grand jury indictment was not a necessary element of due process, being historically intended as a protection against arbitrary and capricious prosecutions by the Crown, rather than such prosecutions by the people. It is significant . . . that the court did not see fit to overrule *Hurtado* v. *People of State of California,* either in *Powell* v. *Alabama* or in *Gideon* v. *Wainwright.* The fact that it rejected its reasoning as applied to fundamental rights, without overruling it, can only be consistent with a conclusion that the court had correctly held that due process does not require a grand jury indictment because the denial of it does not violate those fundamental principles of liberty and justice which lie at the base of all our civil and political institutions.

French law seems to operate successfully on the basic "constitutional" principle that a man is presumed to be guilty until proved innocent. The French judge instruction takes over at the beginning of the hearing. There is less of the adversary system under the continental law than the common law; it is called the "'Inquisitorial" system.

Although Estes and Shepherd recently have attempted to curtail pretrial prejudgment by veniremen, nevertheless practically, in this country, with "freedom of press," a defendant in a "popular" or well publicized case is supposed to be convicted in the press before he gets to trial. Then, too, if defense lawyer can convince the press to call his errant defendant the "errant altar boy" instead of accepting the district attorney's sobriquet of the "black gloved rapist," he's on third base instead of first.

But what of the mechanical means in getting a defendant to trial? If by *information,* then in most states the defendant can cross-examine in the preliminary hearing, can take complete discovery "deposition," if he is adroit, by calling all of the state's witnesses. If the route to trial is by *indictment,* in some states the grand jury is a secret inquisition, and in all states the defendant has no choice of "discovery" by calling other witnesses to the grand jury room since he has no control over the district attorney or the grand jury power of subpoena.

Frequently the improperly drawn information after conviction is *functus officio.* Shouldn't all of the preliminary procedures by which the defendant is brought to trial be *functus officio* once the trial is under way? If the defendant has had his opportunity at testing the sufficiency of the information or indictment, and has had his opportunity at discovery, then the instrument in bringing defendant to trial should really be of no consequence (*functus officio*), saving, of course, purely probative legal questions of, e.g., statute of limitations, etc.

But the calling into use of the machinery by which a defendant is indicted or informed against, is too often dependent upon chance and caprice. I cannot see that we shall ever have an IBM system of selecting the "black beans" from the "white beans" with such efficiency that we're certain (beyond a reasonable doubt and to a moral certainty) that all those who are brought to trial will be convicted. That's the function of the trier of facts, and I see no way of avoiding or correlating, more than we have, the charge to the actual conviction.

FBI statistics would seem to indicate a correlation closer to certainty; that is, 80 per cent plus of those charged by the FBI supposedly are convicted. But rather than prove efficiency, I am afraid that there's an element of prejudgment in these statistics (as well as a self-serving manner in their actual keeping): once the FBI man and the FBI process goes beyond the investigatory and focuses on the accusatory phase of the case of one individual, they do not want to leave anything to the fact trier; and unconsciously, perhaps, their zeal and their own subjective rectitude color their testimony and procedures against defendant. "The man's guilty or we wouldn't have brought him to trial!"

F. The Unanimous Jury. The vital element in the criminal jury system that the United States inherited from Britain is the concept of unanimity. Every juror must be convinced that the prosecution has proved guilt beyond a reasonable doubt and to a moral certainty.

Like so many of the concepts inherited from the British common law, it is being abandoned in the homeland, apparently prodded by a "crime wave" that has sharply increased since World War II. The labour government introduced a criminal justice reform bill in Parliament, one of the elements of which was the ten to two requirement for a criminal jury verdict. Very little opposition was raised and, indeed, Lord Chief Justice Parker argued that the unanimous jury escaped "many, many guilty persons."

I do not agree with him. Whether the analogy is pertinent, I give the experience that we have had just about as many verdicts over on the civil federal side where unanimity is required as on the state civil side where only nine to three is required. Too, I believe the "crime wave" is not related to the population explosion as honest statisticians correlate it.

G. Grand Juries—Transcript Available?—Secrecy of Proceedings. Unlike California, Nevada does not by statute permit a defendant to have or make a copy of the grand jury transcript, nor does it require that a transcript be made. Nevertheless, it is apparent that without a transcript a court cannot determine whether the evidence presented to the grand jury is of the kind and sufficiency to return an indictment, or whether there is sufficient evidence to force defendant to the expense and hazard of trial.

And the Nevada courts have now so held. In *Ivey* v. *State* (1966), court held the defendant's right to be free from restraint if probable cause for trial is not shown to exist necessarily carries with it the right to know what evidence was formally received by the grand jury and supplied the basis for its indictment. (Cf., the apparent Louisiana procedure of the powers of the district attorney before trial.) Writs of *habeas corpus,* prohibition, mandate and other procedures variously test this jurisdiction in such states as California.

The California statute is one procedure; the other is the flat contrary where grand jury proceedings are secret and sacrosanct, and transcripts are not even made.

It would seem to be unfair to allow an attack on the sufficiency of an information and the evidence at the preliminary hearing, but in the same state not allow such an attack when the district attorney chooses the route of the secret indictment.

In such a case as *Brautigan* v. *Miami Herald* (1962), (the case denying *certiorari* on the substantive libel involved before *Sullivan* v. *Times*), the question was presented whether a grand jury had the right to criticize but not indict. The general rule, and that which Florida followed in the defamation case ($100,000 award to Brautigan, then the district attorney of Dade County, Florida) was that a grand jury must indict, that is, return a "true bill" or a "no bill" and cannot take any course in between.

California, Kentucky, Iowa, Minnesota, and New York to a limited degree, have allowed pretrial examination of the grand jury transcript by the accused. Missouri, Utah, New Jersey, and now Nevada have allowed pretrial discovery by decision (*Shelby* v. *Sixth Judicial Dist.*, Nev. 1966).

The trend in the Law Revolution to protect the individual and save him the hazard, harassment and expense, and loss of reputation of an indictment where there is not sufficient evidence is to make the grand jury transcript available for counsel, and trial, and appellate court scrutiny.

Perhaps the most frequently cited justification for the practice of keeping the proceedings secret is found in *United States* v. *Rose* (1954). There the court summarized the reasons for the rule as follows: "(1) To prevent the escape of those whose indictment may be contemplated; (2) To insure the utmost freedom to the grand jury in its deliberations, and to prevent persons subject to indictment or their friends from importuning the grand jurors; (3) To prevent subordination of perjury or tampering with the witnesses who may testify before grand jury and later appear at the trial of those indicted by it; (4) To encourage free and untrammeled disclosures by persons who have information with respect to the commission of crimes; (5) To protect innocent accused who is exonerated from disclosure of the fact that he has been under investigation, and from the expense of standing trial where there was no probability of guilt."

CHAPTER TWELVE

"The D.A. Is My Friend!" (Discovery and Adversary Proceeding)

A. Modification of "Adversary Proceeding" Rule. Common law basically follows the "adversary procedure": "the sparks of conflict shed the light by which justice may be seen."

It was felt that "justice is served, truth will out," if there is vigorous cross-examination and "courtroom battle." But the Law Revolution has changed this "adversary proceeding" philosophy dramatically. In England, Canada, etc., to hear the prosecutor open his case frankly stating evidence inimical to the Crown cause and favoring defendant, makes the American lawyer feel the Crown is only half trying. But not so—he must be fair to judge, Crown, *and* defendant. The old American "ambush procedure" most fully followed under Texas law is now becoming a historical relic.

In *Brady* v. *Maryland* (1963), as we have seen, the Supreme Court held that the *suppression by the prosecution* of evidence favorable to the accused violates due process where the evidence is material either to guilt or to punishment, irrespective of the good or bad faith of the prosecutor. In Brady, the evidence withheld was an extra-judicial statement made by a co-defendant that he and not Brady was the one who actually fired the fatal shot.

Various courts have accepted various tests to determine

whether this conduct results from the deliberate suppression of evidence. Some courts have accepted the "vital and material" test in determining whether the evidence suppressed requires the granting of a new trial. Other courts have accepted a broader, more liberal, rule which strikes a balance between the gravity of the prosecutor's misconduct and the probability of a different result reached by the jury absent that misconduct.

In a recent English case, a barrister was disbarred for failing to disclose the fact that his witness was a convicted felon.

The adversary system has also been further modified by allowing a right of discovery by the prosecution in criminal cases. In *Jones* v. *Superior Court of Nevada County*, the court held that a criminal prosecution is not a "one-way street," but should be based on an orderly procedure, aimed at ascertaining the truth.

In *Levin* v. *Katzenbach* (1966), prosecution's failure to disclose the part of a bank official's statement that might lead jury to entertain reasonable doubt of defendant's commission of grand larceny would vitiate his conviction, even if failure was negligent and not guileful. A number of circuits have recently held that the deception that results from negligent nondisclosure is no less damaging than that which is a product of guile and that such nondisclosure entitles a defendant to relief. We find the reasoning of such cases persuasive and essential to the fair administration of criminal justice especially in view of the disadvantages facing the accused in the trial process. In a comparable situation, ". . . *Griffin* v. *United States* (1947), 1137 (1948), after we had affirmed defendant's conviction of murder, he moved for a new trial on the basis of newly discovered evidence relating to his claim of self-defense . . . the Supreme Court reversed and ordered this court to rule on the admissibility of the evidence. If we ruled that the evidence was admissible, we were to grant a new trial. If we found that it would be 'too dogmatic, on the basis of mere speculation, for any court to conclude that the jury would not have attached significance to the evidence favorable to the defendant had the evidence been before it.' We held the evidence was admissible and, relying on the standards set out by the Supreme Court, ordered a new trial.

"But [this] claim for relief based upon a breach of the prosecutor's duty of disclosure challenges the fairness and therefore the validity, of the proceedings, and relief, either on a motion for a new trial or for *habeas corpus,* may not depend on whether more able, diligent, or fortunate counsel might possibly have come upon the evidence on his own. A criminal trial is not a game of wits between opposing counsel, the cleverer party, or the one with the greater resources, to be the 'winner.'"

It is commonplace knowledge that in our country a man is innocent until proven guilty, and that the burden of such proof is on the prosecution. Thus, it should go without mention that fair trial and due process inherently prohibit the knowing use of false evidence or perjured testimony by the prosecution in obtaining a criminal conviction. Nevertheless, at this late date it was necessary for the Supreme Court to underline this caveat in *Miller* v. *Pate* (1967) in reversing and remanding the conviction of a man sentenced to death for the brutal sexual attack and murder of an eight-year-old girl in Illinois.

An important part of the state's evidence was a pair of men's undershorts, found in an abandoned building a mile from the scene of the crime, which were allegedly stained with the blood of the victim and for that reason had been discarded by the assailant. In a hearing on a petition for writ of *habeas corpus,* the stains were examined by a chemical micro-analyst and found to be paint, not blood.

In *Noland* v. *California State Bar* (1965), a California

assistant district attorney's participation in a plan to remove from the master jury list the names of prospective "pro-defense" jurors was an act of moral turpitude and justified disciplinary action. A conviction was reversed because the prosecutor secreted a witness who would have cast a reasonable doubt upon his case.

Reversing a condemnation decision, the Supreme Court of Nebraska has held that an instruction, given the jury at the end of a five-day trial, to disregard all statements of counsel unless supported by evidence, to draw on conclusions or inferences from counsel's questions or offers of evidence to which objections were sustained, and to give no consideration to evidence stricken by the court, was insufficient to remove the prejudice arising from false statements in the *opening statement* as to what the testimony would show (*Lybarger* v. *State*, 1964).

The Arkansas Supreme Court has ruled an unjust reprimand by the trial judge in the presence of the jury to be prejudicial error. In this recent case, the attorney had been rebuked for exercising his right, under the canons of professional ethics, to interview an adverse or prospective witness without the consent of opposing counsel.

The North Dakota courts have held that the testimony and display of a "known criminal's" book in the identification of defendant was prejudicial and not cured by a cautionary charge for the jury to disregard.

California has held that comment on the failure of a defendant to take a voice identification test (although not within the privilege against self incrimination) was inadmissable unless the police had advised him that his right to remain silent did not include the right to refuse to participate in such a test.

When it becomes apparent that a witness is broadly claiming his Fifth Amendment privilege, the prosecutor cannot continue the use of detailed leading questions to indicate the substance of the hoped for testimony. This deprives the defendant of his fundamental right of confrontation. The trial judge's instructions to the jury not to speculate on what the answers might have been did not correct the infirmity.

B. Discovery in Criminal Case. Justice Peters, in a civil case, *Simon* v. *San Francisco* (1947), philosophizes that a law suit is not an ambush procedure whereby the spoils of victory go to the most technically alert but a method of civilized society justiciably to settle disputes. He was then as a District Court of Appeals justice prognosing the Law Revolution, which later broke out both civilly and criminally in the decisions of the United States Supreme Court. His words were almost as prophetic as were Justice Traynor's in *Escola* v. *Coca Cola.*

With such pronouncements as these and the Dorado and other decisions out of California, it is no wonder that national news media accolade California's appellate courts as being the "best" and "most modern" in the country.

Along with a curtailment of the adversary proceedings, the disgorgement of truth from files on either side, pretrial procedures and Escobedo protection of the individual, there had to come a complete revamping of the laws of discovery, both civil and criminal.

We know now that on pretrial and by deposition or interrogatories a civil litigant may "discover" even to the extent of "going fishing" for irrelevancies which will not even be admissible on the trial.

But on the criminal side, there is the constitutional admonition against defendant being made to incriminate himself. How far we shall be able to go with this caveat remains for decision—or legislation. But we do now know that the criminal defendant in most states and in federal court can demand of the prosecutor that he literally "empty his briefcase" before the trial. No longer is the criminal defendant caught unaware; no longer can he complain surprise of a witness whose name or testimony he did not know, of a recording, a statement, a tape, physical evidence, or demonstrative evidence.

On the face of it, it does seem that with the district attorney having to disgorge everything he has, that the state is put to a disadvantage when the defendant is not made similarly to divulge his fact information before trial. Cases are now coming down in this extremely new development which say discovery is not a one-way street. But we will have to await the federal Supreme Court's decisions to determine how far a criminal defendant can be made to give up on discovery in the face of the Fifth Amendment.

From *Jones* v. *Superior Court of Nevada County* (1962); the *prosecution* in a criminal case is even now entitled to *some* discovery, on the ground that the inherent power of discovery, based on trial administration, is not limited to that which benefits the defendant. The defendant in a criminal case has no vested interest in denying the prosecution access to evidence which can throw light on issues on the case absent some relevant privilege that would forbid disclosure. This case allowed *limited* discovery to prosecution in a criminal case; see the very strong dissent by Justice Peters. The names of alibi witnesses apparently now are discoverable by the state.

Does discovery lie before, during, or after a preliminary hearing?

The Jencks Act provides that after a witness called by the government has testified on direct examination, the court shall, on the defendant's motion, order the United States to produce any statement of the witness in possession of the United States that relates to the subject matter as to which the witness has testified.

Informer's names and identifications are discoverable. The right of the *individual* defendant to confrontation is superior to the state's practical interest of availability and protection of informers.

In *United States* v. *Rhodes* (1966), a parole officer called as witness by a federal narcotics defendant attempting to substantiate entrapment defense was not excused from testifying about a conversation between them by a Justice Department regulation barring disclosure of material in its files.

The court said, "In our opinion the principle recognized and applied in *United States* v. *Andolschek* is equally controlling with respect to the content of the conversation here involved. The government elected to prosecute the defendant, and insofar as conversations between its parole officer and the defendant about matter relevant and material to the defendant's claimed relation to the government's narcotic law enforcement activities are concerned, the government must choose; either it must leave the (conversations) in the obscurity from which a trial would draw them, or it must expose them fully."

C. Criminal Client's Intercepted Letter Admissible. In *State* v. *Grove* (1965), prosecution was allowed to discover a letter which defendant had written in jail to his wife, attempting to exculpate himself from criminal responsibility for the death of his wife's mother, the murder victim. The court held that the privilege protecting husband-wife communications was not violated since the defendant knew that his mail would be censored and did not intend the letter to be confidential. Court held also that a communication was not within the attorney-client privilege, since the lawyer's possession was deemed to be merely an effort to withhold evidence that was incriminating to the defendant.

In 1954 the death penalty judgment against John Santo, Emmett Perkins, and Barbara Graham was affirmed by the California Supreme Court. Barbara Graham, along with her co-defendant, was executed. Later her life and trial were made into a motion picture and Ed Montgomery, crack reporter on *San Francisco's Examiner,* was given a coveted journalistic award for his reporting.

But had this record reached the California Supreme Court on appeal today, the Law Revolution between 1954 and 1966 in many areas would have resulted in its reversal.

First the publicizing of the case, the presence of armed guards obtrusively present in the courtroom during the whole trial, the searching of the spectators (as was done in the Ruby case) created the atmosphere denounced in Estes and Shepherd. But in 1954 the anodyne so pontifically pronounced by affirming justices was made applicable, "Presumably the jurors heeded these admonitions (to disregard) and upon the entire record we cannot hold that because of the publications mentioned the defendant was deprived of a fair trial.

Disregarded was the prophetic language of Mr. Justice Jackson, joined by Mr. Justice Frankfurter in *Shepherd* v. *Florida,* another Shepherd, (1951).

Then this was a pre-Aranda decision, and defendant Graham's contention that a separate trial should have been ordered as to her, because evidence was introduced at the trial which would have been inadmissible if she had been tried separately, was disregarded with one sentence: "The defendant is not entitled as a matter of right to a separate trial—see Penal Code Section 1098. . . . The judge admonished the jury to consider evidence which was admissible against only one defendant in connection with that defendant only."

But the most brutal evidence tricked from defendant Graham was the following: Samuel Sirianni, a policeman in disguise, gave the following testimony, which was offered and received only against Mrs. Graham to show consciousness of guilt and admissions against interest. Sirianni had three conversations with Mrs. Graham while she was in jail awaiting trial. He represented to her that he intended to help her account for her whereabouts on the night of the murder.

During one of these conversations Mrs. Graham admitted that she was with Santo, Perkins, and True. She also said, "Without you as an alibi, I'm doomed to the gas chamber." Sirianni asked when the murder took place; Mrs. Graham replied that it was on March 9; actually she said it was the morning of March 10. Sirianni inquired several times about Shorter; Mrs. Graham said, "He is well taken care of . . . he has been done away with. I assure you he won't be at the trial." In reply to Sirianni's question whether she thought their alibi would be sufficient, she said, "I do—for this reason—there's not one shred of evidence."

Unquestionably, to me, defendant Barbara Graham, being in custody after indictment, was "tricked" by the policeman who represented he was going to set up an "alibi" for her. Is this within the spirit of the "intercepted letter"?

How far can the police go after the initial warning, after custody, after indictment, during incarceration in jail, when defendant, on the eve of trial, or during trial, evinces a desire to set up an alibi or some such faked defense? Will the question be determined on the consideration of who was the instigator, state or defendant? Will these trapping procedures be completely proscribed within the spirit of Massiah, etc.? Certainly, Aranda would now require reversal on the separate trial phase.

CHAPTER THIRTEEN

How Heavy the Lash?

We have seen in the foregoing chapters how courts have extended individual protection throughout the substantive and procedural maze of the criminal process. There are, however, areas still remaining in which individuals may be punished and disabled without constitutional cure.

A gross practical inequity, unequal protection, and lack of due process is trial delay (criminal and civil), the keeping of a man in jail pending trial. Although courts may not set bail in "excess of that usually imposed for crimes of similar severity," the constitutional incantation fails to take cognizance of the financial inadequacy of the indigent accused. The rich man is set free—the poor man still languishes in jail.

Similarly, we may impose the legal, psychological, and financial burden of successive federal and state prosecutions on the individual. (Even Hoffa's ample treasury was severely strained when he went up against the affluent Bobby Kennedy and Uncle Sam.) This, because the double jeopardy provisions of the federal Constitution are not "inherent in the concept of ordered liberty."

But we have made significant advances in related areas. The law now recognizes what the physician and psychiatrist has been saying for many years, that the chronic alcoholic and the habitual narcotics user are not criminals but are individuals who are afflicted with an illness. Thus, the Supreme Court has said that we may no longer make the "status" of narcotics addiction a crime; nor may we incarcerate the chronic alcoholic (although we excuse his alcoholism we don't completely excuse his criminal conduct committed while under the influence).

Finally, we do impose punishment (in some cases more severe than that imposed under our criminal law) on individuals without the benefit of the safeguards of our criminal processes, and we place burdens more weighty than close confinement on those who have been convicted criminally.

Here's where the civil and criminal law converge, and they converge through the imposition of penalties without benefit of criminal processes. We impose exemplary damages and the jury in awarding them really punishes. These civil punishments are really getting more sophisticated; we're not just hitting the individual financially, but we may deprive him of social status and even means of livelihood.

A. Bail. The philosophy of individual rights protection whether one is indigent or "well heeled" is apparent in the new bail procedures, trying to bring this right in *equal protection* to all. Bar associations in many areas are setting up "bail committees" available at all hours to make bail or O.R. (own recognizance) equally available, these following in the wake of the pioneering efforts by the Vero Foundation in New York.

In 1832, Alexis de Toqueville found our bail system ". . . hostile to the poor, and favorable only to the rich. The poor man has not always a security to produce, even in a civil case; and if he is obliged to wait for justice in prison, he is speedily reduced to distress. . . . Nothing can be more aristocratic than this system of legislation."

Bail dates back to the Assize of Clarendon in 1166, the Statute of Westminster in 1275, and the action on debt with its concept of Weggeld. Following the English Bill of Rights in 1688, our Bill of Rights in the Eighth Amendment provides that: "Excessive bail shall not be required, or excessive fines imposed, nor cruel and unusual punishment inflicted."

Justices Jackson and Black pointed out that under our Constitution the judge in fixing bail is not free to make the sky the limit "because the Eighth Amendment gives the individual the *right* to bail" and takes a "calculated risk" that "the accused will take flight."

The attack Bentham and Dickens leveled against jails, bail, and bondsmen in the early nineteenth century won in England; today qualified American observers, Botein and Sturz, find the English system "fairer and wiser" than ours. Sixty per cent of those arrested are released on bail which consists of a contract by their friends and relatives to forfeit a sum of money if the prisoner fails to appear. Thanks to Mr. Pickwick, commercial bondsmen are prohibited and forfeitures are few and far between.

Although the Eighth Amendment is applicable to the states, the problems encountered in applying this amendment are manifest. Much of the problem may be laid on the ambiguous wording of the amendment itself. It seems susceptible to at least three interpretations: first, that where bail is permitted by other authority the Eighth Amendment compels that its application must not be excessive. The absurdity of this interpretation is that the Eighth Amendment carries no force in and of itself.

The second interpretation is that where the court sets bail it may not be excessive—the courts, however, retaining the discretion to grant or refuse bail in any case. In the latter case, *State* v. *Konigsberg* (1960), the defendant was indicted for murder by a New Jersey grand jury and his first application for bail was denied. Upon renewal of the application nearly six months later, bail was set at $25,000. State was granted a stay of release in order to appeal the order fixing bail. The New Jersey Supreme Court continued the stay of bail to enable the state to present evidence to the trial court, bearing on the likelihood of defendant being convicted of first degree murder, which, because a capital offense, is the exception to absolute right to non-excessive bail. Court said: "Guilt or innocence is not the issue . . . the issue of guilt, being the ultimate one, must await jury determination at trial. . . . The just rule for utilization is that bail should be denied when the circumstances disclosed indicate a fair likelihood that the defendant is in danger of a jury verdict of first degree murder."

The problem with this second interpretation of the Eighth Amendment is that it permits judges to do directly what they are prevented from doing indirectly, i.e., they may have the discretion absolutely to deny bail, thereby keeping the accused incarcerated; but if they do decide on bail, the bail may not be excessive.

The third interpretation is that the Constitution simply gives the accused an absolute right to bail.

Even if the latter interpretation is generally accepted, and it seems to be, problems still remain with the definition of "excessive bail." An interesting early case on this question involved one Lawrence, who attempted to assassinate President Jackson. Bail was set at $1,000 but the district attorney objected that the defendant's friends might bail him out so he could try again. Chief Judge Cranch recognized the problem posed by the excessive bail provision. That is, should bail be tailored to fit the gravity of the offense alone, or should it also take into consideration the ability of the defendant to pay it? The Judge said: ". . . To require larger bail than the prisoner could give would be to require excessive bail, and to deny bail in a case clearly bailable by law . . . that the discretion of the magistrate in taking bail in a criminal case, is to be guided by the compound consideration of the ability of the prisoner to give bail, and the atrocity of the offense. That as the prisoner had some reputable friends who might be disposed to bail him, he would require bail in the sum of $1,500. The sum, if the ability of the prisoner only were to be considered, is probably too large; but if the atrocity of the offense alone were considered, might seem too small . . ."

Unfortunately, the courts since Lawrence have for the most part failed to take real cognizance of the problem. This conclusion was supported by the Attorney General's Committee on Poverty and the Administration of Federal Criminal Justice Report, 1963, wherein it was observed that one of the failures of the American bail system was to establish any procedure "to provide the bail setting authority with relevant factual data indispensable to sound bail decisions."

A significant recent case was *Stack* v. *Boyle* (1951), where twelve persons were indicted under the Smith Act and bail was set at $50,000 apiece. The defendants moved unsuccessfully to reduce bail as excessive, thus unconstitutional, and supported this motion with statements as to their financial resources, family ties, health, and prior criminal records. The Supreme Court reversed, holding that federal law unequivocally provides that a person arrested for a noncapital offense shall be admitted to bail, and bail set at a figure higher than an amount reasonably calculated to insure a defendant's presence in court is "excessive" under the Eighth Amendment. "This traditional right to freedom before conviction permits the unhampered preparation of a defense," the court said, "and serves to prevent the infliction of punishment prior to conviction. Unless this right to bail before trial is preserved, the presumption of innocence, secured only after centuries of struggle, would lose its meaning."

Stack is not as promising as it might have been, since the court held that the standard to be used in setting bail is the amount "usually fixed for serious charges of crime," and that individualizing procedures should be utilized only in cases where the amount of bail set is substantially greater than that which is usually imposed in similar cases.

Stack was a federal case and the situation in the federal courts has been substantially altered by the Bail Reform Act of 1966, which provides that any person charged with a non-capital federal offense shall be released pending trial on his personal recognizance; in other words, on his promise to appear in court when required, or upon an unsecured appearance bond, unless the judicial officer determines that such release will not reasonably assure that the defendant will make his court appearances. If, in the exercise of his discretion, the magistrate feels the defendant's promise or unsecured bond is not sufficient, he is then required to consider placing the defendant in the custody of a person or organization agreeing to supervise him, or to consider other non-financial conditions of release before he resorts to the bond of money bail.

Federal Judge George L. Hart, Jr., in releasing eleven criminal defendants on their recognizance under the new Bail Act, quite improperly said, "The good citizens of the District of Columbia had better take cover!"

The intent of the Bail Act, passed in 1966, was to reinforce a long ignored principle: defendants should not be jailed before trial merely because they cannot afford bail. All very well, since many federal criminal cases involve white collar crimes and relatively responsible defendants. But federal jurists such as Judge Hart apparently thought that cities where there has been considerable violence, like Washington, D.C., were not ready for the new bail.

Shortly after Judge Hart's comments, a defendant, while on trial, jumped bail and was jailed. The new law allows judges to jail defendants during a trial to prevent prospective or actual bail jumping. Under the law, except in capital cases, and after conviction, judges cannot consider danger to the community as a factor in no bail proceedings. The law's drafters considered including such a provision aimed solely at Washington, D.C., but dropped it to await developments.

When the amount of bail set is appealed, the appellate courts are reluctant to tamper with the discretion of the court originally setting bail. Usually the defendant must assume the burden of showing that bail is flagrantly excessive. (See *ex parte Morehead,* 1951.) The amount fixed must be shown per se to be clearly disproportionate. In a federal *habeas corpus* proceeding to set aside bail set by a state court the amount must be shown to be "beyond the range within which judgments could rationally differ . . ."

As heretofore demonstrated, the inequity of our bail system falls most heavily on the shoulders of the indigent defendant. An argument could be made that the Supreme Court decision in *Griffin* v. *Illinois* (1956) might make available an equal protection argument to the indigent accused, confined because the amount of bail is outside his reach. (Griffin held that indigents could not be denied access to the state's appellate processes by having to purchase and submit manuscripts of their trial records.)

Pretrial detention is not only offensive to concepts of due process and equal protection, but also as a practical matter it affects the subsequent disposition of the case. Rankin, in

The Effect of Pretrial Detention, 1964, sets forth the following table:

RELATIONSHIP BETWEEN DETENTION AND UNFAVORABLE DISPOSITION

Disposition	*Bail, %*	*Jail, %*
Sentenced to prison	17	64
Convicted without prison	36	9
Not convicted	47	27
No. of defendants	(374)	(358)

B. Cruel and Unusual Punishment. It is interesting to note that the admonition against "cruel and unusual punishment" in the Eighth Amendment which is now, because of the Law Revolution, applicable in state courts and to state citizenships, was in the Bill of Rights linked with bail and excessive fines. Was the philosophy and ideology that refusal of bail and excessive fines (and jailing for civil causes, i.e., debt) could be court determined as cruel and unusual punishment?

Of course, any legislative enactment predicating result upon any reasoning or activity, i.e., "discretion," calls for judicial review and judicial interpretation. But legal language is not a pint, quart, meter, mile, yard, or definite standard. There is also the constitutional requirement of "certainty."

But statutory admonitions are relative things. The best example is the use of the yardstick, which is anything but that, of "discretion," in innumerable statutes and decisions. "Judicial discretion," that most subjective of human commodities in the ratio *dicidendi* is, though paraded as objective, ridiculously subjective.

The revolution has just recently touched, both in the federal and state courts, bail. It is long overdue because a prisoner *awaiting* trial is doing the same "time" that he does if he is *convicted.* If he is innocent, the state does not pay him for this borrowed time. But more importantly, here is the one field of law where there was not equal protection; because the wealthy and socially elite were given bail, i.e., could pay with money or could be recognized ("O. R."), because of social status. But the itinerant, whose guilt or innocence may not be in question any more than the rich man, had to do his time before he owed it, and indeed might never owe it.

But how about the gross, cruel, and unusual punishments themselves? A startling and revealing book, little known, is *The Newgate Calendar*. This is a horrendous account showing man's brutality to his brother through the ages. It almost makes a case that man's nature (since the Garden of Eden) has been bad—indeed sadistic. It has only been relatively recent that drawing and quartering as a punishment, not as an attempt at inquisition for information, has been abandoned. Gibbetting for teenagers for the theft of a loaf of bread and *peine fore et dure* (which some authorities contend was the genesis of jury trials) was not long ago the order of the day.

How now in the revolution, considering modern social evaluations and penology, do we consider cruel and unusual punishment?

Apparently the schoolteacher can still spank the child—to a degree. And apparently the felon can still be whipped. The dignity of man does not prohibit this corporeal or psychic punishment.

But the ideology of the revolution has extended into the following interesting cases. They do reflect, precisely, that the law grows more compatible with, in these instances modern medicine, and psychiatry, and social desires. And perhaps they do prove why these admonitions or definitions of cruel and unusual punishment were not heretofore available—there was not enough scientific fact to justify and require the overhauling of the law still based on the accepted old theories.

The punishment of *lashes* prescribed for specific crimes does *not* violate the *Eighth* and *Fourteenth* Amendments as a "cruel and unusual punishment." Neither the United States Supreme Court, nor any other court, has ever held as a matter of constitutional law that the punishment of lashes is cruel and unusual. "We think that the standards of *present day society* are to be determined by the expressions of that society, itself, and not by an expression of the individual opinions of members of the judiciary. . . . The only manner in which such an expression can be made is through the action of duly elected representatives of the society whose standard is to be applied."

The court added: "The historical development of the laws of this state, therefore, indicates a gradual change in the viewpoint and beliefs of the General Assembly as to what constitutes proper punishment for crime. Indeed, the state of our present law is such that punishments for crime are now limited to death by hanging, imprisonment and fining, and in addition, in some few instances, the imposition of lashes, the sole holdover today of the infliction of corporal punishment for crime.

"It is argued to us that we at this time should recognize the modern view condemning corporal punishment for crime and declare the infliction of lashes as punishment is the remnant of a cruel age, and should be declared to be a violation of the constitutional prohibition against cruel punishments. We think, however, this is not our function. We accept unquestionably that constitutions are living documents in the sense that the phraseology used in them grows and changes with the passage of time. . . . The meanings of words change and grow with the changing sensibilities, beliefs and knowledge of man. We think, however, that this change, this growth, this enlightened meaning of words used in constitutions, comes about by reason of the beliefs of the people themselves. The change may not come solely by reason of the individual belief of an individual judge. What better way is there for the people to express an enlightened attitude toward the punishment of crime than through their elected representatives, the members of the General Assembly who, indeed, hold their office for the very purpose of expressing the will and beliefs of the people who elected them.

"Furthermore, the history of the criminal laws of Delaware demonstrates that this is an effective force to bring about change. If the people feel strongly enough upon a subject, their elected representatives respond to their will. We have no doubt but that the gradual elimination from our criminal law of many punishments now considered cruel was accomplished by the General Assembly pursuant to the will of the people."

A sentence of a prison term, a fine, and twenty lashes imposed on conviction for robbery does not constitute cruel and unusual punishment, *Balser* v. *State* (Del., 1963). But reversed on other grounds; the trial court failed to specify the day on which the punishment of lashes was to be executed.

In *Wilkerson* v. *Utah* (1878), the clause came up again for consideration. A statute of Utah provided that "A person convicted of a capital offense should suffer death by being shot, hanged, or beheaded," as the court might direct, or he should "have his option as to the manner of his execution." The statute was sustained.

The court pointed out that death was a usual punishment for murder, that it prevailed in the territory for many years, and was inflicted by shooting; also that that mode of execution was usual under military law. It was hence concluded that it was not forbidden by the Constitution of the United States as "cruel or unusual." (It might have been argued that it was usually cruel.)

The court quoted Blackstone as saying that the sentence

of death was generally executed by hanging, but also that circumstances of terror, pain, or disgrace were sometimes superadded. "Cases mentioned by the author," the court said, "are where the person was drawn or dragged to the place of execution, in treason; or where he was emboweled alive, beheaded, and quartered, in high treason. Mention is also made of public dissection in murder, and burning alive in treason committed by a female."

The court's final commentary was: "Difficulty would attend the effort to define with exactness the extent of the constitutional provision which provides that cruel and unusual punishments shall not be inflicted, but it is safe to affirm that punishments of torture, such as those mentioned by the commentator referred to, and all others in the same line of unnecessary cruelty, are forbidden by that amendment to the Constitution."

Driver v. *Hinant* (1966) held that the Eighth Amendment, prohibiting cruel and unusual punishments, applies to the *states* through the Fourteenth Amendment.

A petitioner who was a chronic alcoholic, was arrested and sentenced to jail for being drunk in a public place. Court of Appeals held such punishment violates the *Eighth* and *Fourteenth Amendments.*

When that is the conduct for which he is criminally accused, there can be no judgment of criminal conviction passed upon him. Although his misdoing objectively comprises the physical elements of a crime, nevertheless no crime has been perpetrated because the conduct was neither activated by an evil intent nor accompanies with a consciousness of wrong-doing, indispensable ingredients of a crime.

Drunkenness is still no excuse for a crime. All that is excused by this decision is that behavior, which is characteristic of the disease of chronic alcoholism (*Driver* v. *Hinant,* 1966).

The court here excused criminality because a chronic alcoholic's acts were compulsive as symptomatic of his disease, a behavior disorder.

A state cannot stamp an unpretending chronic alcoholic as criminal if his drunken display is involuntary as the result of disease (*Thompson* v. *City of Louisville*, 1960).

The constitutional guarantee against "cruel and unusual punishment" embodied in the Eighth Amendment, applicable to the states through the Fourteenth Amendment, is violated by the imposition of criminal sanctions on a person for the offense of having the "status" of a narcotic addict. Narcotics addiction is an *illness,* and a law which punishes addiction with nothing more *is out of line with modern medical and penal concepts. "Even one day in prison would be a cruel and unusual punishment for the 'crime' of having a common cold"* [italics mine]. (*Robinson* v. *California,* 1962.)

The Eighth Amendment's guarantee against cruel and unusual punishment was not abridged by confining a prisoner, adjudged sane, to an institution devoted to the housing and care of insane or mentally defective federal prisoners. "It is now established that, apart from historical precedent, what constitutes cruel and unusual punishment within the prohibition of the Eighth Amendment is to be judged in the light of *developing civilization, so that what might not have been cruel and unusual yesterday may well be so today"* [italics, not rationale, mine]. (*Austin* v. *Harris,* 1964.)

Mr. Justice Goldberg, joined by Justices Douglas and Brennan, dissenting from a denial of *certiorari* in a rape case in which capital punishment was imposed, felt that the imposition of the death sentence in rape cases constituted cruel and unusual punishment. "In light of the trend both in this country and throughout the world against punishing rape by death, does the imposition of the death penalty by those states which retain it for rape violate 'evolving standards of decency that mark the progress of our maturing society,' or 'standards of decency more or less universally accepted?' " (*Rudolph* v. *Alabama*, 1963.)

Is the imposition of the death penalty for a crime in which human life was not threatened greatly disproportionate to the offense?

Can the permissible aims of punishment be achieved as effectively by the imposition of less than capital punishment in rape cases?

A plaintiff used the equal protection clause of the Fourteenth Amendment to challenge the Oklahoma Habitual Criminal Sterilization Act. An "habitual offender" was one having been convicted two or more times for a felony involving moral turpitude. Under this definition, habitual larceny offenders could be sterilized but habitual embezzlers could not.

Court found there was not a great enough distinction between the offenses to support such a difference in punishment. The equal protection clause protects individuals from state discrimination in the classification of punishment for similar offenses (*Skinner* v. *Oklahoma*, 1942).

Obviously the court was influenced by the unorthodox nature of the punishment and even elderly jurists can wince at this particular prospect.

C. "*Witherspoon* v. *Illinois*: The Final Solution?" It has been apparent for years that a legal execution by twelve citizens of persons who have committed crimes has been out of favor with many judges, particularly those of the appellate courts. In California, where as of this writing some twenty-five men sit on death row at San Quentin, the State Supreme Court has changed the rules at least three times, requiring reversal and retrial of the defendants—at least as to the penalty to be imposed after a finding of guilt. Post-conviction proceedings permitting a convicted defendant access to a variety of delaying tactics so as to delay the imposition of the ultimate sanction have worked virtually to abolish the death penalty as a practical matter in the United States. Nonetheless, in desolate death rows across the land (except in those states which have abolished capital punishment by legislative enactment) sit several hundred men who have as firm a hold on life as the lame duck officeholder after his successor has been elected—and that, the courts are saying, isn't exactly tenure.

The Supreme Court has not often addressed itself to the question of death and the death penalty as such. It has been urged repeatedly by anti-capital-punishment groups that the imposition of the most extreme penalty constitutes cruel and inhuman punishment, forbidden by the Eighth Amendment. (Some do-gooder capital punishment leagues have done excessive harm to their cause.) Although this issue has been presented squarely in recent years, the court has refused to take a position by refusing to grant *certeriori* on such a case.

But even though failing to meet the question head-on, the court nevertheless managed to cast a serious doubt over almost all recent pending death penalty convictions with its decision in *Witherspoon* v. *Illinois*. This was announced by Justice Stewart on the next to last decision Monday of the 1967 term.

The Witherspoon case may be as important for its limitations—expressed in the majority opinion—as for its holding, which was merely that a jury must be "death qualified" before it is allowed to sit in judgment on a capital case.

The so-called death qualified jury is empaneled when all those persons who have "conscientious scruples" against imposition of death have been summarily disqualified from sitting on the case. Such disqualifications come about through the so-called challenge for cause—a venireman who indicates on *voir dire* (pretrial jury examination) that he does not believe in the death penalty can be excused, in most states, by the judge. In Illinois, this process is commanded by statute and defendant Witherspoon was convicted (of killing a police officer) by such a jury. The same jury thereafter decided (in the words of the Illinois law) that the defendant was not "fit to live."

It is interesting to note that the California practice in this area of the law is to employ the bifurcated trial, that is, the issue of guilt is first decided: if the jury convicts of first degree homicide, there must be then a penalty phase trial before the same twelve in which the question of the penalty to be imposed is decided. (A *third* trial if insanity is pleaded.)

The question remains: does Witherspoon signal the end of capital punishment, or will it merely make the death penalty more difficult to get? The answer is not known because the opinion does not shed enough light on the kind of jury selection process that is permissible. The theory of the majority decision is that the "death qualified jury"—one from which all persons opposed to the death penalty have been excluded, is more likely to find the defendant guilty of the offense without respect to penalty. This theory is buttressed by an assortment of sociological studies of the subject (and common sense—sometimes a stranger to the sociologist) which seem to indicate that this is, in fact, the case.

The future of the death penalty, after Witherspoon, is in doubt. If the Supreme Court's theory is correct, the prosecution will be forced to use its limited number of "preemptory" jury challenges to remove prospective jurors having "scruples" about execution. But a jury containing only a *single* member whose attitude toward capital punishment is negative can hang the jury initially on the question of the degree of guilt, thus perhaps forcing compromise verdicts.

What of the status of the several hundred persons who are today on death rows in prisons across the country? Many of them, perhaps the great majority, will now be entitled to have the issue of penalty readjudicated by a new jury panel. This process may impose almost impossible burdens on local prosecutors, especially where the sentence of death was imposed years before, a not uncommon situation. Practically—and very practically to the death row inmate—the best prospect is that the local district attorney will bow to the inevitable and accept a "life" sentence for the defendant.

In some states the Witherspoon case will have no appreciable effect, since the court was very careful to limit its decision in a footnote, to the following: "We repeat, however, that nothing we say today bears upon the power of a state to execute a defendant sentenced to death by a jury from which the only veniremen who were in fact excluded for cause were those who made unmistakeably clear (1) that they would *automatically* vote against the imposition of capital punishment without regard to any evidence that might be developed at the trial of the case before them, or (2) that their attitude toward the death penalty would prevent them from making an impartial decision as to the defendant's guilt. Nor does the decision in this case affect the validity of any sentence *other* than one of death. Nor, finally, does today's holding render invalid the conviction as opposed to the sentence, in this or any other case."

D. Jailing Indigent Unable to Pay Fine—Unconstitutional. In *People* v. *Collins* (1965), it was held that a sentence of $250 fine or one day imprisonment for each $1 of unpaid fine is unconstitutional as applied to an indigent defendant who is unable to pay. Here's what the court said: "The practice of jailing a convicted defendant for nonpayment of a fine is an ancient one but the courts have always held that such incarceration is not part of the punishment but a means of collecting the fine. The commitment authorized by Section

718 for failure to pay a fine does not increase the penalty specified in the criminal statutes to which it is applicable. It follows only upon a defendant's failure to pay the fine and is a means of bringing about collection of the same. It is well settled that this remedy for the collection of a fine is not part of the sentence. A direction in a sentence imposing a fine that defendant stand committed until the fine is paid is not part of the penalty for the offense, but is merely a means of compelling obedience to the judgment of the court." Judge Cardozo elaborated on this by explaining that "The state, when it punishes misdemeanors by fine, is not confined to the dubious remedy of a civil action or a penalty. Imprisonment is another remedy which the state may employ against the offender who refuses to pay. Therefore, it runs directly contra to the meaning and intent of Section 484 of the Code of Criminal Procedure to order a defendant to stay in prison until he pays a fine, when the court knows that he cannot possibly pay it. This is not the use of a lawful means for enforcing payment but is an illegal method of requiring imprisonment far beyond the maximum term of imprisonment allowed by the statute which sets a one year limit on incarceration for a misdemeanor violation. A similar question was put to us in *People* v. *Letterio,* but not directly passed upon. Since imprisonment for nonpayment of a fine can validly be used only as a method of collection for refusal to pay a fine, we should now hold that it is illegal so to imprison a defendant who is financially unable to pay.

"Defendant would have us put our decision on constitutional grounds. He argues persuasively that under *Griffin* v. *Illinois, People* v. *Pride,* and other similar decisions, it is a denial of due process and of equal protection of the law to let a defendant's lack of money determine how long he must be imprisoned. The man who can pay and the man who cannot are not treated equally. Another specification of unconstitutionality suggests itself. Section 5 of Article I of our state constitution, like the Eighth Amendment to the federal Constitution, forbids the imposition of 'excessive fines.' There seem to be no controlling decisions on the question of what is an excessive fine. The phrase 'excessive fine,' if it is to mean anything, must apply to any fine which notably exceeds in amount that which is reasonable, unusual, proper, or just. A fine of $500 for a common misdemeanor, levied on a man who has no money at all, is necessarily excessive when it means in reality that he must be jailed for a period far longer than the normal period for the crime, since it deprives the defendant of all ability to earn a livelihood for five hundred days and since it has the necessary effect of keeping him in the penitentiary far longer than would ordinarily be the case. To make it worse, this fine is to be served out at the absurdly low rate of $1 a day in a state where the legislature has recently imposed a minimum wage of $1.50 per hour.

"We do not hold illegal every judgment which condemns a defendant to confinement if he does not pay his fine. We do hold that, when payment of a fine is impossible and known by the court to be impossible, imprisonment to work out the fine, if it results in a total imprisonment of more than a year for a misdemeanor, is unauthorized by the Code of Criminal Procedure and violates the defendant's right to equal protection of the law, and the constitutional ban against excessive fines."

The new and liberalized bail procedures are exemplary in the field.

An indigent defendant, having pleaded guilty to a misdemeanor, was given the maximum sentence of imprisonment for one year and was also required to pay a fine of $500, which, if not paid, was to be served out at the rate of one day's imprisonment for each dollar remaining unpaid. Reversing, New York's Court of Appeals declared that "when payment of a fine is impossible and known by the court to be impossible, imprisonment to work out a fine, if it results in a total imprisonment of more than a year for a misdemeanor is authorized by the Code of Criminal Procedure and violates the defendant's right to equal protection of the law, and the constitutional ban against excessive fines." (*People* v. *Saffore,* 1966.)

E. Speedy Trial. There are other, and more insidious ways, of punishing than after conviction incarcerations. Until recently, North Carolina had a procedure whereby an individual could remain for an indeterminate period under the threat of imminent criminal prosecution. The device used was the state's *nolle prosequi* with leave, granted by the court and permitting reinstatement of prosecution at an indefinite future date.

In *Klopfer* v. *North Carolina* (1967), Supreme Court first held that the Sixth Amendment's guarantee of a speedy trial was rendered applicable to the states through the due process clause of the Fourteenth Amendment; this, despite the objections of the state that the accused held under the *nolle prosequi* with leave was free to travel, was not required to put up bail, and further, that there was no certainty that the state would go forward with the prosecution. The court, recognizing the duress placed on the petitioner, said: ". . . the petitioner is not relieved of the limitations placed upon his life and liberty by this prosecution merely because its suspension permits him to go 'whither soever he will.' The pendency of the indictment may subject him to public scorn and deprive him of employment, and almost certainly will force curtailment of his speech, associations and participation in unpopular causes. [Klopfer had been prosecuted on a charge of criminal trespass committed by participation in a civil rights demonstration in a restaurant. The jury in his first trial was unable to reach a verdict.] By indefinitely prolonging this oppression as well as the 'anxiety and concern accompanying public accusations,' the criminal procedure condoned in this case by the Supreme Court of North Carolina clearly denies the petitioner the right to a speedy trial which we hold as guaranteed to him by the Sixth Amendment of the Constitution of the United States."

The first articulation of the right to speedy trial was made in the Magna Carta (1215), and this seems to have been derived from the even earlier Assize of Clarendon (1166). Holding that the right to a speedy trial is guaranteed by the states as well as by the federal government is exemplary of the trend restoring ancient rights heretofore lying fallow in legal history.

CHAPTER FOURTEEN

"Let's All Meet at Appalachia!" (Conspiracy)

"Conspiracy" has been the prosecutor's darling because indirectly, through the admission of really inadmissible evidence, all of the conspirators are tarred with the same brush of guilt by association. When evidence is applicable only to one conspirator under the old rules, trial judge would instruct the jury that this evidence which the jury heard could only be considered against the defendant "against whom it was being offered," and could not consider it against any other defendant. I have thought, for a number of years, that this was a most unfair procedure, that a jury could not wipe this information out of its mind and separate the guilty from the innocent.

Recently, in *People* v. *Rock, et al.*, I appeared for two of the defendants (San Francisco Superior Criminal Court). In California, grand jury transcript is made public. For one of my defendants, I brought a writ of mandate in the appellate court while the consolidated cases were pending under indictment in the trial court. By California Penal Code Section 995, I contended that there was not sufficient evidence before the grand jury to hold one of the alleged coconspirators, Simmons, *for trial.* The appellate court, for all practical purposes, agreed (later reversed). It halted the trial as to this one defendant until a date after his trial with the other defendants had begun. I proceeded to trial with the other defendants, one of whom I represented, defendant Ward.

During the course of the trial against these other defendants, a statement was offered which was taken by a police officer against Ward, my now sole defendant, an alleged coconspirator. In that statement there were admissions given by Ward which allegedly inculpated him, *but also inculpated coconspirator Call.* (This was divulged by me on opening statement.) The trial judge ordered that the name Call could not be mentioned because of the Aranda rule. I was ordered to refer to Call as a "nameless one." I considered this deprived me of cross-examination in that I would later have to cross-examine against a "phantom." After two weeks jury picking and opening statements and evidence being taken, Judge Elkington, seeing the problems of Aranda, granted me a separate trial for Ward. The jury, already picked, proceeded only against the one conspirator Call. (Convicted: life imprisonment, murder first degree, on appeal.)

People v. *Aranda* (1965) makes sweeping changes in the old conspiracy procedures and extends the Law Revolution to protest individuals even as much as did Escobedo and Dorado. Significantly, said Chief Justice Traynor, speaking for the California court, "In criminal actions, where life or liberty is at stake, courts should not adhere to precedents unjust to the accused. It is never too late to mend."

The California Supreme Court said further: "In joint trials . . . when the admissible confession of one defendant inculpates another defendant, the confession is never deleted from the case and the jury is expected to perform the overwhelming task of considering it in determining the guilt or innocence of the declarant and then of ignoring it in determining the guilt or innocence of any codefendants of the declarant. A jury cannot segregate evidence into separate intellectual boxes. It cannot determine that a confession is true insofar as it admits that A has committed criminal acts with B and at the same time effectively ignore the inevitable conclusion acts with A.

"In Section 1098 of the California Penal Code, the legislature, while providing that the courts might order separate trials for defendants jointly charged with any public offense, left to the courts the determination of standards governing such severances. The grave constitutional doubts engendered by our present practice of permitting joint trials when the confession of one defendant implicates co-defendants has prompted our *reconsideration* [italics mine] of this practice. Whether or not it is constitutionally permissible, the practice is prejudicial and unfair to the nondeclarant defendant and must be altered.

"When the prosecution proposes to introduce into evidence an extra-judicial statement of one defendant that implicates a codefendant, the trial court must adopt one of the following procedures: (1) It can permit a joint trial if all parts of the extrajudicial statements implicating any codefendants can be and are effectively deleted without prejudice to the declarant. By effective deletions, we mean not only direct and indirect identification of codefendants but any statements that could be employed against nondeclarant codefendants once their identity is otherwise established. (2) It can grant a severance of trials if the prosecution insists that it must use the extrajudicial statements and it appears that effective deletions cannot be made. (3) If the prosecution has successfully resisted the motion for severance and thereafter offers an extrajudicial statement implicating a codefendant, the trial court must exclude it if effective deletions are not possible. Similar rules concerning joint trial have been adopted in other jurisdictions and have been found workable."

A. "Appalachian Conspiracy." The famous Appalachian Conspiracy cases grew out of a "simple meeting of friends" at the house of one Joseph Barbara, a "known racketeer." Police had kept Barbara's home under surveillance for some time, suspecting him of being involved in the illegal manufacture and distribution of alcohol. On November 13, 1957, several cars were observed converging on and remaining at Barbara's house. The police, suspecting some illegal action was taking place in the house, stopped participants on the public road as they came from the estate to determine the identity of the occupants.

While the police were engaged in this activity, the visitors at the estate began fleeing, some on foot through the surrounding woods, others by car. The police stopped and questioned some sixty persons. Over twenty had criminal records. No one was questioned for more than one-half hour, after which each was sent on his way.

In *United States* v. *Bonanno* (1960), the Appalachian defendants contended that the police procedures outlined above constituted an illegal arrest, and moved on that ground to suppress any evidence, of any kind, stemming from those procedures. The district court denied the motion, in a very cogent opinion by Judge Irving Kaufman. Before a finding of illegal arrest, there must be a showing that an arrest took place. The elements of a technical arrest require that there be an intent on the part of the arresting officer to bring in a person so that he might be put through the steps preliminary to answering for a crime. "That every temporary restriction of absolute freedom of movement is not an illegal police action demanding suppression of all resultant evidence is accepted in federal courts, though it is a proposition incompletely articulated. I believe that the relative dearth of authority in point can be explained by the fact that few litigants have ever seriously contended that it was illegal for an officer to stop and question a person unless he has 'probable cause' for a formal arrest.

"While the Fourth Amendment may be construed as encompassing 'seizure' of an individual, it cannot be contended that every detention of an individual is such a 'seizure.' If that were the case, police investigation would be dealt a crippling blow, by imposing a radical sanction unnecessary for the protection of a free citizenry. Under such a theory, a policeman could not stop and question a person standing next to a bloody corpse. If he did so, before having probable cause to believe that he had committed the crime, and then released him, and subsequently decided on the basis of further checking into the individual's activities that he was likely to be the murderer, the policeman could not testify to the presence of the suspect in the vicinity of the victim because it would be testimony about matters learned upon an 'illegal arrest.' "

In another case growing out of the "party" that Joe Barbara threw for his friends at his estate, *United States* v. *Bufalino* (1960), the government prosecuted Mr. Barbara's guests for *conspiracy* to obstruct justice, and conspiracy to commit perjury. The essence of the government's charge was that the several defendants, beginning at the time that they first noticed that the Barbara estate was under surveillance by police officers, until they were called before a grand jury to testify about the purpose of the meeting, conspired to concoct false statements explaining their presence at the alleged meeting. As the Court of Appeals put it: "Indeed, the pervasive innuendo throughout this case that this was a gathering of bad people for an evil purpose would seem to us to rebut any possible argument that only as a result of group action would any individual lie. Even an otherwise law-abiding citizen who is stopped and interrogated by police, and who is given no reason for his detention and questioning, may feel it his right to give as little information as possible and even perhaps to respond evasively if he believes he might thereby be earlier rid of police inquiry. That others may at times go to the brink of truth, or beyond, is likely, particularly when as may have been true in the present case, they know that the existing law does not require them to give a truthful account to police officers."

The whole incident was given much publicity, and the court commented on it thusly: "In the fact of such a hue and cry, it is just as reasonable to suppose that each one present would of his own volition decide that the less he said about Appalachian, and the more innocent his statements made the occasion to be, the better for him."

Thus widespread publicity may not only have the effect of abrogating the right of the accused to a fair trial (Billy Sol Estes and Dr. Shepherd), but may also have the effect of negating any circumstantial evidence of a conspiracy in a case such as this. The court discharged the conspiracy counts because the government failed to show the intent on the part of the conspirators to commit the substantive crimes (about which they conspired), and further, with respect to the conspiracy to commit perjury count, that the government failed to show that at the time defendants were alleged to have conspired they had any knowledge or reasonable belief that they would be called to testify under oath about the meeting.

As a subsidiary point, court commented on the difficulty in evaluating the evidence as to each defendant in a mass conspiracy trial. Again quoting the Court of Appeals: "Courts have long indulged in the somewhat naive supposition that jurors can properly assess such evidence and determine from it the individual guilt of each of many defendants, even when aided by a careful summary of the evidence such as the trial judge gave here. This makes it especially important for trial and appellate courts to determine the sufficiency of the evidence as to each defendant in mass conspiracy trials."

CHAPTER FIFTEEN

M'Naughten Didn't Need a Lawyer—He Needed a Psychiatrist!

In *White* v. *Rhay* (1964), the Washington Supreme Court reaffirmed the application of the M'Naughten rule to the question of criminal responsibility. It stuck to the "right/wrong test" of the M'Naughten rule rather than the Durham rule, the "irresistible impulse" rule or any other legal sanity rule.

The historic M'Naughten rule came about this way: Daniel M'Naughten suffered delusions of persecution and considered Prime Minister Robert Peel his major persecutor. He went to London to assassinate Peel. He would have succeeded, but Peel chose to ride in Queen Victoria's carriage because of her absence from the city. Peel's secretary, Drummond, rode in the vehicle which he normally would have occupied. M'Naughten shot and killed Drummond in error.

After a lengthy trial, M'Naughten, in 1843, was found *not guilty* by reason of insanity. The court was so impressed with medical evidence of M'Naughten's incompetency that the lord chief justice practically demanded a verdict for the accused. But Her Majesty was incensed at the acquittal and the question was "certified" to the House of Lords for a "rule."

The "M'Naughten rule" came down permitting acquittal on insanity only when it was proved that, at the time of the commission of the act, the party accused was laboring under such a defect of reason, as not to know the nature and quality of the act he was doing, or, if he did it, he did not know he was doing what was wrong.

The M'Naughten rule has more or less been accepted by the bulk of the American jurisdictions. So this rule, although completely outdated with respect to modern psychological and psychiatric developments, nevertheless persists as a majority rule.

In the Columbia University Forum (Spring, 1965) William M. Gaylin, M.D., writing on "Psychiatry and the Law: Partners in Crime" said: "When the general population braced itself for the Dallas Dionysia that was referred to by the innocent as the 'Trial of Jack Ruby,' at least one segment of the population that had long since lost its innocence knew that it, too, would be on trial—I mean American psychiatry.

"Criminal activity is a bete noire of the modern psychiatrist. It is the kind of human behavior about which he is most ignorant, and perversely, about which he is called upon to give the most certain opinions—in testimony under oath. The conditions that bind the relationship of psychiatry and the law today are such that confusion and contradiction are guaranteed."

Neil W. Ross in *Issues in Criminology* (1965), applies philosophical analysis to three facets of the debate between law and psychiatry as to the problem of criminal responsibility. These facets are logic, language, and subjectivism—objectivism. Despite contrary appearances, lawyers and psychiatrists are incapable of communication on some issues because the two disciplines, although of common philosophical origin, have in terms of method and symbols taken the diverse paths of pragmatic versus semantic, subjectivistic versus objectivistic, and prescriptive versus descriptive. The logic, language, and orientation of each discipline are in many ways incompatible; some common ground does exist but both disciplines have to redefine their assumptions and methods if successful communication is to be made possible.

The psychiatrist describes the manner of acting; the lawyer how the man ought to have acted. The lawyer is slave to his paragon, the "reasonably prudent person" (an individual or a collection?) in criminal as well as civil law. Really, is the psychiatrist more protective, more definitive, and more concerned with the individual than the lawyer who, despite all his protestations for *individual rights,* worships an "average person"—the median grade—middle intellectual "reasonably prudent person"?

Over the years, various litigants in the United States have tried unsuccessfully to add to the M'Naughten rule what is called the "irresistible impulse" rule. This would take into account the fact that a defendant could not control his conduct in committing a crime even though he knew it to be wrong.

In recent years New York, Illinois, Vermont, and Connecticut, among others, have abandoned the M'Naughten rule in favor of a modified version of the one suggested by the American Law Institute.

The Massachusetts Supreme Court in 1967 ruled that the M'Naughten test, the ability of a person to distinguish between right and wrong, is not a valid standard to determine his legal sanity.

One effect of the ruling may be a new trial for Albert DeSalvo, the self-proclaimed Boston Strangler, who my two friends, Tony Curtis and F. Lee Bailey, both admittedly acted for—but in different fields. DeSalvo was convicted in January, 1967, of sexual assaults on four women in suburban Boston communities and sentenced to life in prison.

This high court, in the decision by Justice Arthur E. Whittemore, said that the American Law Institute's model penal code should be substituted for the M'Naughten rule that is now used to determine legal sanity in Massachusetts.

Some courts in various parts of the country are beginning to follow the ruling of the Court of Appeals in Washington, D.C., which simplified the tests of incompetency to prove that "the act of the accused was the product of a mental disease." The model penal code rule, that of the American Law Institute, provides that "a person is not responsible for criminal conduct if, at the time of such conduct as a result of mental disease or defect, he lacked substantial capacity either to appreciate the wrongfulness of his conduct or to conform his conduct to the requirements of the law."

In *United States* v. *Freeman* (1966), the Court of Appeals for the Second Circuit in a landmark decision discarded the M'Naughten rule completely with this language: "In the past century, psychiatry has evolved from tentative, hesitant gropings in the dark of human ignorance to a recognized branch of modern medicine."

The Court of Appeals, in this decision, adopted the definition of criminal responsibility laid down by the American Law Institute after a painstaking ten year study. The court, in a forty-five page opinion, found the M'Naughten rule too rigid and narrow. The court said: "[It is] not in harmony with modern medical science which, as we have said, is opposed to any concept which divides the mind into separate compartments—intellect, the emotions, and the will. The Model Penal Code formulation views the mind as a unified entity and recognizes that mental disease or defect may impair its functioning in numerous ways. The rule, moreover, reflects awareness that from the prospective of psychiatry absolutes are ephemeral and graduations inevitable. By employing the telling word 'substantial' to modify 'incapacity,' the rule emphasizes that 'any' incapacity is not sufficient to justify avoidance of criminal responsibility but that 'total' incapacity is also unnecessary."

Judge Kaufman writing for the court, stated in his opinion, what could very well be our preface to reflect our very intentions for this book. "The genius of the common law has been its responsiveness to changing times, its ability to reflect developing moral and social values. Drawing upon the past, the law must serve—and traditionally has served—the needs of the present."

Wisconsin's Supreme Court "as an experiment in this perplexing field" has directed that when a defendant pleads not guilty by reason of insanity, presents evidence that as a result of mental disease or defect he lacks substantial capacity to conform his conduct to the requirements of law, desires to be tried under the American Law Institute definition of the defense of insanity, and is willing to carry the burden of proof on the issue, he is to be permitted to waive such statutory provision as place the burden of proof on the insanity issue on the state, and have the jury instructed in terms of the American Law Institute definition.

A Minnesota murder defendant cannot be compelled, under pain of forfeiture of insanity defense, to talk with state's psychiatrist seeking to determine his mental state at time of crime.

In *State* v. *Olson* the defendant sought a writ of prohibition to require the trial court to desist from proceeding with a psychiatric examination. "It has been suggested that inculpatory statements made to the psychiatrist be admitted only on the issue of insanity, and that the jury be so instructed." (*State* v. *Whitlow*, N.J., 1965.) It is difficult, however, to conceive of a jury not considering such evidence on the issue of guilt. In *French* v. *District Court, Colorado*, the court said: a person accused of a crime who enters a plea of not guilty by reason of insanity, cannot be compelled to carry on conversations against his will under the penalty of forfeiture of the defense for failure to respond.

The crux of the issue is compulsion to submit to an examination. Although a statute or court order permitting the prosecution to give a psychiatric examination to a defendant is not in and of itself unconstitutional, its application may be unconstitutional if the defendant is compelled to submit to the examination.

Wion v. *United States* (1963) is exemplary of the problems posed in insanity and criminal responsibility. It is also significant of the modern decision and the sincerity of the modern appellate justice examining all evidence available—the trial record, law books and treatises and even calling in professional societies having to do with the subject under scrutiny. In this case decision by able Chief Justice Murrah, attorney Walter L. Gerash of Denver, Colorado, was called to do an *amicus curiae* (friend of the court) brief for the Colorado Psychological (why not psychiatric?) Association.

At least in this circuit now it appears that in order for a jury to convict, sanity being in issue, the jury must be satisfied beyond a reasonable doubt not only that the accused committed the unlawful act, but that he was criminally responsible for his conduct and that a person is not so criminally responsible if at the time of the act, as a result of mental disease or defect, he lacked substantial capacity either to appreciate the wrongfulness of his conduct or to conform his conduct to the requirements of the law.

The *Fourteenth Amendment* requires, in a criminal prosecution of an indigent defendant previously adjudicated insane, that the court commit him to a mental hospital for examination, or provide funds for employment of a psychiatrist or otherwise make available to the jury and to court-appointed counsel for the defendant evidence as to defendant's sanity.

Intent is a necessary ingredient in most crimes, thus is pertinent in determining the degree of a crime. A premeditated murder is murder in the first degree and carries with it the harshest penalty. It is always the duty of the prosecution to establish the degree of intent in the minds of the jurors and/or the presiding judge.

States like California, having divided trials—the first trial on the question of guilt and then with a guilty verdict the second trial on the question of insanity—found that their nicely divided and departmentalized procedure conflicted with the right of a defendant on the liability of guilt phase of the case to show his insanity or lack of intent.

As a result of the 1964 *People* v. *Wolff* matter, which came out of the California Supreme Court, California must now allow insanity evidence on the intent issue in the first trial, even though insanity is to be tried in the second trial.

After the Denver "Midnight Rapist" had been found not guilty by reason of insanity on charges of burglary, robbery, unnatural and carnal copulation, and rape, the district attorney of Denver chose another case to prosecute against him.

In this second case the defendant refused to "cooperate" with the psychiatrist appointed by the court. (The last time a psychiatrist appointed by the court had examined him, he had found the defendant sane, and whether sane or insane, the defendant at least had practical sense enough to refuse to talk further to a psychiatrist.) Defendant entered another insanity plea, the one found by his former jury, as his defense.

The honorable trial court struck the plea of innocence by reason of insanity, which is to say the court removed the possibility of this plea and attempted to force the case through trial on its merits.

The Supreme Court of Colorado granted a writ of prohibition, a document which in effect agrees with the defendant by prohibiting the intolerable or illegal action against the defendant to take place. In this case, it was held that a person accused of a crime who enters a plea of not guilty by reason of insanity cannot be compelled to carry on conversations against his will under penalty of a forfeiture of the defense or failure to respond to questions or for refusal to cooperate with persons appointed to examine him. The statute which prescribes procedures to be followed upon the entry of a plea of not guilty by reason of insanity cannot operate to destroy the constitutional safeguards against self-incrimination.

Compare with this the edict in the 1966 Ballard case. That defendant who refuses to talk to a psychiatrist is subject to an instruction informing the jury of this thereby giving an inference against defendant. Is this constitutionally valid criminally, even though it may be civilly?

In Colorado, at the time of the French case, it was discretionary in the court to grant a separate or a joint trial. In that case the court has not yet determined whether to grant a joint or separate trial and accordingly if the court did grant a joint trial, any statement made to a psychiatrist would be highly prejudicial if it entered upon a discussion of the merits of the case.

Despite the Law Revolution in other procedural and substantive areas, civil and criminal, in one area Old Mother Law has remained adamant, has refused to change: "expert examination" of a witness. And perhaps for good reason.

We're now learning the "truth serum" still isn't all that it is meant to be, that it's only as efficacious as the operator of the lie detector, the drug, etc., and even then, a great deal remains to be learned.

The old methods of cross-examination (and impeachment by collateral evidence and witnesses—particularly with the availability of the new extended and detailed discovery) seem to be almost emotionally clung to. Perhaps the psychiatrist would (or should) be the first to admit his profession still can't, with any degree of certainty, spot the lying witness.

But some progress in the law is being made as progress is being made in new developments in "truth serum," "lie detectors," psychiatry, and hypnosis. And that's just the point: law is *consonant* with these procedures as they *now* are. It just doesn't want to get *ahead* of them. Then it would not be consonant, it would be *legislating*—prognosing too broadly in policy making for the future.

Ballard v. *Superior Court* (1966) held defendant in a rape case was entitled to have a jury determine the mental and emotional instability of the prosecuting witness through expert medical testimony of a doctor in charge of her case. The jury was entitled to hear such evidence and have it before them as an aid in evaluating her testimony. Court held that a psychiatrist may testify as to the credibility of a witness in rape cases; however, this should rest as a *discretion* of the trial judge. It is up to him to determine whether psychiatric examination of a complaining witness in a case involving sex violation is called for. The court went on to state that a complaining witness cannot be forced to submit to psychiatric examination, but in the event the witness refuses to cooperate, a comment on refusal could be permitted. I believe this latter suggestion, if followed, would be an unconstitutional procedure.

The California Supreme Court in *Cornell* v. *Superior Court* held that a lawyer was entitled to take a history with the aid of a psychiatrist or hypnotist. That is, a client conversely put is entitled to a lawyer for his conscious as well as for his unconscious, and the California Supreme Court ordered the San Diego sheriff to allow a lawyer and psychiatrist to visit, consult, and take a case history of a criminally-charged defendant.

In the matter of *United States* v. *Hiss* it was held that the introduction of a psychiatric testimony on the credibility of a witness is proper. In the Hiss case, the psychiatric testimony was about the witness, Whittaker Chambers, as he was observed in court by a psychiatrist. The court said, "Since the use of psychiatric testimony to impeach the credibility of a witness is a comparatively modern innovation, there appears to be no federal cases dealing with this precise question. However, the importance of insanity on the question of credibility of witnesses is often stressed. There are some state cases in which such testimony has been held to be admissible or which would indicate that if this question had been presented, it would have been admissible . . ."

Expert testimony of this character was excluded in *State v. Driver*. The court's reasoning seemed to be based upon the theory that the witness was to be regarded as a character witness who could only testify as to reputation and not as to his personal opinion. The court indicated that it would not allow him to be qualified as an expert. This was in 1921—before the value of psychiatry had been recognized.

Leading authorities on evidence also advocate the admission of testimony of this character.

CHAPTER SIXTEEN

The Warren Report and Jack Ruby

I should include a statement on *The Warren Report* in this book because the means by which a democracy reports on the assassination of the head of the Republic are exemplary of our system of law.

In the first place, we do not contemplate that our chief executive will be assassinated, though there have been more attempts here than in most countries. Assassination was not a federal crime, and was not made such until after the tragic murder of President Kennedy.

In the second place, there was no legal machinery either for the investigation of the death of the President or procedures to report who did it, guilty or innocent.

So the Republic appointed a commission, and headed it with the chief justice of the United States, a man of unimpeachable integrity, character, ability, and objectivity.

To me, and I hope that I always have been among the first to examine the qualifications of a judge, the membership of the committee was just as unimpeachable. It was political —but our country is run by politicians. If we must say that a man, because he is a "politician" is inept or dishonest or incapable of objective considerations, then at the beginning we are lost.

The report of the Warren Commission answers all of the big questions I have, and I believe that I am as knowledgeable of most of the events of and surrounding the assassination of the late John F. Kennedy and the subsequent trial of Jack Ruby as anyone living.

Perhaps some of the literature of the report could be improved. Perhaps some detailed explanation could be enlarged but I know that no man has ever gone to execution in my own state's public abattoir at San Quentin with more evidence against him than Mr. Oswald, the one and the lone assassin of President Kennedy. I know that Mr. Oswald and Mr. Ruby did not know each other and did not act in concert. I know that Mr. Oswald was deranged of mind, and I know that Mr. Ruby was likewise. I know there was no conspiracy —no conspiracy of any sort.

I know that we American people like the sinister and the ominous, and we are willing to buy books which cast doubt more readily than books which affirm the obvious.

Eighty per cent of the people abroad now believe that there was a "conspiracy" to assassinate President Kennedy. Those abroad will even name the conspirators: President Johnson, Mr. Hunt of Dallas, the FBI, and the CIA. This is utter, sheer rot. But those who fostered these opinions based their arguments in the same manner that I now could make a damn good case that one of President Lincoln's cabinet members assassinated him rather than John Wilkes Booth.

As time goes by, the sinister argument will gather impetus because the living witnesses will be dead.

One living witness said Mr. Oswald used a "Mauser" pistol or gun. The witness so said. But he so said excitedly and without basic knowledge and when he found his errancy, he corrected himself. But those who would cast doubt on the authenticity of the facts of *The Warren Report,* and those who would dispute that it was a lone assassin seize upon such as the original report of the "Mauser" as a basic fact argument to cast sinister doubt.

No matter how well trained a police force, it is not set up to handle or report on events of national tragedy, as the assassination of a President. The police work in Dallas was horrendous, that is, the actual reporting and factual accounting of it. But as time has gone by, I don't know whether I fully believe with United States District Justice Sarah Hughes of Fort Worth that Dallas is the "only city where the assassination could have taken place."

As President Kennedy himself said the morning of the assassination when he stepped on the porch of his hotel in Fort Worth, "How easy it would be to shoot a President of the United States." Bobby Kennedy, talking of his own safety, was just as much a fatalist as his deceased brother.

I am one of those who do believe that District Attorney Wade, the sheriff, and the law enforcement officers had a duty to report to the press all of the events of and around the assassination, so that "we the people" could go about our daily work knowing that there was no "conspiracy." Even though this made it impossible to try the lone conspirator Oswald, here was one instance in which the right of the people of the Republic to know, was above that of the individual to have a fair trial.

The problem was presented in *Rideau* v. *Louisiana* (1963), where the United States Supreme Court sent the case back saying that "[the] kangaroo court proceedings in this case involved a real deprivation of due process of law," and that a trial would have to be had in an unprejudiced community. But suppose the community is completely prejudiced, suppose the crime is so horrendous that a fair jury can't be had in the state, what then? Can a man, e.g., Oswald, commit a crime so horrendous that the Supreme Court would say he couldn't get a fair trial anywhere?

I knew that Jack Ruby couldn't receive a fair trial in Dallas, because Dallas was unconsciously trying itself along with Jack Ruby. And I also knew that Escobedo *et al.* applied to Jack Ruby.

I also knew that the Ruby trial in Dallas was a "kangaroo court" and a "railroad." I so said. In so saying I reported only the language of the United States Supreme Court in *Rideau* v. *Louisiana.*

For my exquisite (and they were—and still are) pains in pointing out the deficiency of justice in Dallas, which deficiencies have been formally resolved by reversal of the Ruby case, *Rubenstein* v. *State* (1966), recently, I was bitterly castigated by a most unethical president of the American Bar Association. (Though I have sued him for defamation I have been unable to "get jurisdiction.") The American Bar Association is still attempting to castigate me for "unethical conduct" in "calling them as I saw them" and ascribing United States Supreme Court language to the conduct of his Honor, Judge Brown, the learned trial judge below in the Ruby case.

I particularly note that my brief was the only brief filed in the appellate court for some two years after the conviction and the principal points raised were failure to change venue and Escobedo, *et al.* I also cited *Rideau* v. *Louisiana* and upon more of these points and this citation the Texas Appellate Court agreed.

It is easy in a brief for the losing party, being vindicated, to say, "I cited." I hope the text above will be read in the spirit that the "I cited" is given, in the context of an objective lawyer being so certain of the objectivity and the goodness of the law that he relied wholeheartedly thereupon.

As far as my being "flamboyant," I'll stand by the Criminal

Court of Appeals opinion in Texas. If that is "flamboyant," if my language was "extravagant," then so is that court's.

I was hired to change venue. I thought I did a lawyer-like job trying to change it. I knew when I couldn't in the trial court, that the case was temporarily lost—but that it would be won in an appellate court. I bought additional insurance by raising Escobedo, *et al.*; when I left Dallas the day after the results of the "kangaroo court" had been announced, I told Jack Ruby that I left him a trial record that would "guarantee" his reversal. With that, my job was done in the trial court, and I would have fired me if I were the Ruby family.

After consultation with the District Attorney's Office and others and with a great deal of fanfare and flamboyancy and bitterness and publicity and intent personally to damage me, the Ruby family did "fire" me. My next act was to buy the transcript at my own expense and in longhand do the appellate brief.

For some reason, known to themselves, the Ruby family delayed the inevitable reversal these two years.

My conscience and that of the trial counsel I led in the trial court must be clear. I knew that Ruby would never have been executed, and I know that Ruby was mentally deranged, and I also know that some "deal" (and I use this in no impropriety) could have been made—that his freedom would have been obtained before long.

Had I remained his lawyer, I would have guaranteed that the freedom that he would have achieved would never have been obtained until adequate mental therapy had been accorded, and had been completed.

I suppose through all of the above runs the personality of the lawyers—in this case, me. I've never proffered myself less than controversial or more than colorful. I've always felt that a lawyer should be heard in court *and out of court*. I've always felt that a lawyer should be a leader in the community, and particularly in community thought on controversial issues.

I've never felt that the function of the lawyer was to be oilcan for an IBM machine, or the "loophole jumper througher" for a conniving corporation.

I'd rather sit next to an honest man who wears a dinner jacket with a red, white, and blue striped necktie in grossly bad taste, than one in impeccable full dress who'd paid for his dinner with counterfeit money!

Just after the Jack Ruby trial, the *Orlando Star* (Florida), a daily newspaper, published a gross defamation against me. The newspaper made statements about an alleged event that was now *nine years old!* The *Star*, interestingly enough, is published in the home town of one counselor McCuen, head of the Grievance Committee of the American Bar Association. The *Star*'s article containing the defamation against me was published just at the time the American Bar Association was bringing charges against me for speaking out against the "kangaroo court" in Dallas. And those charges were petitioned and signed solely by Dallas and a "Southern" insurance company's "lawyers."

That the article was defamatory is not a subjective statement by me. It was admittedly defamatory by the newspaper. They published an abject retraction and apology.

Subsequently *The Saturday Evening Post*, no stranger to the losing side of huge defamatory verdict cases, and *Esquire* published defamatory stories about me. These suits are still pending.

I mentioned the above in context with the Ruby case because a great deal of that case will be retried in *The Saturday Evening Post* and *Esquire* libel suits in San Francisco. I believe facts will be disclosed in those cases which will convince everyone that Dallas was the wrong city in which to have tried Jack Ruby. The trial further should show how national magazines deliberately set out to create an image for circulation purposes.

But Judge Sarah Hughes of the United States District Court in Fort Worth was wrong (and so was I for the same reason) when she said Dallas is the only city in which a President of the United States could be assassinated! Now Senator Robert Kennedy, a man who was very close to the presidency, in Los Angeles.

And there was some distorted newspaper reporting about a lawyer for Sirhan Sirhan. Shortly after the assassination it was reported that my friend F. Lee Bailey and I had "volunteered our services to represent Sirhan." The next story was that Sirhan had "rejected" our services. The truth was that neither of us knew Sirhan, neither of us "volunteered" our services; Lee Bailey being in Boston during the time and I being in the Republic of Haiti! But it made a good newspaper story.

A. A Divergent View—Jim Garrison's Report. I report here a divergent view of mine on *The Warren Report,* that of the capable and respected New Orleans District Attorney, Jim Garrison, a good friend of mine. I hold with *The Warren Report,* until Jim can otherwise convince me—but what he says does disturb me. The following is his "With Liberty and Justice for All" (September 1, 1967).

"The hallmark of the superstate is its readiness to conceal from the people facts which might make them restless. In order to maintain power its officials must keep the populace believing that it is living in the best of all possible worlds.

"Consequently, those in control of the governmental machinery sometimes find it necessary to rewrite history as fast as it happens. The truth becomes not what occurred but what they announce to have occurred. Reality becomes just another government controlled commodity.

"If the official myth to be presented is particularly unbelievable, it may be necessary to have honorable men study it and announce that they have found it true. This is not really as difficult as it sounds because there is nothing to which honorable men joined in an honorable cause will not stoop in the name of duty. As a general rule of thumb, the more unbelievable the story, the more honorable should be the men assigned to attest to its veracity.

"In 1939, after having invaded and conquered western Poland because of alleged Polish atrocities committed against German individuals, the German government appointed a committee to make careful study to determine the fact with regard to the claimed Polish misconduct. The final printed report of the study contained much documentary evidence, including not only photographs, affidavits, and countless medical certificates, but an authenticated quotation for the year 1598 to the effect that barbarous cruelty was one of the vices of the Polish people. The report confirmed that the Poles indeed had committed atrocities against Germans, and it indicated that things would have been even worse were it not for the timely arrival on Polish territory of the German rescuers. The conclusions of this painstaking study by a government appointed committee meant that Adolf Hitler would not have to withdraw his armies and apologize to Poland. See: "Polish Acts of Atrocity Against the German Minority in Poland," German Library of Information, New York, 1940.

"Until fairly recently, the leading example of the correction of history to fit present political needs was to be found in George Orwell's *1984*. In Oceania, that dismal land presided over by Big Brother, the power of the government had become gargantuan and the rights of individuals virtually had vanished. In order to maintain this imbalance, the Ministry of Truth continually was engaged in the improvement of history to make it more harmonious with government pronouncements. This was justified on the ground of 'national security,' a relatively honest rationale inasmuch as the government could not have survived without such wholesale concealment of facts.

"If, for example, Big Brother made an error which was exposed by statistics, the offensive statistics were destroyed and more satisfactory statistics were published. If books or newspapers described facts which were embarrassing to the government, they were merely rewritten so as to conform with official legend. The original troublesome material was simply filed in the 'memory hole,' a chute leading down to the incinerator. The government's policy of vaporizing into nothingness unpleasant facts contributed in great measure to the calm of the populace of Oceania. This was helped by the fact that individuals who interfered with the public calm also were vaporized.

" 'Who controls the past,' said the official slogan of the superstate, 'controls the future.'

"It now appears that, twenty years ahead of Orwell's schedule, the United States has succeeded in producing the classic model of rewriting history to conform to official needs. It is hard to assay this accomplishment when we are still so close to it, but when our contributions to civilization are added up this well may rank ahead of our invention of napalm.

"When the President of our country was executed on a public street, one would have thought there would have arisen an uncomplicated desire on the part of everyone to catch the assassins and to bring them all to justice. After all, there was sufficient information available concerning the strange movements of cars behind the grassy knoll immediately prior to the assassination, the fusilade of rifle fire coming from that sector, and the rapid departure of men on foot and by car from that point following the shooting. Apparently, however, it was not as simple as that. It appears that when a President's heart stops beating, considerations of power and policy take over.

"Instead of running down the men who killed John Kennedy, the United States government has simply ratified his execution and moved on to more important matters. With regard to the men who actually killed him, because of their displeasure with his foreign policy, the assassination has been treated not as an offense but as a mandate for change.

"The young man who so promptly was nominated by the Dallas police force was duly elected as the lone assassin. He had, if one did not look too closely, excellent qualifications. He wore the tag of a "communist defector" who had spent three years in Russia. He had been murdered, which assured that there would be none of the time-consuming problems of proof which a live defendant would have presented. And his gun and three empty cartridges had been placed on the sixth floor of the book depository.

"In spite of these conveniences there was a slight problem. The overwhelming weight of legitimate evidence clearly indicated that he could not possibly have fired a shot at the President.

"There was, to begin with, the fact that the rifle originally brought down from the book depository at 1:05 P.M., and briefly exhibited as the assassin's rifle, had—unlike Lee Oswald's rifle—no telescopic sight. There was the fact that his Marine shooting record showed that Oswald could not hit the side of a barn. There was the fact that the nitrate test had indicated that Oswald had not fired a rifle of any kind on that day. There was the fact that the ancient Italian rifle, which Oswald was supposed to have used, could not conceivably have accomplished the ballistic miracle with which it was credited—particularly driving a single bullet to inflict seven different wounds, including bone destruction, in two different men. There was the fact that the President had been hit from several different directions and that his fatal wound quite obviously had been received from his right front, from the area of the grassy knoll.

"To make matters worse, there were probably more witnesses to President Kennedy's murder than any in history and the great majority of them were very conscious of the fact that most of the shots came from in front of the President. There was also the embarrassing evidence that Lee Oswald had been an employee of the Central Intelligence Agency and had acquired his stigma of Communist defector while in the service of the United States, and as the result of instructions given him by the United States government.

"These problems were approached with aplomb. Most of the embarrassing evidence was simply buried at the outset in a swift funeral devoid of ceremony. The autopsy photographs and X rays, for example, which would have revealed that the President was struck from a number of directions, were whisked away and have been kept hidden ever since.

"Dr. Robert N. McClelland, at Parkland Hospital, examined the President and concluded that the cause of death, was a gunshot wound of the *left temple.* Similarly, Dr. Mahlon Jenkins recalled, in his testimony before the Warren Commission, that there was a wound in the *left temple,* right in the hairline. The book depository, although it may since have been moved, at the time of the assassination was located to the rear of the president. At all events, it does not appear likely that the original autopsy photographs and X rays will ever be seen by the public. By now there has been time to construct new photographs and X rays which more closely harmonize with the official myth.

"Hundreds of significant government files and memoranda have been secreted away in vaults where they cannot be seen. Among the hidden Central Intelligence Agency files alone are to be found such titles as: 'Oswald's Access to Information about the U-2,' 'Reproduction of Central Intelligence Agency Official Dossier on Oswald,' and 'Information on Jack Ruby and Associates.' Inasmuch as we have been assured by honorable men that neither Oswald nor Ruby had any connection with the Central Intelligence Agency it probably would be unpatriotic to speculate on what these secret files contain.

"As bad luck would have it, a rash of conflagrations swept away other vital evidence in the government's custody. The only notes known to be taken during the long twelve-hour interview of Lee Oswald after the assassination appear to have been burned. Notes taken by a federal agent who interviewed Oswald before the assassination also went up in flames. A secret Central Intelligence Agency memo concerning Oswald, written prior to the assassination, went up in smoke while being thermofaxed. This phenomenal instance of spontaneous combustion occurred in Washington the day following the assassination. The autopsy notes describing the President's wounds were cremated in his fireplace by the attending Navy pathologist.

"This is not to say that the government has not shown concern for the people's right to know. For those citizens who are curious about how and why their President was killed, the Ministry of Truth has made available the dental charts of Jack Ruby, photographs of Russian scenery, grammar school records of Oswald and Ruby, a careful analysis of Oswald's pubic hairs, irrelevant letters, irrelevant telegrams, picture postcards showing bullfights, a copy of the proceedings in an unrelated divorce case, a list of traffic citations received by Jack Ruby, and an excellent photograph of an unidentified man.

"For those whose curiosity about the assassination may not have been satisfied with this frank display of evidence, it has been announced that even the secret files will be made available. There will, however, be a slight delay of seventy-five years before they can be examined. This farsighted provision not only assures a long period of national tranquility with regard to the assassination but also substantially reduces the danger of the involved government officials being lynched.

"Of course, there is no real guarantee that, even if you are very patient, you will actually get to examine these files in seventy-five years. New concerns by the government with regard to national security may require an additional seventy-five years delay, and it even might come to pass that one day it will be announced from Washington that actually no assassination ever occurred. In time, it can be explained that John Kennedy really never existed at all and that Dwight Eisenhower was followed by Grover Cleveland or Calvin Coolidge, depending on which selection best suits the government's purpose at the time. Any of these announcements would be every bit as accurate as the official myth that Lee Harvey Oswald, the lone assassin, killed President Kennedy.

"In the superstate, it really does not matter at all what actually happened. Truth is what the government chooses to tell you. Justice is what it wants to happen.

"In Dealey Plaza reality destroyed illusion, the illusion that we were living in the best of all possible worlds. The fairy tale of the lone assassin represents an effort to resurrect the illusion, to legitimize it by proclamation and to impose it by muscle.

"In the interest of tranquility the decision has been made somewhere, that it is better for you not to know what really happened. It is better for you not to know that at midday on November 22 there were many men in many places who were glancing at their watches. It is better for you to believe that the successive murders of the President of the United States, Officer Tippit, and Lee Oswald were simply three meaningless incidents which happened to occur one weekend in Dallas.

"Above all, it has been decided that you are not to know of Lee Oswald's relationship with the Central Intelligence Agency. Nor are you to know that a number of the men actually involved in the assassination had been employees of the Central Intelligence Agency. You are not to know about those matters because of something called 'national security.'

"When national security is used as the excuse for concealment of the essential facts surrounding a disaster, it usually refers to the security of the men who allowed the disaster to occur. Actually, the greater threat to national security is the cynical concealment of such facts from the people.

"Behind the facade of earnest inquiry into the assassination is a thought control project in the best traditions of *1984.* Major news agencies, whose role in the Establishment and whose failure to conduct any effective inquiry has given them a vested interest in ignorance, have thrown themselves into the frontline of the defense against the truth. They look away from the widespread evidence that something is wrong just as Russian news agencies in the thirties looked away from Stalin's extermination of his political opponents, just as the members of the Warren Commission looked away from the autopsy photographs and X rays of the murdered President. This evidence could have clarified once and for all the number of times the President was shot and the various directions from which he was shot. The commission, however, loyally refused to play Russian Roulette with the "lone assassin" theory. The unviewed autopsy evidence was locked away behind concrete walls and the Dallas police department scenario duly was adopted as the official myth. Tranquility, the time-honored message reads, is better than knowledge.

"In the authoritarian state, it is regarded as a self-evident truth that the control of history is an inalienable right of government. All words are created free and equal.

"If it is proclaimed in Washington tomorrow that the moon is made of Limburger cheese, a horde of honorable men can be produced to attest to that fact. If it is proclaimed that an elephant can hang from a cliff with its tail tied to a daisy, a phalanx of experts will appear to confirm it. Anyone rash enough to question these official verities can expect to be exposed as a villain or a fool. The name of the game is not truth—it is power.

"The Ministry of Truth has announced that the assassination of John Kennedy was investigated exhaustively, that no evidence of a conspiracy was found and that the matter should now be considered closed.

"The greatest lies are told in the name of truth. The greatest crimes are committed in the name of justice.

"The American people have suffered two tragedies. In addition to the assassination of the President by dishonorable men, there is occurring the assassination of our national integrity by honorable men. It does not matter what the rationale is—whether to calm the public or to protect our image—the fact remains that the truth is being concealed.

"The United States Constitution, assuming that it has not accidentally been burned to a crisp, does not give anyone the power to rewrite history. The fact that this is happening should be evidence enough that it is far later than any of us have dreamed.

"The question now is whether we have the courage to come face to face with ourselves and admit that something is wrong, whether we have the will to insist on an end to deception and concealment with regard to the execution of John Kennedy—or whether we will let the official fairy tale be told and retold until the truth itself fades into vagrant rumor and finally dies forever.

"If we will not fight for the truth now—when our President has been shot down in the streets and his murderers remain untouched by justice—it is not likely that we will ever have another chance."

CHAPTER SEVENTEEN

Conclusion

While this may seem to be a book about constitutions, laws, and courts, really it's a book about lawyers. And my basic premise is that most lawyers are "good" in the sense that most priests are "good."

By this I mean that there may be some "bad" lawyers and priests, but even agnostics must admit that the great majority of priests are "good," in that they want to "serve" their fellowman. And that quality of service is the goodness in lawyers.

As a profession, principally we must serve or we're not lawyers because we cannot practice law on ourselves, only on our clients. If our only motive for service is money, still we must serve well or we won't make money. If another motive for service is ideological goodness, then the only quarrel with some of my serving professional brethren is that their service in pursuit of their goodness is misconstrued, i.e., left-wing goodness, extremist goodness, and such may not be true goodness.

The "Unfriendly Ten" Hollywood writers who were ostracized and labeled "Communists" in an earlier day, were not motivated by money. They were motivated by a desire to serve. Indeed, they had plenty of money and the course they took was the hardest one to follow. But their "service," their "goodness" was not accepted by society since they were "subversive." (Some of today's "subversives" are tomorrow's majorities—so it is with minority opinions.)

Some say that after Adam and Eve and the garden, man's basic nature is evil. I don't agree. I think man's basic nature is good, that there is a *de rerum natura,* a natural law. It's the concept of man that provides, without legislatures or constitutions, a natural or conscientious law which is "good."

This "goodness" is not an immutable one-age goodness, but extends through history so that it is a contextual "goodness," dependent upon the time, age, and country.

England has no constitution, yet it has the concept of a law as being "unconstitutional," i.e., against natural law and natural goodness. This natural goodness is an unwritten law that resides in the breasts of men. I like to think that at any age in any country at any time "right will be done," or if it is not, men of goodwill quickly will come to the awareness that the "law" is being broken.

Into the Fourteenth Amendment of the Constitution of the United States we wrote that we must be governed by due process of law. This amorphous concept of natural law, i.e., "due process," is as ambiguous a phrase as could be written for a prescription for human action. Yet most lawyers now understand it, and I think most laymen are beginning to understand it, but only because they know what is natural goodness, i.e., what is right, what is fair.

Plato, in his *Republic,* ultimately determined that "justice" was "doing unto others as you would be done by." This is a sort of *de rerum natura* due process of law.

The vigilantes in my home city of San Francisco, when courts became corrupt and the process of law and order had broken down, gave their own brand of justice (which was not "vigilante justice" as the term has come to be known), really a return to "due process" justice.

I dedicated the legal volumes of this Law Revolution to

". . . those tough cases which made the five to four decisions. They controverted, fomented, and promoted the Law Revolution, thereby making a better life and law for all of us. Furthermore, they're a lot more interesting than these bland nine to zero sandlot baseball games."

For the layman I should be more explicit. The Law Revolution really has been in the *state* courts, not the *federal* courts. Escobedo and these household word case names had applied federal-wise, but it was only by bringing those first ten amendments of the Constitution which had applied to the federal government to the states that there was a Law Revolution in all our courts.

That procedure was the process of the Law Revolution. There will be two volumes to this work as there were in the law edition; the first criminal, the second civil. In both it will be shown that the *result* of the Law Revolution is to make our law modern, in context with today's living conditions. Today's law is where the action is. We've tossed out the "whereases" and dusted off the law books, and we're as modern as missilemen and anatomical transplants. But in our due process of law we're concerned not with numbers or collectives. Like the surgeon, we don't operate on a whole ward, we operate only on one individual at a time. Like the surgeon we take the patient as we find him. Furthermore, I hope, like all surgeons, we're just as concerned for the least of us as we are for the greatest of us. As long as the Supreme Court is concerned with the least of us, because so many of us are in that class, I'm certain the most of us, more fortunate, will be safe.

APPENDIX

Appendix
The Bill of Rights and the Fourteenth Amendment

We've spent a good deal of time talking about the Bill of Rights. Following are these first ten amendments to the United States Constitution for easy referral:

AMENDMENT I

Congress shall make no law respecting an establishment of religion, or prohibiting the free exercise thereof; or abridging the freedom of speech, or of the press; or the right of the people peaceably to assemble, and to petition the Government for a redress of grievances.

AMENDMENT II

A well regulated Militia being necessary to the security of a free State, the right of the people to keep and bear Arms, shall not be infringed.

AMENDMENT III

No Soldier shall, in time of peace be quartered in any house, without the consent of the Owner, nor in time of war, but in a manner to be prescribed by law.

AMENDMENT IV

The right of the people to be secure in their persons, houses, papers, and effects, against unreasonable searches and seizures, shall not be violated, and no Warrants shall issue, but upon probable cause, supported by Oath or affirmation, and particularly describing the place to be searched, and the persons or things to be seized.

AMENDMENT V

No person shall be held to answer for a capital, or otherwise infamous crime, unless on a presentment or indictment of a Grand Jury, except in cases arising in the land or naval forces, or in the Militia, when in actual service in time of War or public danger; nor shall any person be subject for the same offence to be twice put in jeopardy of life or limb; nor shall be compelled in any criminal case to be a witness against himself, nor be deprived of life, liberty, or property, without due process of law; nor shall private property be taken for public use, without just compensation.

AMENDMENT VI

In all criminal prosecutions, the accused shall enjoy the right to a speedy and public trial, by an impartial jury of the State and district wherein the crime shall have been committed, which district shall have been previously ascertained by law, and to be informed of the nature and cause of the accusation; to be confronted with the witnesses against him; to have compulsory process for obtaining witnesses in his favor, and to have the assistance of counsel for his defence.

AMENDMENT VII

In Suits at common law, where the value in controversy shall exceed twenty dollars, the right of trial by jury shall be preserved, and no fact tried by jury, shall be otherwise reexamined in any Court of the United States, than according to the rules of the common law.

AMENDMENT VIII

Excessive bail shall not be required, nor excessive fines imposed nor cruel and unusual punishments inflicted.

AMENDMENT IX

The enumeration in the Constitution, of certain rights, shall not be construed to deny or disparage others retained by the people.

AMENDMENT X

The powers not delegated to the United States by the Constitution, nor prohibited by it to the States, are reserved to the States respectively, or to the people.

And here is the "Glorious Fourteenth," the Fourteenth amendment to the Constitution, which makes due process and the Bill of Rights binding on the fifty states as well as the federal government.

AMENDMENT XIV

Section 1. All persons born or naturalized in the United States, and subject to the jurisdiction thereof, are citizens of the United States and of the State wherein they reside. No State shall make or enforce any law which shall abridge the privileges or immunities of citizens of the United States; nor shall any State deprive any person of life, liberty, or property, without due process of law; nor deny to any person within its jurisdiction the equal protection of the laws.

Section 2. Representatives shall be apportioned among the several States according to their respective numbers, counting the whole number of persons in each State, excluding Indians not taxed. But when the right to vote at any election for the choice of electors for President and Vice-President of the United States, Representatives in Congress, the Executive and Judicial officers of a State, or the members of the Legislature thereof, is denied to any of the male inhabitants of such State, being twenty-one years of age, and citizens of the United States, or in any way abridged, except for participation in rebellion, or other crime, the basis of representation therein shall be reduced in the proportion which the number of such male citizens shall bear to the whole number of male citizens twenty-one years of age in such State.

Section 3. No person shall be a Senator or Representative in Congress, or elector of President and Vice President, or hold any office, civil or military, under the United States, or under any State, who, having previously taken an oath, as a member of Congress, or as an officer of the United States, or as a member of any State legislature, or as an executive or judicial officer of any State, to support the Constitution of the United States, shall have engaged in insurrection or rebellion against the same, or given aid or comfort to the enemies thereof. But Congress may by a vote of two-thirds of each House, remove such disability.

Section 4. The validity of the public debt of the United States, authorized by law, including debts incurred for payments of pensions and bounties for services in suppressing insurrection or rebellion, shall not be questioned. But neither the United States nor any State shall assume or pay any debt or obligation incurred in aid of insurrection or rebellion against the United States, or any claim for the loss or emancipation of any slave; but all such debts, obligations and claims shall be held illegal and void.

Section 5. The Congress shall have power to enforce, by appropriate legislation, the provisions of this article.